Preface Books

A series of scholarly and critical studies of major writers intended for those needing modern and authoritative guidance through the characteristic difficulties of their work to reach an intelligent understanding and enjoyment of it.

General Editor: MAURICE HUSSEY

Available now:

A Preface to Wordsworth	JOHN PURKIS
A Preface to Donne	JAMES WINNY
A Preface to Milton	LOIS POTTER
A Preface to Coleridge	ALLAN GRANT
A Preface to Jane Austen	CHRISTOPHER GILLIE
A Preface to Yeats	EDWARD MALINS
A Preface to Pope	I.R.F. GORDON
A Preface to Hardy	MERRYN WILLIAMS
A Preface to Dryden	DAVID WYKES
A Preface to Spenser	HELENA SHIRE

Titles in preparation:

A Preface to Dickens	ALLAN GRANT
A Preface to Conrad	CEDRIC WATTS

A Preface to Spenser

Helena Shire

Longman London and New York

LONGMAN GROUP LIMITED
London and New York
Associated companies, branches and
representatives throughout the world

Published in the United States of
America by Longman Inc. New York

This edition first published 1978

Library of Congress Cataloging in Publication Data

Shire, Helena.
  A Preface to Spenser.

  (Preface books)
  Bibliography: p.
  Includes index.
    1. Spenser, Edmund, 1552?–1599.   I. Title.
PR2363.S5   821'.3 [B]   76–23272
ISBN 0 582 31511 5 Cased
     0 582 31512 3 Paper

Printed in Hong Kong by
Sing Cheong Printing Co. Ltd.

HELENA SHIRE is a student of medieval and renaissance literature
of Scotland and England, instigator of research into court-song of
Scotland, author of *Song, Dance and Poetry of the Court of Scotland under
King James VI* and publisher and editor of the series 'The Ninth of
May', anthologies of earlier Scots poetry which include many pieces
hitherto unknown.

  Formerly Senior Research Fellow in Arts, the Carnegie Trust for
the Universities of Scotland, now Foundation Fellow of Robinson
College, Cambridge, pre-elected.

Contents

Acknowledgements

A general and introductory book such as this must needs draw upon authorities in many fields. Books I have found particularly useful are included in the Bibliography. If anywhere I quote a passage without such acknowledgement I offer sincere apologies. I owe a debt of gratitude to Miss Helen M. Roe, whose vivid conversation first led me to see Spenser 'from the other side of the water', and whose vast knowledge of Ireland's antiquities has informed my steps; also to two professors of Spanish, Arthur Terry and Frank Pierce who showed me the renaissance lyric and heroic poem in European dimensions, and to my brother Professor Duncan M. Mennie for support in ventures into Gaelic of Ireland. Discussion with several generations of university pupils played a lively part in this book's development. My unending gratitude goes to the series editor Maurice Hussey and the publishers for their unending patience with a book that was so long agrowing.

H.M.S.

The passages from Spenser in this book are in the text of the Variorum Edition—with minor modernizations of spelling for clarity in incidental quotations only.

The author and publisher are grateful to the following for permission to reproduce photographs:
Lord Bath, page 46; Bodleian Library, Oxford, page 172; Ruth Brennan, page 62; Irish Tourist Board, page 28; City of Manchester Art Gallery, page 38; National Portrait Gallery, pages ii, 20, 70 and 86; National Trust, page 116; Staatliche Museen Preußischer Kulturbesitz, West Berlin, page 52; University Library Cambridge, pages 8, 13, 18, 22, 24, 34, 36, 50, 54, 66, 96, 97, 100, 101, 160 and 173. The illustration *Coeur D'Amour Épris* by René d'Anjou reproduced on the cover is by courtesy of the Austrian National Library, Vienna.

Foreword

The concept of the European renaissance provides historians with what is called a problem of periodization. It springs up in different countries at different times between the 14th and 16th centuries, and when it does it is never entirely distinct from the Middle Ages that preceded it. In England, at any rate, it came late. Not yet evident in the work of Chaucer, the full force of artistic innovation (is there such a thing as *progess* in the arts?) is delayed until the time of Shakespeare two hundred years later. This was also the time of Spenser, the most distinguished non-dramatic poet of the English renaissance and the subject of this book.

Helena Shire's *A Preface to Spenser* details the growth of a renaissance poet and scholar's mind, revealing how much he owed to a formally structured education and how much he built upon this foundation as he extended his range in both ancient and recent models and created for himself an eclectic body of knowledge in literature, symbolism and art. In the process he prepared himself as philosopher, moralist and even philologist as well as courtier, lover and poet. If, however, he was to make the most of these gifts, he needed patronage to offer him room at the top and political and diplomatic arts to keep him there. In Spenser's case, as we see, the outcome, a post in Ireland, was a liability as well as a reward, yet it had the virtue of providing for him a political reality with which to test his academic studies of a god-possessed universe.

Extreme care, attention and clarity mark the expositions in the following pages. All readers, no matter how experienced, will find the intricate diagrams a fascination; visual aids that enhance and sharpen the sensitive explication of the poetic texts. They are the true maps of the renaissance. Throughout this distinguished book so many concepts are presented: the poetry of the cosmos, the symbolic nature of the months of the year, the hidden meaning of numbers and the imaginative and intellectual constructions that went to the full language of the renaissance arts. Religion, morality and monarchy are all enshrined there and Spenser's long poems were built out of them.

A Preface to Spenser is the fruit of an intense commitment to the literature of the Middle Ages and the Renaissance. The sensitive awareness and erudition that inform it provide an outstanding intellectual and artistic preparation for the student not only of Spenser but of the entire poetic tradition of more than two centuries and of the whole western world.

MAURICE HUSSEY General Editor

Introduction

The aim of this Preface is to bring Spenser's poetry into touch with the modern reader so that he can share the enjoyment, the stimulus to mental and moral questioning and the experience of 'learning' and enlightenment that an Elizabethan reader felt:

> Thy muse hath got such grace and power to please
> with rare invention bewtified by skill
> As who therein can ever joy their fill!

For a short book on a great and complex writer of an age long past this is no easy matter. It concentrates therefore on the needs of a generation who know no Latin and seldom can 'derive' a word in their heads to try to get at the poet's full meaning, who must seek many a mythological reference in an encyclopaedia and who will not easily relish an implied quotation from Vergil—but who have a serious interest in the past as relevant to the present (and the agony in Ireland is writ large in Spenser's poetry and prose), who have a lively interest in astrology and symbols, and who may find that an imaginative excursion into an ordered universe gives deep satisfaction to a mind under pressure from disintegration and the threat of chaos.

With this aim in mind I have shown how words are made to work under Spenser's hand and how new concepts find expression in pun or name conceit. (The reader who has sampled James Joyce's *Ulysses* will find he is on known ground.) I have tried to show how to read allegory from the inside—to 'ride with the Knight', not appraise from a critic's stance—and to learn from that revealing experience how to make deeper and wider judgments about good and evil in man and society, in the process coming to know oneself better. For a reader of Orwell or one eager to tackle Kafka the challenge is exhilarating.

The passages for particular study are of necessity long, as above all what is new for today's reader is the need to be constantly aware of the whole as the part is entering his mind—to be conscious of the form of the poem as an aspect of its meaning. Diagrams are included as they help here, enabling the reader to 'see' the poet's whole meaning, the interaction of part on part in a complex artistic creation. In that 'seeing' lies the 'truth' aimed at by a renaissance poet, the 'delight' and 'instruction' experienced by his reader.

In reading Spenser we have to be 'wary and wise' like Guyon, and all the time. The best word is E.M. Forster's: 'Only connect!'

H.M.S.

List of Illustrations

Eudoxa to Irenaea

Spenser's Poetry

...it is learned wythout hardnes, such indeede as may be perceived of the leaste, understoode of the mooste, but judged onely of the learned.

Introductory Epistle to *The Shepheardes Calender* 1579

Spenser in what he saith hath a way of expression peculiar to himself; he bringeth down the highest and deepest mysteries that are contained in human learning to an easy and gentle form of delivery...which showeth he is master of what he treateth of, he can wield it as he pleaseth. And he hath done this so cunningly that if one heed him not with great attention, rare and wonderful conceptions will unperceived slide by him that readeth his words, and he will think he hath met with nothing but familiar and easy discourses.

Sir Kenelm Digby, 1638

Part One
The Background

Chronological table

(Thick vertical dividing line indicates Spenser's presence in Ireland)

LIFE	EVENTS
1552 Edmund Spenser born	Reign of Edward VI Ronsard *Amours*; sonnets and odes Raleigh born
1553 1554	Accession of Mary Tudor Mary marries Philip of Spain Philip Sidney born
1557	Tottel's *Miscellany*—plain style iambic poetry
1558 1559	Accession of Queen Elizabeth Act of Uniformity Act of Supremacy Homily of Obedience
1560	Puttenham *Art of English Poetrie*
1561 Foundation of Merchant Taylors' School in London. Spenser a scholarship boy	O'Neill's rebellion in Ireland
1564	Sack of Antwerp: refugees in London Shakespeare born
1566	Translations: Turberville *Mantuan's Eclogues*; Drant *Horace's Art of Poetry*; Golding *Ovid's Metamorphoses* Revolt of the Netherlands
1568	Mary, Queen of Scots, abdicates, flees to England, is imprisoned there Accession of infant James VI Clement Robinson *A Handefull of Pleasant Delites*

2

1569	A Theatre... of Voluptuous Worldlings Spenser at Pembroke Hall, Cambridge	
1570	Friendship with Harvey	Pope excommunicates and deposes Elizabeth as heretic and bastard Ascham *The Schoolmaster* Castelvetro *Poetica d'Aristotele*
1572 1573	Spenser graduates	Camoens *Os Lusiádos*: Ronsard *Franciade* Du Bartas *Judith*; Tasso *Aminta* Gascoigne *Hundred sundry flowers* Massacre of St Bartholomew's Night
1574	Plague in Cambridge Spenser leaves...	
1575		Ronsard *Sonnets pour Hélène* Tasso *Gerusalemme Liberata* Sidney's 'Arcadia' begun Anabaptists burnt in England
1576	Spenser graduates M.A.	The Theatre built in London Sack of Antwerp Frobisher's voyage
1577	Spenser visits Ireland 'in the north parts'— Northamptonshire, Lancashire	Execution of Morrogh Obrien Drake's voyage round the world Blackfriars Theatre in London
1578	Secretary to Young, Bishop of Rochester 'Dreams, Legendes, Pageants, sonetts, Court of Cupide'	Lyly *Euphues* Du Bartas *Sepmaine*

3

1579	In London—service of Lord Leicester: perhaps a continental journey Exchange of letters with Harvey *The Shepheardes Calender* 1579/80	Catholic influence in Scots court Simier in London, on behalf of Alençon Jesuit mission to England Leicester married to Lettice Knollys Countess of Essex, falls from royal favour
1580	Married by April (to Machabyas Chylde?) To Ireland, Secretary to Lord Grey	Sidney *Arcadia*, first version Penelope Devereux marries Lord Rich 'Astrophel and Stella' Battle on River Ure. Siege and massacre at Smerwick
1581		Alençon in England Mulcaster *Positions*
1582	Leases New Abbey, Kildare Birth of a son, Sylvanus	Sidney's *Arcadia*, second version Mulcaster's *Elementarie* Return and disgrace of Lord Grey
1583		Du Bartas; second *Sepmaine* Death of arch-rebel Desmond
1584	With Sir John Norris ? birth of a daughter Katherine ? death of his first wife	Raleigh's failure in Virginia
1585	Deputy to Bryskett as Clerk of Council of Munster	Hooker's sermon *On Justification* 'Munster a graveyard' Norris leaves to serve under Leicester in the Netherlands
1586	Sonnet to Harvey *Foure Letters and Certaine Sonnets*	Settlement of Munster Babington Plot Trial and execution of Mary, Queen of Scots Sidney dies at Zutphen Composition of Connacht Webbe *Discourse of English Poetrie*

1587	Sarah, Spenser's sister marries in Munster	Marlowe 'Tamburlaine' Pope proclaims a crusade against England Drake at Cadiz
1588	Spenser acquires Kilcolman	The Armada Fraunce *Arcadian Rhetoric* mentions Spenser's 'Faerie Queene'
1589	Raleigh visits him there Journey to England 'The Faerie Queene' Bks I–III entered December 1	Marlowe 'Jew', 'Faustus' Drake and Norris to attack Spain
1590	Litigation with Lord Roche Brief return to Ireland (May 30) *The Faerie Queene I–III*	Sidney *Arcadia* Victory of Henri IV at Ivry
1591	*Complaints:* Ruines of Time Teares of the Muses Virgil's Gnat. Prosopopoia or Mother Hubberd's Tale. Muiopotmos, Ruines of Rome (du Bellay), Visions of the World's Vanitie (of Bellay, Petrarch) *Daphnaida* *Shepheardes Calender* (4) Spenser granted a pension	English forces aid Henri IV Sidney *Astrophel and Stella*
1592	Harvey *Three Letters; Four Letters*	Sylvester tr. *Sepmaine—* Bartas *Weekes*
1593	Litigation	Henri IV becomes a Catholic Hooker *Laws of Ecclesiastical Polity* Sidney *Arcadia* (revised) Shakespeare *Venus and Adonis*
1594	Marriage to Elizabeth Boyle	Shakespeare *Lucrece* Daniel *Delia* (sonnets)

5

1595	*Colin Clout's Come Home Againe* 'Astrophel' *Amoretti and Epithalamion* Peregrine Spenser born	Raleigh's voyage to Guiana Southwell executed Sidney *Defence of Poesie*
1596	*Fowre Hymnes* *Prothalamion* *Faerie Queene I–III, IV–VI* *Shepheardes Calender* (5) 'A Vue of the present state of Ireland'	Raleigh and Essex storm Cadiz Spanish aid to the Irish King James protests at 'Duessa'
1597		Bacon's *Essays* 'Second Armada' dispersed
1598	'A Vue' entered for printing but not passed Appointed Sheriff of Cork Kilcolman sacked Return to London	Sidney *Arcadia*; *Astrophel and Stella* Philip II dies. Edict of Nantes. Tyrone rebellion Spanish fleet for Ireland dispersed by gales
1599	Died in London	

6

1 Spenser's Life

'Why Colin since thou foundst such grace
With Cynthia and all her noble crew
Why didst thou ever leave that happie place
In which such wealth might unto thee accrew?
And back returnedst to this barren soyle
Where cold and care and penury do dwell.'

Colin Clout's Come Home Againe 1591

'That there may be an Art of our English Poesie
as well as there is of the Latine and Greeke.'

George Puttenham, *The Arte of English Poesie* 1560

'The great contentment I sometimes enjoyed by his Sweete society,
suffereth not this to passe me, without Respective mention of so true
a friend.'

Robert Salter (1564–1646),
from *Wonderful Prophesies from the Beginning
of the Monarchy of this Land* (1626)

'Mery London, my most kindly Nurse'

The full life story of Edmund Spenser is difficult to tell for several
reasons. Over the first twenty-five years, one half of his life-span,
records or personal documents are sparse. His fortunes and feelings
from childhood on can be glimpsed in certain passages of *The Shepheardes Calender*, printed in 1579; but these facts, happenings and
opinions have been woven into a grand design of poetic art and are
difficult to disengage from it. For the second half of his life his career
as a civil servant in Ireland has left traces in official documents, some
from his own pen, and the general course of his fortunes can be
followed in terms of offices held, properties owned and legal business
transacted. His political treatise written in 1596, *A Vue of the Present
State of Ireland*, illuminates his subject, but the concern is general, not
personal. Our information is such that over his lifetime an important
fact may be known—his passing from the service of the Earl of
Leicester in London to take up an appointment in Ireland—but we
cannot interpret it. We cannot tell for certain why this came about,
either for what reasons or to what end; nor can we ascertain whether
the choice was his, or what disappointment, acquiescence, gratitude,

7

anxiety or satisfaction it aroused in the young poet. Yet the event rightly understood may be the key to his life story.

Most fortunately, however, this poet published his works in print and for the most part appears to have seen them through the press in person. In so printing his poetry he was breaking new ground. Contemporary poets of distinction were men of rank or position: Sir Philip Sidney, Sir Walter Raleigh, Sir Edward Dyer or Fulke Greville. Their work circulated in manuscript among friends and in wider circles of courtiers and men of learning. They did not feel it was either fitting or needful to have their poetry printed. Spenser was of no rank and much humbler condition. The poetry he set himself to write was public poetry, meant for the attention of all educated men in England, treating of issues of state and religion that affected the common weal and, with *The Faerie Queene*, 'fashioning XII moral vertues'—aiming indeed to 'fashion a gentle man or noble person in vertuous and gentle discipline'. The medium of print was essential to his aims and the work of the poet is, with one major exception, on perfect record, virtually as he wished it to be.

A biographical table, then, can record the life of the poet Spenser as his country saw him, through a sequence of works in verse, printed as they became ripe for publication. Against these are plotted the few known facts and dates of his personal life, the main phases of his activity as an official, his contacts with patrons or with other writers. Behind this the inner history of his life can only be divined. His love poetry arises from personal experience but it is not primarily about himself, but about love: the psychic discipline of courtship in the *Amoretti*, the cosmic joy of marriage in the *Epithalamion*. His were 'apprehensions free from personal worry'; they were for mankind, for true religion and for the common weal.

Education: schooldays

Edmund Spenser was born, as far as we know, in the year 1552 in London, child of a merchant family. Without doubt he was exceptionally gifted, and for such a boy, no matter if his family were of very modest means, the way to a fine education was now opening in some parts of Britain. The Renaissance with its revival of classical learning had stimulated new thinking about what children should be taught and how they should be taught it. Change was in the air as it is today; indeed we are witnessing the close of an era that was then in its first vigour, where the grammar school, offering Latin and mathematics as basic subjects, was for the gifted boy the highway to knowledge and opportunity.

Merchant Taylors' School, Suffolk Lane (probably much as it was in Spenser's day): engraving by Sheppard.

These years were marked by an enthusiastic movement to found new schools. Men of wealth and influential and prosperous bodies of citizens devoted time and money and thought to projects of children's education, believing that to do so was to serve the common weal of the realm. The year 1561 saw the foundation of The Merchant Taylors' School, in London, by the Company of Merchant Taylors of that city. Its first master was Richard Mulcaster, an enthusiast and idealist, original in mind and strong in character, and distinguished as a classical scholar. To his new school, possibly in the first year of its existence, Spenser went as a scholarship boy. No greater luck could have befallen him.

Mulcaster's régime was intelligent and liberal if to modern eyes it may appear authoritarian. Spenser's schooling is glimpsed in a contemporary account.

> In a morning [Mulcaster] would exactly construe and parse the lessons of the scholars [that is he would go over their essays and translation exercises]; which done, he slept his hour (custom made him critical to proportion it) in his desk in the school: but woe be to the scholar that slept the while! Awaking, he heard them accurately and Atropos might be persuaded to pity as soon as he to pardon, where he found just fault.

He had a love of order and system, thoroughness and discipline. Penalties were exacted according to a fixed code for 'school faults' such as swearing, lying, truancy or tardiness; and the penalties were stripes—strokes of the birch 'immutable though not many'. In this he was of his day, but in many matters he was advanced. He believed in physical education, because 'soul and body were co-partners in good and ill' and 'we cannot afford to have one strong and the other feeble'. He may or may not have included physical training in the curriculum, but he advocated the value of music as a subject and taught it to his boys. He also regarded acting as important and he presented plays every year before the court in which his boys were actors; this taught them 'good behaviour and audacity'.

He was a master of Greek and Latin but had a regard for the English language that was unusual in those days: it went beyond the teaching of correct and accepted vocabulary and style to an interest in old and regional or 'dialect' words. Poetry had its place in the scheme of studies, and for those boys with an aptitude for creative writing he prescribed wider and fuller reading of it; 'the whole books and arguments' of poets were laid before them. Typical of his liberality of mind was his concern for the education of women, uncommon in those days: 'they have little time to learn much because they haste still on toward husbands'; but he did not doubt their capacity and he believed they should have higher education where their state and circumstances permitted.

How much this was fertile ground for the growth of a poet is obvious. Clear too is the good atmosphere of the schooling Spenser received, the honour and affection in which Mulcaster was held by him and how well his natural gifts for creative writing were trained and fostered while he was at school. When Spenser writes of himself as a poet we can discern through the unfamiliar mode of expression— the 'world of shepherds' in which the actual world is portrayed— something of the early days of a boy attending school in a London from which it was only a short walking distance to open countryside.

> Whilome in youth, when flowered my joyful spring
> Like Swallow swift I wandred here and there:
> For heate of heedlesse lust* me so did sting,
> That I of doubted danger had no feare.
> I went the wastefull† woods and forest wyde
> Withouten dreade of Wolves to bene espyed.

> I wont to rainge amydde the mazie thickette
> And gather nuttes to make me Christmas game:
> And ioyed oft to chace the trembling Prickett
> Or hunt the hartlesse hare til shee were tame
> What wreaked I of wintrye ages waste,
> Tho deemed I, my spring would ever laste.

> How often have I scaled the craggie Oke
> All to dislodge the Raven of her neste:
> How have I wearied with many a stroke
> The stately Walnut tree, the while the rest
> Under the tree fell all for nuts at strife:
> For ylike to me was libertee and lyfe.

> And for I was in thilke same looser yeares
> (Whether the Muse so wrought me from my birth
> Or I tomuch beleeved my shepherd peres)
> Somedele ybent to song and musicks mirth.
> A good old shephearde, Wrenock was his name
> Made me by art more cunning in the same.

Thus speaks Colin Clout, Spenser's name for himself in the pastoral world of shepherds. And Wrenock is Mulcaster—a diminutive of 'wren', *regulus* in Latin, 'a little king'. Apparently Mulcaster was small in size, commanding great authority.

Spenser, then, was in debt to Mulcaster for many attitudes and qualities we shall find in his character and writing: enthusiasm for the

* lust—vital energy.
† wasteful—undeveloped.

widely educated and finely trained individual, respect for discipline and self-discipline, faith in the English tongue in all its variety, and a desire to extend and enrich the language in which English poetry was written (especially by drawing on native sources), an eager ambition to produce illustrious works in English, and a zealous patriotism.

In 1569, his schooldays over, Spenser was ready to pursue his studies further at a university. But in the very year he went up to college at Cambridge at the age of, say, seventeen, verses of his appeared in print. While encouragement from his schoolmaster must have contributed to making this come about, the fact that Spenser was a London boy at this particular moment in history was also an important factor. London was flooded by Protestant refugees from the Netherlands, after the sack of Antwerp by the Spanish overlords there. The refugees fought back with words in print and the school-boy's skill in verse composition was elicited in the publication of literature of propaganda. It is seldom that a poet *as poet* is brought so young into close contact with international crisis and international controversy in political and religious issues. It was new that a poet so young should see his work published in print.

Catholic Spain—the occupying power in the Low Countries—was rendering liberty of conscience impossible for some of the subject people, the Protestant Dutch and Flemings. These refugees were of all walks of life, many of them men of talent and skill, intellectuals, writers, poets and master-craftsmen such as printers and engravers. Among them was the poet and propagandist Jan van der Noot. In London he found freedom to issue in print poetry for which he was already known. It now appeared in his native Dutch and also translated into French and English. The volume that contained his work was entitled in English *A Theatre wherein be represented as wel the miseries and calamities that follow the voluptuous Worldlings, As also the great ioyes and pleasures which the faithfull do enjoy* (an argument both profitable and delectable to all that sincerely love the word of God). This book was an exhortation against worldliness and at the same time an attack on the shortcomings of the Roman Catholic Church. (Who 'the faithfull' were was in no doubt.) To render the message as effective as possible the book had pictures and poetry, the pictures matched to the poetry in a style that was already familiar on the continent but now reached print in England for the first time. This style was that of the Emblem Books, of which we shall have more to say.

Van der Noot's *Theatre* was made up of a sequence of 'visions' meant to set the vanity and perishable nature of worldly things vividly before the reader's eyes, to demonstrate change and its moral and spiritual significance. The poetry was famous poetry, some of it undeniably proceeding from the earlier Catholic world. There were six visions of Petrarch, great poet of fourteenth-century Italy, showing the death of 'Laura', and Laura meant poetic fame as well as the beloved ideal lady. There were ten visions of Joachim du Bellay, a distinguished writer of the new Renaissance poetry of France; these were pieces showing the ruins of Rome, poems written on the decay of the ancient city of the Roman Empire, symbol of antique civilisation, but as presented now they pointed towards the downfall of the Church of Rome. Finally there were four visions by van der Noot himself, of themes drawn from the Bible, the Book of Revelations, where phenomena of St John's apocalyptic vision were read as foretelling the destruction of the Catholic Church. The verses and engravings show several images that figure in Book I of *The Faerie Queene*.

The engraving for Sonet 7 from du Bellay shows the Tiber as river-god and spirit of ancient Rome, crowned with laurel and bearing palm for victory and olive-branch for peace. Beside him is the she-wolf that suckled Romulus and Remus, Rome's legendary founders—the heraldic arms of the city. The buildings in the background include the Coliseum, to be used symbolically in the first woodcut of *The Shepheardes Calender* (p.100).

An extensive commentary in prose by van der Noot made sure that the pictures and poetry drove home his message. The whole work is strange to modern eyes, but to that generation it was urgent in message and novel and striking in presentation. There had not been

*Rome, the river Tiber
—from A Theatre:
the buildings show the
Coliseum.*

13

many books of poetry with pictures before. For the edition of it in English the poetry in three languages had to be translated into English verse and it was for this that the talents of the young Spenser were drawn on. Fourteen of the verse translations are from his pen. He must have been given learned help with some texts, and he improved several of his versions before giving them for print again. But already there are lines that have the true Spenserian sound.

> But many Muses and the Nymphes withall
> That sweetely in accorde did tune their voice
> Unto the gentle sounding of the water's fall . . .

How profoundly the nature of this first poetic commission influenced Spenser's habit of thought and mode of expression we shall later see. It took him in one step into the heart of religious controversy, Protestantism against Catholicism, among people who faced death or exile for the sake of freedom of worship according to the form of Christianity they regarded as the true one. It brought his mind into close contact with great poetry of the Renaissance from earlier Italy and from contemporary France, Petrarch and du Bellay. It set him to work on verse whose meaning was already matched to pictorial representations. He drank in the allegorical way of thinking and feeling about moral and spiritual truths rendered in visual terms, in pictures and symbols. He found himself deeply involved in expressing the theme of stability and instability, what was eternal and unchanging and what was subject to time and decay, to the mutability that was to be his deep concern throughout his poetic life. And he saw the stupendous visions of the Apocalypse linked with the realities of sixteenth-century Europe, the battle of beliefs and creeds that issued in armed strife between individuals and nations. This battle of beliefs and creed still issues in bloodshed in our modern world, still rooted in territorial anxieties and national consciousness. Look only at the papers for the news from the Near East or from Northern Ireland.

'*My mother Cambridge*' *1569–76*

Cambridge in Spenser's day was a centre of learning isolated from the rest of England by its fenland situation and the difficulties of overland travel in winter. Access was by waterway. For the nine months of the academic year the student's college would be his home in term and vacation alike. Spenser's college, Pembroke Hall, was a 'little' college numbering in all about a hundred persons in residence—teachers, students and servants. His studies would be pursued there but also in the university, as he would listen to lectures by senior members of other colleges as well.

What did he study? According to the statutes the student devoted his first year to rhetoric in Latin or in English, learning to express his meaning effectively, how to marshal his thoughts and shape an argument, with the examples before him of great writers of antiquity such as Plato and Aristotle (probably in Latin translation) or Quintilian and Cicero. In his second year he studied logic; in his third philosophy, the course being based on works by Aristotle, Cicero, Pliny and Plato. He would learn how to argue a case, answer objections and defend or attack a point of view. He would have to practise in public speechmaking and disputation. Such a course completed to the satisfaction of the examiners, he would graduate as Bachelor of Arts. For a further three years he might continue studies in philosophy as well as learning drawing, astronomy and Greek, both the language and the literature.

Living at close quarters in his college with dons and fellow-students and mixing in lectures with men from other colleges, the student was perforce involved in the controversies that were agitating senior and junior members alike: issues of religion and politics, of this or that theory or mode of education, this or that view of values in learning and scholarship. By the same token students are involved today in controversy, in moral, political or economic theories, and are exposed to religious enthusiasm and partisan loyalties in a variety of forms that now extend far beyond Christendom.

At the time that Spenser went to Cambridge sharp differences of opinion in respect of religion and Church government were dividing college from college and severing members of a college from one another. (It should be realised that almost all dons were in religious orders.) Elizabeth soon after becoming Queen had turned the country from the Catholicism of her sister Mary back towards the Protestantism of her brother Edward, Mary's predecessor on the throne. She had honestly sought a religious settlement that would content the majority of her people; but with characteristic diplomacy she had taken a middle way, approving an organization of the church and ritual that would remind her Catholic subjects of a church they still venerated while at the same time providing a system of doctrine satisfactory to her Protestant subjects. Extremists however, Catholic or Puritan, continued to hold their views with determination. Voices were heard within the university loudly championing both poles of opinion.

Outstanding personalities of the day were Thomas Cartwright of St John's College, Professor of Divinity and a Presbyterian eloquent in preaching that point of view. Against him were ranged the Masters of two colleges, Grindal, at that time Archbishop of York, and John Whitgift, later to be Archbishop. Whitgift was passionately loyal to Elizabeth's establishment and also an eloquent preacher. On the other hand, the Master of Caius College was Roman Catholic in creed and sympathies. Both sides of the Cartwright/Whitgift controversy expressed their convictions in a war of pamphlets for or against the establishment. The dispute was carried to 'Whitehall', as it were, in an appeal to the Chancellor of the University. Cartwright the Presbyterian who had a vigorous and vociferous following among the students, was suspended.

Such personalities and issues could not but make their impact on the student Spenser: witness the fact that ten years later they were to feature prominently in his first major work, *The Shepheardes Calender*, his first essay in mirroring in poetry the realm, the common weal and man's lot in it.

In the year 1572, Spenser's third year of study, Cambridge was rent by dissension that centred on new statutes devised for the University. Their provision for the wearing of caps and surplices became touch points for confrontation of establishment by dissenters. In the greater world outside the political climate was thundery, as we shall see, because of the proposal of a match for the Queen with a prince of Catholic France. In the August of that year the whole of England was horrified by reports of the 'massacre of St Bartholomew's night', where in one night the men who were the mainspring of the Huguenot (Protestant) party in France had been treacherously done to death. Opinion in England hardened against the Catholics as Huguenot refugees brought to London details of the horror. In Cambridge Puritan voices were raised in anger and there was a violent demonstration against the Catholic Master of Caius College, with public burning of mass books and treasures of ecclesiastical art. In this atmosphere Spenser was formulating his thoughts about creed and conscience, about values in government of Church and state.

Graduating as Bachelor of Arts in 1573, Spenser continued at Cambridge to study for a higher degree. And now for the first time we begin to have direct information about his personal friendships and loyalties. The first of these was with Gabriel Harvey, a young don of Pembroke Hall, newly elected Fellow in Spenser's second year there. He was handsome, ambitious, devoted to the study of Latin and Greek literature, and interested also in English and Italian writers. Others found him egotistical and eccentric, but over a number of years a firm friendship between these two gifted young men is recorded in letters passing between them—some of these private communications, some more self-consciously literary pieces composed with possible publication in view. From now on Harvey's ambition, his desire to achieve as Machiavelli recommended, can be felt behind the young poet. Harvey 'is' Hobbinol of *The Shepheardes Calender*:

> Fro thence I durst in derring doe compare
> With Shepheards swayne, what ever fedde in field:
> And if that *Hobbinol* right judgement bare
> To *Pan* his owne selfe pype I neede not yield.
>> For if the flocking Nymphes did follow *Pan*
>> The wiser Muses after *Colin* ranne.

In plain prose, Spenser was writing poetry during his years at Cambridge as were other students. Pastoral poetry (verses written in the convention of 'the world of shepherds') was the popular mode, and Harvey found Spenser's work in it outstanding. Another friend of thòse days was Edward Kirke, who was in on the preparation of *The Shepheardes Calender* and indeed may have contributed towards the commentary that was to accompany the poetry when it appeared in print.

In 1574 the plague appeared in Cambridge and, as far as we know, Spenser's presence there is not recorded thereafter. There are several mentions of his being in poor health. He may have tried for a College Fellowship and not been successful. (Being elected to a fellowship meant that the successful candidate became a senior and permanent member of his college, residing there, retained to do teaching and to pursue advanced study.) We know only that he graduated Master of Arts in 1576, his place in the class lists not being a distinguished one. From his poetry and from the letters we learn that during these last years began a love affair between the poet and a lady who features in his verses as 'Rosalind'.

For the next few years of Spenser's life we have no certain knowledge of his whereabouts. The love affair with 'Rosalind' continued and she was someone whom Harvey knew, so she may have belonged to the Cambridge region. At some point Spenser apparently gave up writing poetry for a while—we do not know why. He was for a certain period far away, 'farre estranged', as the preface to the *Calender* tells us. A journey to Ireland and back during this period is probable if we discern personal record in his writings. The *Calender* shows one Diggon Davie returned in rags from a sojourn in a land where 'was all of miserye' and in Spenser's prose treatise (in dialogue form) one of the speakers was present at the execution of a notable Irish traitor (or hero of the resistance) which took place at Limerick in 1577. Another possible journey of this time was to north-east Lancashire, where a local tradition has it that he resided while writing *The Faerie Queene*. Here there was a family of Spencers that have been claimed as forebears of the poet.

That we may relate what actually happened to Spenser to what is presented in his verses is supported by one important passage in the *Calender*. The June Eclogue, which gives Colin Clout's lament at the loss of Rosalind, has Hobbinol counselling Colin:

> Then if by me thou list advised be
> Forsake the soyle that so doth the bewitch...
> And to the dales resort, where shepheards ritch
> And fruictfull flocks bene every where to see.

The commentary notes: 'This is no poetical fiction but unfeygnedly spoken of the Poete selfe, who for speciall occasion of private affayres

Bishop's Palace, Bromley, Kent, 1756. Spenser was secretary here to the Bishop of Rochester in 1578.

(as I have bene partly of himselfe informed) and for his more pre-ferment removing out of the Northparts came into the South, as Hobbinol indeede advised him privately.' The 'Southpartes where he nowe abydeth' is Kent. In plain prose, Spenser had for a while continued in or near Cambridge without preferment in academic life and with a love story that ended unhappily. Taking the advice of the worldly-wise Harvey he now sought advancement in the London region, near the centre of affairs.

The 'Southern Shepherd's Boy'

In Spring 1578 Dr John Young, distinguished London clergyman and at the same time Master of Pembroke Hall, became Bishop of Rochester. The Bishop's Palace was at Bromley in Kent, in those days lying deep in country woods and fields, yet only two hours' ride from London. At some point during Young's first year as Bishop, Edmund Spenser became his secretary, at the age of about twenty-six. He would now be aware of affairs of Church and state at closer quarters. For a couple of years the Bishop's secretary found Rochester not too far from the capital of the realm. He was now a young man of fashion, 'a young Italianate signor and French Monsieur', bearded and moustachioed, frequenting the theatre with other lively wits.

All this we learn from letters of Harvey. The two friends had a long discussion on how a young man might best advance his fortunes in England. There was only one answer in those days, through patronage. Spenser had no distinguished family connections, though he apparently claimed some kinship with the wealthy Spencers of Althorp in Northamptonshire. But he was finely educated and he was by vocation and training a poet. His hope lay in winning recognition for his poetry. And that meant finding a powerful patron to back him. It necessitated his production for publication of a substantial work that could be dedicated to this patron, a work in nature and quality such as would redound to his patron's credit. This exigency was new for a poet, as we saw. The printing of poetry by living authors was a recent development. Such verse as reached print was often 'useful' in matter, or was translation or imitation of the classics. The volume of verses by Thomas Howell, his *Arbor of Amity* of 1568, was a rare precedent—and he was an official in the service of the Sidney family, and therefore modestly in touch with the cultivation of poetry at its very centre. Gascoigne and Breton had published 'handfuls' of lyrics, and Gascoigne a substantial poem. But Spenser's way was not quite clear.

The men of rank and power with whom we know Spenser to be at least in touch were, first and foremost, the Earl of Leicester, the great favourite of Queen Elizabeth and a champion of Protestantism; then Philip Sidney (beloved nephew of Leicester) and Sir Edward Dyer, a close friend of the Sidneys. Philip Sidney was himself a distinguished poet in the 'sweet new style' caught from the poetry of Italy. Dyer, an older man, was a poet too, if of an older fashion. Something like a 'school' of poetry, certainly a literary circle, had grown up round Sidney, his sister (the Countess of Pembroke) and his friends. A third poet member was Fulke Greville, and we can see in the works of those three how they exchanged poems or chose a theme for each to write on. No account of the circle survives; but apparently it was called the 'Areopagus' and was modelled on the poetic academy of Florence under Ficino, as were the academies of poetry in contemporary France. Spenser for a time served Lord Leicester and was on a friendly footing with Sidney and Dyer, but there is no trace in Spenser's works of his inclusion in the poetic activities of the aristocratic circle. He was on the outer fringe only of the wellborn company who attended the court of Queen Elizabeth.

In order to fulfil his vocation as poet, of which he was by now quite sure, Spenser had to find apt employment that promised advancement but would leave him some leisure for study and writing. In October of 1579 we hear in a letter that he was in high hopes of being sent to France and even farther afield on some mission in the service of the Earl of Leicester. He is looking forward to this as exciting in itself and promising well for the future, but he is in love and does not

Robert Dudley, Earl of Leicester: by Nicholas Hilliard, 1576.

relish the thought of leaving his beloved behind. He has a poetical work of some substance ready for publication and is worrying whether he may or may not fitly dedicate it to Leicester. (Dedication was a chancy business, a work recently dedicated to Philip Sidney had not been well looked on by that gentleman.)

Spenser may indeed have gone to France on a short mission. But the extended continental service for Leicester did not come to pass. Whether the projected mission abroad itself fell through, whether it was declined by Spenser or his employment on it was spectacularly cancelled by Leicester, we do not know. And this uncertainty is tantalizing if we seek to understand the whole pattern of Spenser's life as it was now unfolding. Certainly the year 1579 (March to March for in those days the year was reckoned in this way) was momentous for the young poet. His love affair prospered into marriage with a lady called Machabyas Chylde; it was celebrated at St Margaret's, Westminster on October 27. And on December 5 his poetical work *The Shepheardes Calender* was entered for printing and appeared before that year ran out—perhaps indeed by January 1, certainly by the March to follow, when 1579 'old style' ran out.

The volume did not bear the name of Edmund Spenser on its titlepage, and it was dedicated not to Leicester but to 'M. Philip Sidney . . . most worthy of all titles both of learning and chevalrie'. The author was named as 'Immerito', which can be construed as the modest 'undeserving' but also as 'he who has not yet been rewarded or recognized'. The book was a notable success. And Spenser in 1580 went to Ireland as secretary to Lord Grey, who had been newly appointed Lord Governor there. This chance of employment Spenser owed in all probability to recommendation by Philip Sidney whose father had earlier held the same office, that of the Queen's representative in Ireland.

Is the story so far a straightforward one of advancement in the career of a young man who was a poet of some distinction and great promise? Or should we note a change of patron and a disappointment of early hopes of travel on the continent and widening cultural horizons, a non-occurrence of appointment on a minor diplomatic errand that might have been a first step to a placing within sight and sound of the Queen's court? Was this posting as a secretary in the wild and troubled country of Ireland a second-best, amounting indeed to a kind of banishment from London and the court environment? We cannot tell for certain how he regarded it at that time, but he came to see it as 'my lucklesse lot/That banisht had my selfe like wight forlore/Into the waste, where I was quite forgot.'

The whole story of the crucial year 1579 has not come to light. Offence was given to 'a great peer', we gather. Spenser's composition of *Prosopopoia or Mother Hubberd's Tale* could understandably have given offence to Lord Burleigh. His publication in print of *The Shepheardes Calender* was singularly unfortunate in its timing in so far as it touched on private affairs of Lord Leicester, as we shall later see. Spenser's humbler fortunes were interwoven with events and personalities at the very highest level of state and policy. To follow them we need to understand the dynamics of society in the realm of England under Elizabeth Tudor: the character of the Queen as woman and monarch, the court and the system of royal or noble patronage as focus of endeavour for any man of talents or ambition, the relation in which England stood to the European power struggle in this era, and the part Ireland played in all this. Only then can we appreciate how a distinguished poet fared, who wrote for England the great national epic that every nation hoped for at the Renaissance but who yet failed to win the reward of place, title, lands and position in his native land that his achievement and service might seem to have merited.

With Lord Grey: Dublin to New Abbey

The new Lord Deputy, Arthur Lord Grey, stepped ashore in Ireland in August 1580 and with him, we must think, his new secretary. From now on Spenser would be much in his master's company, in Dublin Castle where lay the seat of administration or journeying with him up and down the country. Spenser and at least one other secretary were responsible for the official correspondence, the

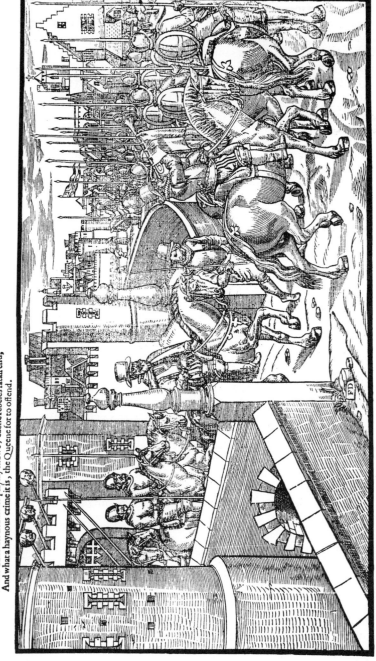

These truncles heddes do playnly showe, eache rebeles fatall end,
And what a haynous crime it is, the Queene for to offend.

recording and copying of documents, but they would have aman-
uenses (copyists by hand) under them. That much we know from the
presence of the poet's own handwriting which has been identified and
traced through items in official papers that have survived.

To envisage Spenser's way of life in his new surroundings we follow
Lord Grey, which will of necessity trace the story of unrest in the land,
and we take note of the process by which over the same period the
secretary consolidated his position in the new country, winning
additional appointments which were often sinecures, brought into
contact with matters of leases and grants of land and himself setting
down roots in the soil of Ireland. There is also a glimpse of his leisure,
his friends, his interests, studies and conversations. And all the while
the busy secretary is pushing on with the composition of his great
poem. These are not separable concerns. They intertwine all the way.
Spenser was energetically engaged on both courses to which Bel-
phoebe/Gloriana summoned men to her service in *The Faerie Queene*
—'Abroad in arms, at home in studious kind'.

Spenser had not been long in Ireland before he met congenial
company. In a cottage near Dublin lived Lodowick Bryskett, civil
servant and man of letters. The son of a Genoese merchant settled in
London he had studied in Cambridge (entering in 1559) and he had
companioned Philip Sidney on the grand tour of Europe made by
that young nobleman. He was now Clerk of the Council in Dublin.
We find a secondary appointment passing from him to Spenser as
Bryskett moved on to one more gainful. He too was on his way to
become a land-holder, an 'adventurer' or 'undertaker' in the process
of Elizabethan settlement of the land, and in the end a 'landed
gentleman'—in Irish terms. He too was anxious to conserve some
time for his writing.

Soon after the poet's arrival we find him recorded in Bryskett's
company, spending happy hours in discussion of issues philosophic
and 'scientific'. Bryskett was making a version in English of an Italian
work by Giraldo Cintio on the education of a gentleman; it was
eventually published in 1606 as *A Discourse of Civil Life*. As was
customary with such a writing, a background was sketched in, giving
the circle of friends and the subjects they discussed. Thanks to those
pages we know that Spenser had offered to teach Bryskett Greek and
that the company now requested the poet to discourse to them on 'the
great benefits which men obtained by the knowledge of Morall
Philosophie—and in making us to know what the same is, what be
the parts thereof, whereby vertues are to be distinguished from vices'.
Spenser countered this:

Sir Henry Sidney, Lord Governor, rides out from Dublin Castle.

The house built by the abbey ruins may date from Spenser's time.

I have already undertaken a work tending to the same effect, which is in *heroical verse* under the title of a *Faerie Queene* to represent all the moral vertues, assigning to every vertue a Knight to be the patron and defender of the same, in whose actions and feats of arms and chivalry the operations of that vertue whereof he is the protector, are to be expressed, and the vices and unruly appetites that oppose themselves against the same, to be beaten down and overcome.

He therefore begged to be excused, but turned the compliment by suggesting that Bryskett read from his work in progress and that they discuss it. A lively desire to read Spenser's poem was engendered and indeed 'some parcels' of it were already in circulation among them. The sentences recorded from Spenser here provide an important view of the purpose and method of his heroic poem now in process of composition.

The leasing or granting of property to English officials was a recognised mode of acknowledging loyal service rendered by them to the Crown. Such properties were in Crown control because they had been forfeited by rebels or had been in English hands since the dissolution of the Irish monasteries. Spenser in 1582 had a house in Dublin that had belonged to (the rebel) Lord Baltinglas. As a personal venture he bought and sold the lease of a number of other properties. In 1582 he leased the site of a house of friars called New

Abbey in County Kildare 'with appurtenances including an old waste town' adjoining, which was in the Queen's disposition since the earlier 'Desmond' rebellion (p. 24). This lay near the banks of the Liffey and bordered on the Bog of Allen. Spenser took up residence at New Abbey and just before Lord Grey left Ireland the lease passed finally into his hands. By this time Books I to III of *The Faerie Queene* were completed and the Liffey and the Bog of Allen had found their way into the pattern of his imaginings. By 1583 he was Edmund Spenser of New Abbey, Kildare, responsible as a gentleman for the muster of arms.

Spenser's work as secretary was not safe and sedentary. Following Lord Grey meant travelling widely in Ireland, on horseback in wild country, seldom by made roads but by tracks through bog and glen, mountain and forest, the landscape varying from rich pasture and farmland and orchard to tracts of once fertile territory laid waste and now overgrown, ruined by war, spoliation, famine and depopulation. Spenser was now witnessing at close quarters the work of an administrator who sought in the name of the Crown to execute justice in wellnigh impossible conditions; to keep law and order in the small part of Ireland under English occupation of long standing and to protect that part from the hostility of the rest of the island.

Grey's first exercise was to deal sharply with English troops in West Meath, of whose extortions the people were complaining bitterly. (The English forces in Ireland were less an organized army than bands of men who had been recruited locally in England and were now ill-paid, ill-clad for the climate and often hungry. The pattern of recruitment was still not very different from that glimpsed in Shakespeare's histories.) This year was a time of peril in Ireland. Bryskett reported to Walsingham at home that the crisis was urgent. Indeed in the far south-west of the land a force of six hundred mercenaries from Italy under Spanish officers—sent as they declared themselves by the Pope and the Catholic King of Spain to whom the Pope had granted Ireland—had made a fortified place in Elizabeth's realm, in the fort above Smerwick harbour. To dislodge them Lord Grey and Walter Raleigh hastened there in substantial force. With English support at sea the besieged were doomed men, for no help came to them from the Irish rebels. An unconditional surrender was forced and was followed by a massacre. This was notorious conduct in terms of 'honourable warfare' but the obvious course of a weak administration terrified by the dangerous combination of 'malice domestic and foreign levy'. Grey's forces were outnumbered by their prisoners and Irish help might arrive at any moment. This clash of wrongs resounded in Spenser's imagination and echoed in his Book of Justice.

Both within the Pale and without, rebellion was muttering. In the south Munster under Lord Ormonde had not been subdued, while to the north in Ulster the O'Neill in power pretended friendship but plotted revolt. Lord Grey appealed to Elizabeth for money and troops to meet the threat, but instead she sent a general pardon. Hamstrung, Lord Grey sent home a request to be recalled. An expedition south as far as Wexford, the oldest colony of the English dating from the Norman Conquest of Ireland, resulted in Ormonde's command in Munster being terminated. At the same time it revealed to Spenser the way of life of the 'old English' in Ireland, whose costume was antiquated and whose language was English of an earlier time, by now much mixed with Irish. On an expedition to Ulster Grey attempted pacification by friendly negotiation, and Spenser saw the beauty of the northern region, its mountains, lakes and pasturable lands. He saw too its strategic importance and the enormous potential for civilized development of a region that had once been the most important part of the English Pale. When Lord Grey turned south again to Munster he found the south devastated by what we now call 'scorched earth policy' and, to make matters worse, pillaged by persistent rebels.

Not only was Lord Grey frustrated in his course of enforcing order by strong measures because denied the means to do so, but also he was assailed in England by complaints that he was rewarding too freely those under him who were loyally furthering his policy. The year 1581/82 saw the execution of notable rebels 'chiefly for ensample sake' in hope of quelling the hundreds who remained untaken. Whether he proceeded with severity in the hope of frightening disaffected elements into quiescence, whether he attempted to consolidate by rewarding loyal service, or whether he of necessity appealed for more money and more troops, he could not please the Queen. Devastation in the south continued under the great rebel, the Earl of Desmond.

In August 1582 Lord Grey set sail for England. It had been made clear that his appointment was at an end. In London he met with strong expression of royal displeasure, fierce censure by critics and slanderous attacks by enemies. Spenser admiring the man and upholding his policy from firsthand knowledge of the issues, defended his conduct in the treatise 'A Vue' and in poetic fiction featured him in *The Faerie Queene* as an aspect of the Knight of Justice, Artegall.

Why did Spenser remain in an Ireland so perilous, so liable to burst into flames of rebellion? Why did he not go back with Lord Grey? The issue must have arisen. To return to England as one who had served Lord Grey faithfully, and been rewarded for it, would be to share in his disgrace, to be without prospects of appointment or office, to have a black cloud of disfavour as climate in which to publish his heroic poem, his life's work as a poet. It was surely better to stay where he had some footing and a reputation for work well done, and in a land whose countryside he had come to love for its surpassing beauty and whose antiquities and legends had seized his imagination. He would be no more at the hub of government affairs in Ireland; but, only a day's ride from Dublin, he had the chance to be a man of substance, a landed gentleman—if in Irish terms. Bryskett, disappointed in official advancement, had already made his choice, to reside at his place in Wexford and 'pick a living from the soil'.

The new Lord Deputy was Sir John Perrot, committed to winning over the Irish by conciliation. Now begins in our story the fatal pattern of events that Spenser traces in his treatise—vacillation of Crown policy in the government of Ireland through alternation of policies—severity or conciliation—as one Lord Governor succeeded another.

With John and Thomas Norris: Munster

Spenser's decision to stay soon yielded fruit; he became deputy to Ludowick Bryskett who was now Clerk in Dublin to the Council of Munster. (Munster, Leinster, Ulster and Connacht were the four administrative regions of Ireland.) The appointment meant for the poet close attendance on the President of Munster (governor of the province) an office now held by Sir John Norris and later by his brother Thomas. Sir John Norris was a distinguished soldier of European experience; he is celebrated in a sonnet prefacing *The Faerie Queene*. After a vigorous campaign against the rebels in the north he faced his task in Munster, to 'bring order into a land of corpses'. (The arch-rebel Earl of Desmond had met his death in a private feud in 1583.) A professional soldier, Sir John Norris had little stomach for this task and was soon transferred to martial command against the Spanish forces in the Netherlands.

Survey of Munster had convinced authority that the only possible course was resettlement of the region by 'undertakers' from England. 'Plantation' was pursued with vigour. What this entailed is explained in the chapter on Ireland.

In 1588 the Spanish Armada sailed, was defeated by the seamanship of the English and was 'scattered by the winds of God'. Alliance in the cause of the Apostolic faith and in enmity to the Tudor power did not save the lives of Spanish troops shipwrecked on Ireland's savage coast. Many of them were murdered and spoiled. The hour of the Armada was not matched by an organized Irish rising as had been dreamed. Mary, Queen of Scots, had been executed; but Spain could now muster a Catholic pretender to the English throne and might strike again.

As the decade closed enthusiasm for the plantation was waning. It proved more difficult to persuade English families to come over. It is not surprising that a number of the 'undertakers' (colonizers)

acknowledged failure and withdrew from the project. But it is worthy of note that one, Sir William Herbert, in Kerry, was praised by some (and maligned by others) for his good understanding and courteous handling of Irish in his region. We should recall this as we pass in *The Faerie Queene* from The Book of Justice to The Book of Courtesy, where a gentler 'savage man' appears, as well as ferocious brigands, and a gentler way with the 'savage man' is envisaged.

It is in this context of history and geography that we must see Edmund Spenser's move to become undertaker of an extensive seigneury in Munster, where his lands would neighbour those of Sir Walter Raleigh (some 20,000 acres wide), with those of Sir Christopher Hatton beyond. At Kilcolman in County Cork he became, by 1590, master of an extensive property of hill, forest and pasturable and cultivable land, and of a ruined castle that had been the home of a Desmond. There a house had to be built, according to the undertakers' agreement. The region is of great beauty, richly forested, watered by the Rivers Blackwater, Awbeg and Bregog and stretching up to the Galtee Mountains, to which in his poetry he gave the 'old' name of 'Mole' (see page 62). And nearby was Aherlo, or Ar.o, a fastness of mountain and forest, notorious as a refuge of rebels, outlaws and the dispossessed.

Kilcolman 1590

Spenser, approaching forty years of age, was now a landed gentleman of extensive property. His heroic poem was so far towards completion that a manuscript of its opening Books was circulating in London among discriminating company. Christopher Marlowe had read it and had paid it the compliment of stealing a verse. Abraham Fraunce in his *Arcadian Rhetorike* (1588) had quoted a stanza from Book II, naming Book, canto and author. Spenser's *Calender* was in vigorous circulation reprinted in 1581 and 1586; it had been warmly praised by William Webbe in his *Discourse of English Poetrie*. Spenser had been abroad in the savage island for eight years, but his reputation as a fine poet was very much alive in London.

At his house of Kilcolman Spenser had with him two children of his first marriage, Sylvanus born about 1582 and Katherine, probably younger. Of his wife there is no record: presumably she had died some time before. There is mention of his sister Sarah, who at some point had come over to Ireland, where she married and settled in Munster. The years had not been without difficulty. There was a persistent feud with Lord Roche, an Irish neighbour who queried at law Spenser's title to some of his lands.

Kilcolman Castle, Co. Cork: an ancient stronghold of the Desmonds, 'granted' to Spenser.

The atmosphere in Ireland at that time can be readily gauged. A spell of comparative quiet had ensued but now 'if it was changing, it was for the worse'. The year 1590 saw a mutiny in the English forces by Sir Thomas Norris's company of foot, who marched from the south to Dublin and confronted authority, demanding arrears of pay—to be met by a demonstration of that authority with display of the Sword of State. There was a new Lord Deputy, Sir William Fitzwilliam. In Ulster the lordship of the O'Neills had passed to Hugh O'Neill created by Elizabeth Earl of Tyrone, a brilliant and formidable personality whose story will be told later.

The time was now ripe for some part of *The Faerie Queene* to be published; of that the poet was convinced by Sir Walter Raleigh, who visited him at Kilcolman and persuaded him to come to London. In Raleigh's company he made the journey, spent some months in England and saw through the press *The Faerie Queene*, Books I to III. At the same time he saw published a volume of *Complaints* and a short pastoral elegy *Daphnaida*.

As author of *The Faerie Queene* he was introduced to the court and to the Queen's presence and was rewarded for his heroic poem in February 1591 with a pension of £50 a year as long as he lived. Dazzled by the presence of Elizabeth his monarch and the 'Gloriana' of his poetry, delighted to pay tribute to the poets who served her and the gracious ladies who attended her, he yet was not blind to what was false or vicious in court life: flattery, conspiracy, backbiting and long suing for favour by merit that went unrewarded. This whole experience was deeply moving and disturbing and he transmuted it into poetry in *Colin Clout's Come Home Againe*. The particular and personal experience becomes 'ideal' as he searches out the essential meaning and expresses this in moral and spiritual values. Pastoral tradition offered him the perfect vehicle: two favourite themes of the pastoral are intertwined—the shepherd's journey from 'shepherd-land' to sophisticated society and back (with meditation on the experience), and the singing match where shepherds sing in contest on the theme of love. The stay in England had included time spent in wooing 'Rosalind' and the wooing had not won acknowledgement of his devotion in love returned, but his faith in love is unshaken, his devotion undying. This poem is an exploration of love on earth in all aspects—abuse of love in incestuous lust punished by oblivion, love-service of sweetheart and love-service of Queen-monarch, love conceived 'philosophically' in myth of classical antiquity as a cosmic force creating and holding creatures in harmony; behind this last is glimpsed the working of love divine, God's love in Christian terms. *Colin Clout's Come Home Againe* was written after his return to Ireland that spring and the dedicatory letter that stands at the head of the printed poem is subscribed, 'From my house of Kilcolman the 27 of December, 1591'. The entitling of the poem raises the query, which was now 'home' for the poet Spenser, England or Ireland? He was back in his countryside of wood and water that he loved and wove into his poetry; things were quieter in Munster but the night-alarum, wailing and sudden death were never far away, and he was struggling in litigation with Lord Roche. The coming of a new Lord Deputy of whom he thought highly, Sir William Russell, was offset by the renewal of rumours of invasion.

Love and marriage

Spenser, whose first wife had died some time before, had been wooing a lady called Elizabeth Boyle who came from a region of England no distance from the ladies of Althorp. Part of the courtship may have taken place in England during the poet's recent stay there but Elizabeth and her brother had come over to the neighbourhood of Cork apparently under the guardianship of an uncle who was a power in the region. The courtship and its course of love, with joys, rebuffs, delays, absence, and delight in beauty, laughter and gracious company is written into a sonnet sequence, the *Amoretti*. It is Spenser's story, but it traces for everyman a deepening experience of love as a discipline of the soul. And when it was printed it culminated in the splendid celebration of love fulfilled in marriage in the *Epithalamion*.

We are not completely sure of the year in which Spenser married Elizabeth Boyle; it was probably 1594. But the place was pretty certainly Cork, and the day was 'St Barnabas' tide', midsummer, propitious as the summer solstice, the zenith of vital energy in the universe. The poem is a paean of cosmic joy in sexual vigour and fulfilment, the universal superbly at one with the particular and personal. In 1595 it was printed in London, in *Amoretti and Epithalamion*, as was the pastoral *Colin Clout's Come Home Againe*. Spenser himself was again in London, spending there the winter of 1595/96. Of *The Faerie Queene* Books IV to VI had been completed before this marriage. Their printing was now afoot and, along with Books I to III revised, they were published in 1596.

By this year storm clouds were gathering darkly in Ireland. Sir John Norris was sent for to take command over all the forces there and he found the army in desperate plight. In the north Hugh O'Neill had been declared a traitor. For long he had manipulated his double loyalties, as Earl of Tyrone in the Tudor régime as well as 'the O'Neill', the high title of lordship in the north in Irish terms. His clever policy of duplicity, feigning contrite surrender after acts and accusations of rebellion, had served him well. At that time he was building up a formidable muster of fighting men in his impenetrable territories and 'importing lead to roof his houses', which he soon turned into an arsenal of ammunition.

During 1596 Queen Elizabeth, realizing that Spain was preparing a second Armada, sent an expedition under Raleigh and the Earl of Essex to prevent the project. They returned in triumph to loud popular acclaim, but Elizabeth was not pleased with the expedition's execution. Spenser, ever loyal to the house of Leicester and Essex, celebrated the 'heroick parts' of Essex in *Prothalamion*, a piece in honour of a betrothal that was held in Essex House. (This is discussed in detail in the critical analyses.)

Spenser must have been in England for about a year, and we do not learn that his heroic poem, now printed in all six Books, had won him further financial reward. It may have earned him promise of office, but in Ireland. (His appointment as Sheriff of Cork seems to have come somewhat late, at the moment of his despairing flight from Kilcolman and his final departure from the island.) During this visit his political treatise was written or completed, the dialogue *A Vue of the Present State of Ireland*, for the Lord Deputy there mentioned is Sir William Russell. The work is discussed in the chapter on Ireland, where it is made clear that Spenser's well-informed and severe criticism of crown policy was such as would cause disquiet and anger at the centre of affairs. It was entered for printing in 1598, but failed to pass the censorship.

Spenser, returning to Ireland about the late autumn of 1596, found authority at odds with itself. Lord Russell was committed to a policy of appeasement while Sir John Norris, Vice-President of Munster, was attempting to rebuild the ruined armed forces in preparation for defence or attack. Trouble was brewing in Connacht. In the north Tyrone had submitted again, but no reliance could be placed on his word. Munster, however, was the most peaceful region of Ireland, despite alarms, and with peace had come a measure of prosperity and fertility restored to the soil. Little is known of Spenser's doings during the next year or so. It is presumed that he was living at Kilcolman and writing—perhaps 'The Book of Constancy'; of which portions survive, that would bring his cosmic poem to a close. (We should bear in mind that there may have been much more. Papers of his in charge of a servant after his death are understood to have been lost in a shipwreck.) References in records recently discovered but not yet published suggest that he was planning to acquire properties nearer to Dublin, perhaps sensing danger even in a prosperous Munster. Certainly he acquired lands in the region of Kildare for his young son, Peregrine, born of his second marriage.

The new Lord Deputy died after a few months in the land. In summer 1597 rumour of a second Armada was again heard of from Spain; it sailed in October but was scattered by autumn gales. Tyrone was ready to act; in summer 1598 he fired the gunpowder trail of insurrection from one end of Ireland to the other. The dispossessed and the outlawed were to get back their lands and the Catholic faith was to be restored. Patriotic and religious issues were by now fused in the Irish mind. In the north the English army, ill-disposed at a strategic point, were routed at the Battle of the Yellow Ford. This spread alarm in Dublin and throughout the Pale and it fired hope in the Irish forces waiting to rise. Munster was alerted, the English to stand ready to defend their lands. But readiness to arms had waned with prosperity.

The rebels made forays and many of the population went over to their side. The rising gained strength, the 'undertakers' despaired and those who could fled to shelter in the few walled towns. Cork was crammed with refugees. Kilcolman was despoiled. Spenser was probably already in flight when he heard that he had been appointed Sheriff of Cork—if he heard at all in Ireland that his later services in poetry had at last been rewarded with office. He left Ireland bearing urgent letters to Whitehall, which he delivered to the Council on Christmas Eve 1598. For this, his last service, he was well paid. But two weeks later 'Spenser, our principal poet, coming lately out of Ireland, died at Westminster'.

Shocked after acute peril and personal disaster, with few material possessions salvaged, a library and much writing in all probability destroyed, Spenser finished a course in strenuous endeavour and fortitude—and exhaustion. Legends accrue to great persons and to disaster: 'he died because of neglect and want' may express a fellow-writer's indignant sense of *loss*. Another tale, that Lord Essex had sent twenty pieces to him but he sent them back and said he was sorry but he had no time to spend them, rings true in its dignity and sense of irony. The gesture sounds like a friend in high places told too late of urgent need and approaching death, and a poet's proud comment on patronage. For patronage is support of a creative writer so that he may write his poetry, 'grace coming and grace returned'.

This figure from Sphaera Civitatis *(1588?) by John Case shows correspondence between macrocosm and microcosm: the spheres each with the apt virtue of government. Queen Elizabeth in the ninth sphere is prime mover; sphere eight, of the fixed stars, has the star-chamber court, judges, heroes and councillors; then come Saturn, Jupiter, Mars, Sol, Venus, Mercury—and Luna as fertility of creatures and plants. At the centre the earth, immovable justice.*

2 Political and Historical Background

The realm of Britayne, the commonwealth

> The ideal of the Commonwealth, as Shakespeare and his contemporaries understood it, was not, in our sense, a political ideal. It was an ideal of justice, of duty, of unity rather than the freedom to differ, of the manifestation of the will of God.
>
> Philip Styles

England

Englishmen of the sixteenth century thought of themselves as belonging to a commonwealth, in which the common weal—well-being, prosperity of all members—was realized. The commonwealth was an aspect of *the sacral universe*, a term we shall use from now on. Its pattern corresponded to the cosmic pattern and to its law. It was a cosmos in little, a microcosm. Authority was of God and from God; the administration of justice was the reason of the state's being. Christian rulers, whether monarch or magistrate, must think themselves 'to be God's officers ordained by God to be his ministers unto the people, for their salvation, common quietness and wealth; to punish malefactors to defend innocents and to cherish well-doers'. Thus ran the Homily of Obedience of the year 1559, preached in all churches of the realm.

Obedience was the duty of all members, for obedience to higher power was implicitly obedience to God. The ruler was appointed by God as part of His divine plan; obedience to him was a Christian duty, so in a sense his power was absolute; but the ruler's duty was absolute obedience to God and His laws. The ruler, then, interpreted and transmitted God's providence to the members of the Commonwealth. Duty of obedience was not withdrawn when he ruled badly, as suffering under misrule might be part of God's providence. The sole exception was this: 'When laws are made against God and his word, then I ought more to obey God than man.' A man might disobey the wicked law and suffer the penalty, but he might not rise up against the ruler.

All administrative power resided in the prince (*princeps*, the first). But

> The most high and absolute power of the realm of England consisteth in the Parliament...for every Englishman is intended [understood] to be there present either in person or by procuration

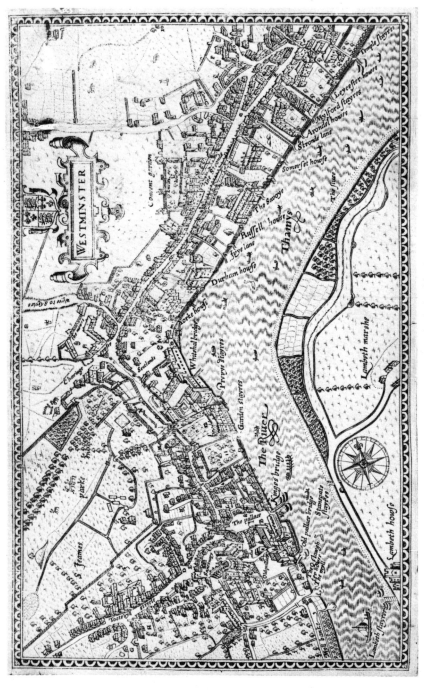

Westminster 1593, by John Norden

and attornies, of what pre-eminence, state, dignity or quality soever he be, from the Prince (be he King or Queen) to the lowest person of England.

Thus Sir Thomas Smith in *De republica anglorum* of 1583.

In the High Court of Parliament was the prime seat of justice and in it the laws were fashioned. The wishes of the monarch and the wishes of Parliament might clash, as they did over the question of marriage and succession, yet Parliament was jealous of its privileges and played a powerfully important part in framing the model of Elizabethan life. At Westminster also were other courts, where civil matters were considered.

The monarch was God's minister, servant and server. The monarch was also, from Spenser's childhood onwards, Supreme Governor of the realm in spiritual affairs, the very head of the Church being Christ himself. Elizabeth had been made so in the spring of 1559, when Parliament passed a Bill of Uniformity and a Bill of Supremacy. All but one of the bishops who had served in the reign of the Roman Catholic Queen Mary resigned, followed by a number of the minor clergy. There was no persecution or bloodshed. There had been Catholic martyrs in the past and blood had flowed under Mary Tudor. But Elizabeth, though pressed again and again by Parliament to apply the law severely against Catholics, maintained her 'middle way' of wide tolerance of extreme opinion. Recusants (those who refused to worship in the parish churches) still heard mass in the privacy of a private chapel. 'I make no windows into men's souls,' she said. Puritans found the Anglican Church government and modes of church service savoured too much of popery. They placed great emphasis on the individual conscience and on each man's reading of scripture, unguided by the ordered liturgy of the Church of England. Their interpretations of scripture and 'prophesyings' were looked on with disfavour by authority.

On a wider front affairs of Church and state could not be so peaceably resolved. The neighbours of England were Scotland and Ireland. The Prince of the independent realm of Scotland was in the 1570s a child being educated in the Reformed faith. In his realm the Kirk was Presbyterian and the discipline Calvinist. His mother Mary, still Queen of Scots in the eyes of many and in Roman Catholic eyes rightful Queen of England also, sat since 1568 in prison in England, a focus for hope and for conspiracy. Ireland was a country of ancient culture, alien in laws and traditions to England, since the times of Henry II part-conquered and part-colonized by the English. Irish resistance to English domination was now reinforced by zeal for the Church of Rome. Elizabeth in Catholic eyes was illegitimate and she was a heretic, 'deposed' and excommunicated by the Pope in 1570. On both counts rebellion against her was deemed justifiable.

'The Head of Spenser' is one of a series of 'Heads of the Poets' prepared by Blake for the library of his friend Hayley. The likeness is based on a portrait-tradition deriving from an original now lost. (The Pembroke College painting is another example.) Blake has added a 'medal' worn at the poet's throat—an Elizabethen gold sovereign. He has enwreathed the portrait-head with laurels, then with a ring of fairies for poetic imagination. On the poet's right appears 'Elisa, Queen of shepheards all' decked with flowers—here seated in the crescent of her Belphoebe personality. The crescent moon as a vehicle belongs to Blake's own repertory of imagery, the moon-boat of woman's love, or God's love, for man. Above Elisa the sky is clouded. On the poet's left hand stands a bard or seer with wand, a severe patriarch over whose head shine two stars, perhaps Castor and Pollux for intellectual endeavour. The poet is between two powers. The stern regard of the seer abashes the 'lady' of love-service and royal patronage. The line of that regard passes through the lips of the poet. Blake's illustration for The Faerie Queene is on page 116.

Farther afield again, on the continent of Europe, there were being waged wars of religion and of resistance to foreign domination, notably in the Netherlands, as we have seen. It required all Elizabeth's diplomatic skill to keep the issue of religion in England from becoming a matter of serious international tension.

When war did break out with Spain (the champion of militant Catholicism) the Queen and her policy were attacked at home by the fanatical extremes of Catholic conviction and Puritan sect, the two ends of the gamut of creed. Nevertheless Elizabeth and the Church of England were loyally served by a majority of her subjects and the last decade of the century saw the system translated into philosophical terms and nobly expounded and defended in Richard Hooker's *Lawes of ecclesiastical politie*. The ideal there expressed was of course fallen short of in the actual and general conduct of the Church, where there were failures and abuse. But the measure of tolerance and liberation achieved in England had their virtue in a European scene where in many places passion and persecution had their way.

Elizabeth's conduct of policy, whether in the long years of peace she maintained or in the decades of threatened invasion, was based extensively on voluntary service. Both on land and at sea the Queen's expenditure was frugal and the appeal to endeavour in loyal service or championing of a right cause extended the forces in action or at call. She improved her naval forces in design and strength. The spirit of the age of discovery and the tradition of seamanship worked in her favour. But the real strength lay in private enterprise, the gentleman- or merchant-adventurer who would furnish and equip a vessel, find skilled hands, financial backing and a cargo.

By the same token there was no standing army as such; but the enthusiasm of the adventurer or of the partisan in a 'right cause' went far to supply the lack. Volunteers—Raleigh in his 'teens is an example —were fighting on the Protestant side in the civil wars of religion in France at a time when Elizabeth was non-participant. When forces were mustered for service overseas, in the Netherlands or in Ireland, we know that there were many unenthusiastic soldiers in the ranks. But the Queen and her Council had a list of trusty gentlemen who could be called on to raise a band. And there were among the host of unprovided younger sons a store who saw in volunteering for armed service a first step in advancement, to promotion and possible gain in ransom money or, in Ireland, eventual reward in a grant of lands. We shall see the same pattern of private enterprise encouraged, in the plantation of Ireland.

Tribute has here been paid to the ideal of the commonwealth and will be paid to Elizabeth's outstanding success in making the 'model' work. In her service there stood by her right hand the wise senior statesman, Lord Burleigh. Behind the scenes worked the highly efficient intelligence service of Secretary Walsingham. When we later review the function of the poet in the princely commonwealth we should remember that Christopher Marlowe, Renaissance poet of the popular theatre and secret agent, also had his political place in it.

The Queen

Can a realm flourish under a ruler who is female if, in the order of nature the female is inferior and naturally subject to the male? In Scotland John Knox under Queen Mary answered the question with a trumpet blast of 'No', against 'the monstrous regiment of women'. There was, however, an exception made to nature's great order, where a woman is the rightful heir to the throne and is therefore God's appointed. The triumph of Elizabeth Tudor was her vindication of this exception. It was a personal triumph. She was remarkably intelligent, her mind trained and her talents developed by a fine education in scholarship and languages, in history and law. 'I thank God I am endued with such qualities that, if I were turned out of the realm in my petticoat, I were able to live in any place in Christendom.' Her will was indomitable and her wisdom deep.

She presented herself as in all aspects woman, exacting loyalty as 'love-service'. The lady had done thus in the medieval code of love; but Elizabeth, in very fact unattainable great lady and virgin queen, played both roles with consummate skill. She declared herself wedded to her people: at her coronation she 'wedded' England with a ring and the anniversary of her accession was kept as a festival on 17 November, 'Queen Elizabeth's wedding-day'. Exacting love service, she gave in return unswerving devotion to the wellbeing of her realm, the common weal.

> I do assure you that there is no prince that loveth his subjects better, or whose love can countervail our love: there is no jewel, be it of never so rich a prize, which I prefer before this jewel: I mean your love, for I do more esteem it than any treasure or riches—for that we know how to prize but love and thanks I count inestimable. And though God hath raised me high, yet this I count the glory of my crown—that I have reigned with your loves. This makes me that I do not so much rejoice that God hath made me to be a queen as to be a queen over so thankful a people.

Dealing with a monarch who was altogether woman had its difficulties.

> By art and nature together so blended, it was difficult to find her right humour at any time. Her wisest men and best counsellors were oft sore troubled to know her will in matters of state, so covertly did she pass her judgement as seemed to leave all to their discreet management: and, when the business did turn to better

40

advantage, she did most cunningly commit the good issue to her own honour and understanding but, when aught fell out contrary to her will and intent, the Council were in great straight to defend their own acting and not blemish the Queen's good judgement. (Sir John Harington, 1594)

The Queen's projection of her personality as virgin lady and monarch was masterly done. First, consider the image of monarch in the cosmic order. The sun was the figure of the male monarch, *sol justitiae*, the light shining alike on all. In the order of nature the sun was masculine, but the moon of feminine gender. Queen Elizabeth was moon: the moon gave light by night when light was most needed; it waxed and waned and calculation was required to find the better time or worse to profit from its light and power. So she turned an inscrutable and capricious aspect to good account. As moon she influenced the waxing and waning of plant, or project, or courtier. As moon she had power over the tides and waters of the world; she was mistress of the sublunary region of the cosmos, the region of change on earth. As moon she was constant to the earth, though wielding rule through her power to be inconstant in her aspect. She reflected the light of the sun of justice. Where the generosity of the sun was the largesse of the male monarch, her parsimony was the thrifty housekeeping of a woman. As ruler in cosmic terms she could be figured also as *primum mobile*—of which an illustration is included. As God was prime mover of the macrocosm, so she was of the microcosm.

Tudor propaganda knew how to develop and display the 'legend' of the Queen. When a monarch was received in state on progresses through the realm, the royal entry to the region was marked by ceremony of welcome, by decoration of gateways and streets, by pageantry, speeches, music and entertainments. For all of these the image of the monarch furnished a basic theme for the expression of the welcome. The range of emblem, symbol or analogue was enormous: figures from the Old Testament or the New, mythology or legend from the antique world, astronomy, history, the language of heraldry or of the emblem books. When Elizabeth entered the City of London in state the day before her coronation she was hailed (among a wealth of symbols used) as Deborah, who in the Book of Judges brought succour to the distressed people of Israel. The scattering of flowers in the way was an age-long gesture of tribute, and as she grew older she was greeted especially with the flowers of spring to signify the eternal spring her presence brought to her realm.

In such pageantry the Queen herself played the principal part. The monarch's showing himself to the people in his estate royal was understood to spread wellbeing abroad. As Elizabeth with her magnificent company moved residence from one to another of her palaces, or as she visited regions of her realm in progress, the spectacle was rich and splendid. At the Renaissance with its emphasis on array the presentation of the person through costume was of signal importance. The portraits of the period repay careful study, above all the likenesses of Elizabeth as Queen. In every one her dress and jewels are breathtaking in value and beauty. The royal account books show the fantastic number and costliness of her dresses and jewelled ornaments, of which the portraits show only a few. Look always for the symbol or emblem, on jewel or dress or in the objects associated with her pose. She will have a fresh rose pinned at breast or shoulder, a rose of red streaked with white for the Tudor plant-badge or the single white rose, the eglantine, which she chose as her personal emblem, a rose with a difference. She had a pelican jewel, showing the pelican in its piety of biblical and medieval lore, who wounded her breast that her blood might nourish her young; so the Queen sacrificed her strength that her people might prosper. One gown was embroidered with eyes, ears and mouths, for the sovereign is aware of all and speaks for all. She may have a rainbow behind her, or a window may open on a view of her ships at Tilbury while she holds in her hand the globe showing the old world and the new. She may hold a sieve in her hand or a live ermine on her wrist, both emblems of virginity. The 'Ditchley portrait' (frontispiece) shows the Queen in cosmic setting of four elements. She stands on a map of her island realm, her feet resting on Oxfordshire, thunder on her left, on her right sunlight and clearing air. The last was a theme in the entertainment made for her visit to Ditchley, which this portrait commemorates. She wears a *rosa mundi*.

None of these was invented in the modern sense of the word. Each was invented in the Elizabethan sense, sought out and displayed, 'discovered' from among the ordered significances available in the great web of meaning. For each there was authority, in hierarchies of plant or animal each with its own 'use to man', in the properties of tools or instruments often taken from scripture. The eglantine was novel but devised from the rose as Queen of flowers, the Tudor plant badge and the singleness and whiteness of purity. The devising of the eglantine, the devising of the pageants on progress show the same thought process by which Spenser in his poetry devised the flower garland for Eliza, Queen of shepherds or the person, mien and array of Belphoebe in *The Faerie Queene*. (These will be found quoted and discussed on pages 132–8, 153–6, 162.)

The poet writing in a Queen-centred realm had, then, an enormous repertory of imagery to draw on. He could vary, combine, interpret anew by taking some fresh bearing, or find correspondences not observed before. A court play by Lyly shows Endymion a shepherd loved by Cynthia, the moon, in a devising developed from classical legend, pastoral convention and the Queen as moon figure. Sir Walter Raleigh, poet and sea adventurer was Cynthia's servant, her 'shepherd of the ocean'. His Christian name, pronounced in his west country speech, lent itself to Walter Raleigh. His long poem of love service, of which only a portion has survived, was 'of the Ocean to Cynthia', showing her power over him as man and as servant in that element, but revealing also a 'ten years war', the tensions of personality, passion and pride in a relationship of 'love-service' between great courtier and his sovereign lady. At the humbler level of popular song and ballad sheet the love the people had for their Queen hailed her as Bess:

> Come over the bourn, Bessy to me
> and I will thee take
> and my dear Lady make.

To this she replies 'Here is my hand, my dear lover England...'

There were, however, dissident voices though few and muted. In the covert poetry of Catholic dissent, which became vocal in private at the time of Queen Mary's execution, Elizabeth was Isabel (the Spanish form of the name). Isabel was Jezebel, or, in anagram, reference could be made to the story of Abel and Cain.

The image of the Queen is explored and expounded in Spenser's great heroic poem, as we shall see. Gloriana, his new name-of-glory for her, was the majesty of *The Faerie Queene* over all. The Books of the poem reveal in turn aspects of the Queen in relation to the Virtue of each: Una, Belphoebe, Britomart, Belphoebe twinned with Amoret; Astraea and Mercilla for the Book of Justice, Cynthia and Diana in Book VII. Some are drawn from the repertory of imagery already current; some are fresh devisings where name conceit renders tangible the abstract idea.

The Queen was the ultimate patron to be served and glorified in poetry, God's agent on earth through whom grace descended on her realm and her people. Poetry was loving tribute, a returning of that grace. Yet Spenser is not afraid to champion those he loved and admired who had suffered her displeasure unfairly. His poetry works towards the restoration of such to the Queen's grace: Raleigh and Lord Grey in the epic, a bishop in the *Calender* and in his last poem, *Prothalamion*, Lord Essex of the house of Leicester, to which also he owed loyalty and thanks.

Within the heroic poem as it developed over years may be traced the growth of disenchantment with the earthly and fallible aspect of the sovereign lady. Astraea, cosmic figure of heavenly justice, departs from earth early in Book V. Its pages show, besides Mercilla, the tyranny of a female ruler in Radegund the Amazon Queen, humiliating Artegall as Omphale humiliated Hercules: this at a salient point (V.v.25). Domination of the male by the female is profoundly against nature even though the Queen, God's appointed, be excepted. A poem conceived as a build-up for the female ruler comes to figure forth disquiet that is not divorced from her female sex.

As Elizabeth aged and the question of succession remained undecided the deep anxiety felt declares itself in the images of portrait or of poetry. She is painted contemplating a death's head. In the last Cantos of *The Faerie Queene* Cynthia is in eclipse. But the depth of that anxiety is a measure of the dependence on their Queen that her realm and people had known for so long.

The court and patronage

> By wide distribution of favour the Crown and its Ministers sought to link to themselves the interests and hopes of the great majority of the English governing class.
>
> Professor W. T. MacCaffrey

Elizabeth's government, a 'model' on earth of the Kingdom of God, depended on obedience. The possibility of violent resistance had to be reckoned with. There was no army or body of officialdom to enforce the will of the monarch. Elizabeth's art of government consisted in persuading her subjects that the decisions taken at top level were in the interest of their common weal. As from God flowed the plenitude of his will and grace, so from the Queen could flow favour and advancement. Such favour under Elizabeth was distributed widely, extending to the great majority of 'the English governing class', the gentlemen of England.

It has been reckoned from the rolls of 1591 of 'Principal gentlemen of the shire' that there were some 2,000 of such persons. For them the way up was through service of the Queen at court. It helped to be born of distinguished and landed family; for men of rank there was the prospect of command in land or sea forces or appointment as Lord Lieutenant of the county, ambassador or magistrate. Below these were the gentry who had lands and influence in their regions, and beyond them were the lesser gentry and the hundreds of younger sons. For such as these advancement lay through the professions, the Church or the law, and meant long education and training. But entrance to the Queen's service offered a chance for a young man of good birth and little wealth to enter on the obvious way to win fortune, place and lands.

For this there was a recognized programme: to enter the service of a social superior and obtain education and training in his household, thereafter to make his way further through introduction to court circles and recommendation to the Queen by the noble patron. Or he might capture the notice of the Queen by personality and character, by evidence of capability or handsomeness of person and bearing. We recognize the path taken by Walter Raleigh, son of a Devonshire squire. We recognize the path embarked on hopefully by Edmund Spenser, born of plain people and extremely interested in tracing family links with noble persons of his name. For him it lay through excellence in studies, in service under a bishop then under a nobleman, and in supplying evidence of capability in his poetic work, by 1579 in print and only partly anonymous.

The nobleman in whose service he hoped to rise, the Earl of Leicester, was as Robert Dudley already a friend of Elizabeth before she became Queen. On her accession he was made Master of the Queen's Horse. He was married, but his wife did not come to court: she was sick of 'a malady of the breast'. (She met her death in 1560 by a fall, in circumstances of mystery and some suspicion at the time—but research suggests that the fall was indeed accidental, proving fatal because she was frail from advanced cancer.)

By virtue of his office Leicester was every day in close contact with the Queen, in charge of the large body of horse needed by the Queen and her household as they moved from place to place. By birth and breeding, by stature, handsome looks and imposing presence, by natural gifts and by training as a courtier he was well fitted to make the most of his station and office, 'to ride next behind the Queen'.

From the first he enjoyed her confidence and intimate friendship. When, stricken with smallpox she believed herself on her deathbed, she asked her Council to make Lord Robert Dudley Protector of the Realm. After the death of his wife it was always possible that the Queen might marry him, her subject, and that possibility survived through recurrent projects of a royal match with a princely suitor from abroad. Dudley, raised to Earl of Leicester in 1564, was notably Protestant in sympathy, and though he had personal enemies he enjoyed during his lifetime a large measure of popular support.

When Spenser wrote to Gabriel Harvey that he hoped soon to be sent abroad in Leicester's service his foot was on the second rung of the ladder to advancement at court. But the year 1579 saw Leicester secretly married, and by November that marriage discovered to the Queen. It saw the immediate consequence, Leicester's spectacular fall from royal favour. It saw the project of a royal match with a French Prince dissolved. And that year's winter saw Spenser's *Shepheardes Calender* in print, perhaps by January 1579/80. The crisis of timing must have been agonizing to the poet. He had been adding passages to the eclogues after September—references to events in the Scottish court that only happened then. His serious pastoral bears traces of references to Leicester that became unpropitious after the favourite's fall. (There are signs of changes and erasures.) But there remained in the *Calender*, however discreetly wrapped in allegory, teasing references to Leicester's love affair with the lady he had secretly married in September, Lettice Knollys, Countess of Essex

Lettice Knollys, Countess of Leicester—formerly Countess of Essex.

recently widowed—'Lettice' glossed as 'a country lass', of the amorous eclogue for March. Furthermore there was an odd reference to an old ewe with a bandaged leg who broke her neck by a fall, surely a glance at the death of Leicester's first wife. The episode features the hawthorn-bud, Leicester's plant badge. There was no mistaking.

In the wisdom of hindsight this is seen as the most appalling indiscretion. Even had Leicester not married the lady it was playing with fire to intrude thus on a great patron's privacy, and to publish teasing references to it in print. And he had married, been discovered and suffered the penalty. This permanent record must have incurred the extreme anger of the Lord and his Lady, to say nothing of offending the Queen. It seems highly likely that Spenser was simply removed from the scene, sped on his way to outlandish Ireland. What is more, in a poem written then but published only after Leicester's death he pleads his avowed intention to warn Leicester of maligning tongues. The fable was of *Virgil's Gnat*, the helpful gnat that sought to waken the sleeping shepherd (when a serpent of poisonous tongue was poised to sting him,) but was brushed away and killed for its pains. Perhaps the 'warning' went astray partly by ill luck in the turn events took. But it seems obvious that the young poet, untrained in the art and tact of a courtier, presumed indeed in touching on affairs of state at this personal level and badly misjudged the relationship of poet to patron.

This was not the only time that Spenser overplayed his hand as serious poet intent on treating of the realm's affairs. His verse fable *Prosopopoia or Mother Hubberd's Tale* (printed in 1591 but written earlier) featured Lord Burleigh in unflattering terms and offence was taken. The volume of *Complaints* that contained it was called in. Burleigh was a generous patron of men of letters, serious writers of chronicles like the lawyer Camden. Love poetry he evidently rated as trivial, possibly noxious, and Spenser's early draft of *Hymnes to Love and Beauty* may well not have been to his taste; hence in part the refashioning of these poems as precursors to Hymnes of Heavenly Love and Beauty, published late in the poet's life as *Fowre Hymnes*. The conclusion of The Book of Courtesy speaks sadly of the enduring enmity of a great peer.

On the other hand Spenser's poetry, apart from the disaster of 'Lettice', bears witness to a relationship with noble ladies that was both delightful and profitable. Three daughters of the large family of Sir John Spencer of Althorp in Northamptonshire extended gracious patronage and 'bounty' to the poet. These Spencers were granted a new coat of arms in 1595 allowing a connection with ancient baronial Despencers; hence the 'house of ancient fame' of *Prothalamion* to whom the poet traced his name, a link apparently allowed by the ladies of Althorp. When in *Colin Clout* Spenser pays tribute to fair ladies at court three Spencer sisters are named in pastoral terms. Elizabeth is 'Phillis the fair'; she married Sir George Carey and at Carisbrooke Castle in the Isle of Wight dispensed hospitality and patronage to writers. A sonnet to her is among those prefacing *The Faerie Queene* and to her Spenser dedicated his delicate fantasy *Muiopotmos: or the Fate of the Butterflie*. Anne, 'bountifull Charillis', was three times married to a husband of rank and to her as Lady Compton, a beautiful young widow at court, Spenser dedicated *Mother Hubberd's Tale*. 'Amarillis' is Alice, who married Lord Strange; to her was dedicated *The Teares of the Muses*.

In Sir Walter Raleigh Spenser found a patron who was both fellow poet and distinguished servant of the Queen—indeed over a long period her intimate friend though not at all times in her personal favour; he was, moreover, a neighbour landowner in the plantation of Munster. He was a discriminating and sympathetic critic of the poet's works in progress. His kind service in taking Spenser to court to present the first part of his great poem in print was repaid by the poet's loving loyalty—witness his championing in *The Faerie Queene* of Raleigh, figured as Timias, 'misdeemed' by Belphoebe, an aspect of Elizabeth's royal person.

When *The Faerie Queene* came to be printed in its six Books it was prefaced first by Raleigh's sonnet in commendation, where Spenser's praise is sung beside Petrarch and Homer 'Me thought I saw the grave, where Laura lay...' A pageant of sonnets was devised by Spenser to introduce the national epic, a sequence of eulogies dedicated to great ones of the realm and to persons to whom the poet owed a debt of gratitude. While the book was in the press the sequence was extended and Burleigh was included. Addressing him Spenser pleads there is serious value in 'these ydle rimes'. This sequence can be read as an illustration of the way patronage and dedication operated. The aptness of each piece of eulogy is admirable. Sir Christopher Hatton, Lord High Chancellor of England, had his lighter moments; he is said to have made his way into Elizabeth's favour by his skill in dancing. Lord Burleigh is 'impatiente with ydle rimes' but *The Faerie Queene* will reveal deep and serious matter. The Earl of Oxford is a poetry lover and will find his own ancient ancestry celebrated in the poem. The great lords of the north are honoured, the Admiral of England victorious against the Spanish fleet, and Hunsdon who defeated the rebels in the north. Those who knew Ireland and had suffered there are honoured also, not omitting Lord Grey (at that time in disgrace); so were Raleigh whose own poem for Cynthia/Elizabeth was not for public eye, and Mary Sidney, Countess of Pembroke, who had encouraged Spenser's early writing. The sequence places *The Faerie Queene* as epic of national import, as poetry to be judged by fellow poets and as the work of Spenser, who was most loyal and deeply grateful. Inclusion in this sequence was a courteous request for serious attention in great ones near the sovereign. At the same time it conferred honour, for the work was to win everlasting fame.

Ireland: the other island

> What can be sayd but that the secrett Judgment of God hangeth over this soyle, that causeth all the best endeavours of these that labor the reformation thereof to came to naught?
>
> Ludowick Bryskett: a letter to Walsingham, 1583

> Fubuń on ye, O race of the Gael*
> Not one of ye has any life in him
> While the Foreigner is sharing out your country
> Ye are like a fairy host.
>
> *The Bard of the O'Carrolls*, 1542, from the Irish

Neutrally regarded, Ireland of earlier times was an island on the westernmost fringe of Europe where the conquering power of the Roman Empire had never penetrated. It was inhabited by a people largely Celtic in race, into which had been absorbed waves of incomers, conquerors of seaboard regions, who had settled there. The people spoke a Celtic language and followed still an ancient pattern of life related in origin to that of Gaul before the Romans came. Christianity had come early to the people in the Dark Ages and had spread thence into northern parts of Great Britain at a time of heathen English settlement. From these early days Irish Christianity, with its emphasis on hermit, saint and scholar, retained a timbre different from the rest of the ordered, organized medieval Christendom centred in Rome. The 'otherness' of Ireland was very real. It presented to medieval feudalism a challenge and a core of resistance. For the emerging nation-state of the Renaissance world both challenge and resistance persisted and indeed became more marked. Ireland, in fact, could seldom if ever be regarded neutrally.

Ireland is a potent presence in the life and work of Edmund Spenser. To understand either aright we must come to terms with several differing attitudes to the island and its people, beliefs held in different quarters about the nature of the land and its inhabitants, and policies pursued—in determined conflict one with another—as to their destiny. Our main guide, though not of course an impartial one, is the prose treatise that Spenser himself wrote, or completed, in 1596 in London: *A Vue of the Present State of Ireland*. It is written as a dialogue, a favourite Renaissance form. The speakers are Irenaeus, a man who knows Ireland well, and Eudoxus, a well-educated Englishman who knows nothing of it but desires to learn. The dialogue

---

*a dire curse.

is a model for our modern form of communication, the interview on broadcast media between the specialist and the intelligent layman.

Spenser writes as one experienced over years both as a government official, widely travelled with firsthand knowledge of official business and as an Englishman possessing extensive lands in Ireland, who has made his home there. He is also a poet and a scholar of the Renaissance era, interested in 'antiquities', in patterns of human history, in ethics, law and religion. And he is a partisan Protestant. Reading the dialogue we realize how completely ignorant of things Irish the typical Tudor Englishman was and how extensive and detailed was the information of Spenser himself *as far as he could discern*. Following his exposition, we realize how ill-informed and misconceived he could show Crown policy in Ireland to be, how deeply he had come to love that beautiful land, and how deeply also he despaired of its condition and its future. We shall not find in his treatise any inside knowledge of Crown policy at a high level or any appreciation of the reasons why Elizabeth was reluctant or unable to disburse vast sums to maintain substantial military forces there. And we shall find no sense whatsoever that the Irish had a right or an understandable determination to persist in their ancestral life-pattern and to maintain their form of the Christian faith, resisting the presence in the land of foreign overlords, who were intent on subduing them and colonizing the island completely. Yet Spenser the scholar knew that the Irish were a language people of ancient culture who had inhabited the island for many centuries, that they were 'lettered' earlier than the English, and that their way of life made sense to them. (The entity of the Irish as a people lay in their language.)

For Spenser's England and its Queen Ireland was 'part of Britayne by right', by conquest and treaty of long standing. 'When the Kings of England conquered all the realme they there by assumed and invested all the right of that land to theyr heyres and successours for ever', Spenser's speaker says. But on what authority was that right based and for whom was it valid?

The Lordship of Ireland had been granted by Pope Adrian II to Henry II, who was King of England and master of wide territories on the continent. He was encouraged to go into Ireland and bring order to that turbulent country. The 'Norman Conquest' in Ireland, however, was not complete nor was it a lasting success. It took in much of the north but never penetrated westwards beyond the Shannon. Monarchic feudalism was introduced into the conquered part, land grant backed by reciprocal service and land tenure by primogeniture, the whole based on agriculture and a peasantry tied

An Irish Chief, MacSweeney, dines in the open air—with a gentlewoman, a friend and two friars, one saying grace (B). The beef is cut from the carcase (A) and boiled in the hide (C) while his bard and harper entertain (D).

51

Irish galloglas and their attendants, 1521: drawing by Albrecht Dürer.

to the land. But Norman barons among whom the conquered territory had been parcelled out intermarried with the Irish from the first and many of them soon rivalled the Irish themselves in 'Irishry'. A hundred years later an effort was made by statute to conserve an English domination there by defining an area under English law (the 'land of peace'—the King's peace).

Beyond an uneasy borderland under march law lay the far areas acknowledged as Celtic and continuing under their own ancient Celtic law system (known as 'brehon law'), a complex and effective one and unique in Europe. 'The Pale', the English area marked off by ditch and palisade, shrank in time to a region of the south-east, one modern county deep along the eastern seaboard from Dundalk to Waterford (map p. 58). Even so the inhabitants of the Pale were by no means all English in stock, in language or in sympathies.

How did 'the matter of Ireland' look to Tudor eyes? Within living memory of an older Elizabethan Henry VIII had declared himself King of Ireland. His policy was one of conciliation and he received a 'grand submission' of certain Irish chiefs. This was disavowed by the Irish people as invalid according to the non-hereditary aspect of their ancient clan laws. Chiefdom of a clan, Kingship of the four regions of the Isle and High-Kingship were all elective. (The High-Kingship was offered at one point to King James V of Scotland, a Catholic prince: he declined it.) There were thus two distinct views as to whether Ireland and the Irish belonged to the commonweal of Elizabeth's realm.

An English poet of 1578, John Derricke, saw Ireland as land surviving from the ancient wars of the giants against Olympus, an outpost of Chaos whence chaos always threatened to return. He published his poem in 1581, illustrating it by a series of handsome woodcuts—*The Image of Ireland*, from which several plates are included here.

The confrontation dating from Henry II's time was of two cultures in almost every aspect inimical to one another. Opposed to monarchic feudalism was elective lordship, the system called 'tanistry'. The land belonged not to the chiefs but to the people; a clan had not absolute ownership of a region but had regional rights of territory. Values were warrior values. The strength of a clan lay in its fighting men, among whom a caste system prevailed—horse and foot, followers and attendants, from the *galloglas* or heavy-armed warrior, the *kerne* or light foot-soldier down to the horseboys. One of the warrior caste would not put hand to a plough. The warrior caste was supported by tribute in kind for sustenance of man and beast. Blood kinship ranged the clans in patterns of alliance, or contest and hostility, that presented to feudal eyes a picture of perpetual and endemic unrest.

The way of life was primarily pastoral. Wealth lay in herds, bulls, beeves and milch kine, and in horses, sheep and swine. Being pastoral

it was mobile: stock was moved seasonally or as an area of pasture was exhausted. There were freemen and unfree churls who were concerned with tilling the soil for oats and barley to provide straw and corn, from which also whiskey, ale and rough cake were made. What was the role of the freeman is difficult to determine, but tilling of the land was undertaken on short rent, at most a year or two on end. There was also a caste of skilled craftsmen working in wood, leather and metals, often to a distinguished standard. And there were the learned castes—law-givers, leeches, priests and poets, who contributed their professional skills to the system and were maintained by it.

The warrior-pastoral way of life was well suited to the terrain of forest and mountain, bog, lake and river, with rich natural pasture-lands, that could yield a good short-term crop of corn. There were very few made roads or bridges, but an extensive system of 'paces' or paths for passage of man and beast, over plain, through boglands into forest or mountain and over river by fords. At points there were castles and tower-houses of stone, and there were isolated cottages of wood; but habitation was often in temporary or quickly devised shelter. There were fine natural havens, some of which had been developed by earlier Viking settlement into trade-posts; through these passed trade with England and the Continent, especially with Brittany and Spain. But of these havens only a few were walled towns. Other towns there were none, though inland there were centres of learning such as Armagh.

Food was fundamentally the proteins of a pastoral society that also hunted and fished, but not systematically. The Irish, then, lived on flesh, milk, cheese and the plentiful cresses that were there to gather. The pattern of warrior society with its strong element of contest related to the pastoral pattern in the phenomenon of the cattle raid, which was undertaken at the promptings of scarcity or in order to impoverish a rival.

This antique way of life retained its own system of laws and law-giving, of lawmen and assembly, of medicine and leeches, and of bards who were trained as poet and annalist. The learned castes were itinerant of habit. There were renowned centres of learning, but schooling in poetry and history, medicine and law was pursued largely by the group of learners under masters moving from place to place. A chief would have with him his priest or friar, his bard, his storyteller and harper, perhaps his adviser in medicine also. The bard served the warrior culture, proclaiming genealogy of kings and valorous deeds of heroes, defending the chief's honour and attacking his enemies by fierce invective and satire. Naturally powers of exhortation and invective were directed against the presence in the

An Irish cattleraid on an 'old English' homestead.

island of foreign overlords and settlers.

Dress belonged to the way of life, the terrain and the weather. The thickly woven all-covering mantle of wool and fur served as cloak, bed and blanket, indoors or out. It made possible life by day and night in a mild but rainy climate and made feasible campaigning in a wild land with few houses. Armour, harness and mode of fighting were 'other' than those derived from feudal chivalry, but in their geographical context they were efficient, and murderously effective against 'superior' arms. The traditional *glibb* or thick matted growth of hair over the men's foreheads was good defence in combat and afforded a ready disguise of identity. When a great chieftain paid a formal visit to the early Tudor court in his own full costume of state with warrior train the apparition was regarded with as much wonder and sarcasm 'as if they were from India or China'.

For Renaissance Europe interested in the great variety of man the Irish and their way of life were a fascinating case. Travellers came from as far as Bohemia and wrote descriptions of land and people. The 'otherness' was recorded in drawing and print. The discovery of the new world from accounts of returning voyagers had stirred up a lively interest in 'savage man' and attempts were made by scholars to account for their state and to place them in the scheme of world history. Two main views were current in Spenser's time. Either they were seen as living in primal innocence—naked, friendly, subsisting on natural resources and 'having a sense of deity'—or, where experienced as hostile, they were cruel, licentious and idol-worshipping—degenerate man. A parallel between Indians of America and the Irish was frequently drawn, especially for warlike valour and horsemanship. However viewed, both kinds of savage people were ripe for reformation and their lands for occupation and colonization.

Parallels were also drawn between 'savage' people and peoples known from the writings of classical antiquity, especially the Scythians; there was a correspondence in customs and modes of warfare. Spenser with the enthusiasm of a Renaissance scholar studied the indigenous people of Ireland. He did not learn to speak Irish but he must have had translated for him the Irish names of natural features and the 'place lore' that explained them. (The Lord Governor always had an interpreter in attendance.) He did not know their written annals, but he had contact with their bards, with whom, of course, he could converse in Latin as these were learned men. He had some of their poems translated for him and he granted that these had a certain quality. Yet he could not admit to equal footing 'bards, whom they have in place of poets'. But he noted that they were honoured and feared, that their words were heeded and that they had no need to sue for patronage or earn a living by other means. Since the bards exhorted the people to hold to the ways of ancient Gaeldom and defend their land from the foreigners' rapacity, they were arch-enemies, traitors, forces for unrest and champions of chaos.

So profound was the antipathy of culture to culture that comment, by traveller from afar or by antiquarian scholar resident there, is almost all of the same pattern. These men are savages, their marriage customs and acknowledgement of bastards are heinous. Their way of life must be dismembered and destroyed. Their assemblies for law-giving must be proscribed: their mode of settling blood-feud by blood-money encourages murder. Their bards must be put down, that eloquent exhortation silenced. The great forests must be cut through by rides, fords destroyed and bridges built, for bridges are defensible. Roads must be cleared of those of itinerant habit, be they learned men or craftsmen plying their skills, strong vagabonds, dispossessed unfortunates, loose women or wandering minstrels. The *glibb* and mantle must be forbidden. How to effect all this was the problem.

For the reform of the savage people it was necessary somehow to harness to the Tudor power structure the loyalty of clan to chief. Descendants of the feudal barons, such as Fitzgerald Earl of Desmond or Butler Earl of Ormonde, held great sway in the land. Ormonde of Elizabeth's time was kinsman to the Queen through the Boleyns and came to court; but he could not or would not 'solve the Irish problem' for her. Desmond had a blood-feud with the monarchy since the betrayal and execution in 1467 of a forefather who had been the King's friend. In the north Elizabeth hoped to turn to her service a young O'Neill of Tyrone, who might become chief in time, by having him fostered in England with the Sidneys and educated as an English aristocrat. Of him we shall hear more. A system had been evolved of 'surrender and regrant': a chief who might be faring badly in inter-clan hostilities was encouraged to surrender his native 'title' to his lordship and accept in its stead a feudal title from England's monarch, say 'Earl of Tyrone', which could then be hereditary. Thereby he was to gain support from the English. But this action cost him the trust of his fellow chiefs and disaster usually followed, with little lasting loyalty accruing to the Crown under the non-hereditary law of *tanistry*.

The reform of the savage people to a Tudor system of life entailed—from Henry VIII's time if not under Mary's short reign—a bringing in of Protestantism. But such pastors as could be persuaded to go to Ireland made little headway. The dissolution of the monastic houses was deeply resented. Destruction of sacred treasures like the stained-glass windows of Ossory was resisted by the local population in stone-throwing force. The 'middle way' of the Elizabethan settlement did not seem a middle way in Ireland. Not only the 'mere Irish' (the indigenous unconquered Celts) but also many of the 'old English' (the early Norman settler stock) stubbornly persisted in the 'old

Ireland

ULSTER

Never

penetrated

●Armagh

CONNACHT

Dundalk●

Drogheda●

Boyne R

●Trim

Bog
of Allen

Liffey R

DUB

Kildare●

Glenmalure

Kilcullen
(New Abbey)

Shannon R

O S S O R Y

LEINSTER

Oure R

Limerick●

Slaney R

MUNSTER

●Tipperary

Awbeg R

Galtee Mts

Clonmel●

●Kilcolman

Suir R

Wexford●

Smerwick

Mallow●

Castletownroche●

K e r r y

Blackwater R

Lee R

●Cork

Youghal●

	The Pale 1500
	The Pale 1580
✂	Site of battle

religion'. The zeal of Roman Catholic priests, many of them Irishmen trained on the continent, contrasted with the ineffectiveness of Protestant propaganda. Preaching in English to people who spoke a different tongue was as unrewarding as trying to exact tithes from a hostile population. Elizabeth in Catholic eyes was illegitimate and had no claim on them as sovereign. When she was excommunicated by the Pope in 1570 the Irish could claim that they were rebelling not against the crown but against the bastard and heretic Tudor who wore it.

When Spenser set foot in Ireland only one-twentieth of that island was firmly under English rule and occupation; beyond the Shannon was wild Irishry; and all between, the main body of the land from north coast to south, was territory England was seeking to keep or bring under control by pact or treaty, by acts of warfare, and by a policy of plantation, renewed with vigour in Elizabeth's reign. Over this Ireland, whose population ranged from mere Irish or old English to recent planters and settlers, the body of English officials and the army, the representative of English rule was the Lord Deputy or Lord Governor. The four traditional regions each had a President and Council, but Connacht was 'mere Irish' and Leinster largely contained the Pale. The authority of the Presidents of Ulster and Munster was somewhat theoretical. The seat of government was in Dublin, the only substantial city in the realm and possessed of a strong castle. There was a Parliament of Ireland that met there, and in Dublin were maintained colonial versions of the main courts as existing in London, except the Mint.

The post of Lord Deputy was an arduous one that had destroyed the spirit, health and reputation of a series of determined men. They were faced with a multiple task that was virtually impossible: to maintain the Queen's peace in the Pale, to defend that peace from attack, which could come from anywhere in the wide area under march law, and (it was hoped) to come to terms eventually with the Gaelic region beyond. In addition they were to be ready to counter any attempt by foreign powers to win foothold or support in Ireland, be they Spanish in the south and west or Scots pirates in the north. The mere Irish in the stronghold of their impenetrable forest, bog and mountainland could not be brought under subjugation. Large areas of the intervening territory could be 'granted and planted'. But the English overlords or their immigrant tenants—'undertakers' who undertook to develop the regions—could not defend their lands from persistent and revengeful clansmen dispossessed of them. The cost of maintaining English forces in Ireland bore heavily on the 'old English' of the Pale. And Elizabeth, in Spenser's lifetime, would never disburse funds generous enough for effective garrisoning or decisive warfare.

Over the years a pattern of events had evolved, of rebellion by the Irish, then a savage and purposeful campaign of subjection, extirpation, laying waste and confiscation of territory. This was then 'granted and planted' and held as long as the Irish were terrorized and as long as English families could be persuaded to emigrate or to remain in Ireland once they had sampled the conditions there. Where English farmers failed, Irish were perforce accepted in their place as the land must be cultivated according to contract. This of course had inbuilt dangers. Treaties might be made but no trust could be engendered where cruel destruction had been experienced and blood-feud initiated. Revenge smouldered until time was ripe for rebellion again.

A corresponding rhythm can be traced in relations between the Lord Deputy and the Crown. Once a victorious campaign was reported at home, funds for supply of the armed forces were drastically reduced, which set at hazard once more all that had been gained. What is more, an outcry against savage oppression would reach the Queen's ears and her 'mercy' invoked; the Lord Governor would be chidden and might be recalled in disgrace, or he might resign in despair. A new Governor would, for political reasons, reverse the policy of his predecessor.

Spenser watching and experiencing events in Ireland is not cold or unmoved. Scenes of horror he witnessed when Munster was laid waste in his first year of service are described in *A Vue* and must have haunted him thereafter; the fearful face of starvation, the voice of despair, the distress of fertile countryside ruined, barren and over-grown make themselves felt in his poetry. Both in *A Vue*, where he hopes to influence policy, and in his poetry where he is searching out moral truth it is not enough to react with pity and anger. In poetry the root of evil must be found and in the political treatise a way, however stern, must be prescribed *to stop it*.

Spenser's treatise is a carefully marshalled exposition of the distressed and deeply disturbing state of Ireland, with urgent recommendation that the only remedy be applied immediately: despatch of English military forces in strength, offer of a general amnesty followed quickly by a major campaign well planned and efficiently executed. One winter campaign, he says, would finish the dreadful business for good and all. The inevitable suffering would be sharp but soon ended. The policy of Lord Grey, he maintained, had failed because the Crown failed to support him.

A Vue must have occasioned deep disquiet and displeasure when the manuscript circulated in high places in London. Small wonder that it was not published then, and saw print only in 1633 and in Dublin. By then the recommended policy had indeed been carried out, with the ruthless and efficient campaign of 1600 under Mountjoy, then the end of the old Gaelic order with the 'flight of the Earls', and the subsequent wholesale plantation of Ulster with Protestant

Scots in King James's reign. 'Poetry is more philosophical than history.' *A Vue* records and interprets the course of events as personally experienced and understood on the spot. *The Faerie Queene* explores and expounds the essential nature of moral and spiritual values by showing them in an action. At times an exemplar is taken from current events—for instance Raleigh's fall from royal favour (Timias in Books III and IV). By the same token the terrain in which the hero acts is at times identifiable though still of exemplary force—as when, in a painter's portrait of the Queen, a view of recognizable landscape is glimpsed through a window behind her or seen mapped and spread under her feet.

The presence of Ireland in Spenser's poetry is now actual, now of exemplary force. *Epithalamion* celebrates his actual wedding in Munster at midsummer, but both latitude and date are woven into the cosmic design of the poem's meaning. The journey in his eclogue *Colin Clout's Come Home Againe* is a favourite theme of pastoral poetry used to contrast simple with sophisticated culture; and it is an actual journey made by the poet from Ireland to London and back. The title is cryptic: it raises the question 'Which was *Home* for Colin Clout?' The piece is superscribed 'From my house of Kilcolman'.

The presence of Ireland in the poetry of *The Faerie Queene* is felt only momentarily in the earlier Books, which, we believe, had been substantially composed before Spenser took up work there. In canto ix Book II it appears by name in the torment of gnats in the Bog of Allen, figuring intolerable subjection to guerrilla attacks against which there is no defence. It has moreover been suggested that the topography of Guyon's voyage to destroy the Bowre of Blisse, devised in symbolic terms and designed to bring to mind the voyaging of classical hero towards his objective, bears also a curious resemblance to the approach by sea to Smerwick harbour, scene of the massacre in war. (The conflict of values, the suppressed guilt, mind and spirit steeling itself to wreak utter destruction, is comparable in psychological terms?) Timias/Raleigh in royal displeasure with Belphoebe appears

> in wretched weedes disguiz'd
> With heavy glib deform'd and meiger face
> Like ghost late risen from his grave agryz'd.

Spenser's fear and horror of the alien Irish and the face of their misery is betrayed in the choice of the image (IV, viii 12). As Book IV draws to its close the marriage of Thames and Medway is celebrated— river as natural resource united with river of use to man in commerce. It has a pageant of attendant rivers of Britayne and overseas. The rivers of Ireland are called in. The poet catalogues them in an ordered sequence that delineates England's contact with Ireland, and his own. He displays with affection their beauty, variety and fruitfulness; but terror is not absent.

The first, the gentle Shure that making way
By sweet Clonmell adornes rich Waterford. . .
The spreading Lee that like an Island fayre
Encloseth Corke with his devided flood
And balefull Oure, late staind with English blood.

Book V of Justice, after a series of adventures that are theoretical
'cases' as in a law-book, advances to the practice of justice in
international affairs, which brings the glimpse of mapped terrain.
From scenes that reflect issues in European politics and continental
wars of religion the hero moves by boat westwards, to attempt at last
the long-delayed rescue of Irena which was his appointed Quest.
(He had been deflected from it to take part in continental issues, as
Norris had from duty in Ireland to service in the Netherlands.)
Grantorto, the great wrong of rebellion, whom Artegall then fights
in single combat, wears the armour of an Irish *galloglas*. Irena, who
is met in terror and despair, is rescued—but for the time being only.
And after his strong and determined action her champion is disgraced
and savaged by the arch-enemies of justice, the Hags Envie and
Detraction. The fate is that of Lord Grey. Irena is peace, Irene, and
she is Ireland, Eire. (We recall that The Pale was known as 'the land
of peace'.) The rescue of Irena for good and all is an impossibility
as the inbuilt irreconcilables in her name declare. The poet shows
Ireland in a context of issues that were Europe-wide, blindly and
violently contended in the name of territorial right, national identity
and true religion. He could not perceive a parallel in abstract justice
between the revolt of the Netherlands against Spain's dominion and
the rebellion of the Catholic Irish against Elizabeth's sway. But who
of that epoch could?

The presence of Ireland is felt again in Book VI, of Courtesie
which takes over where Book V had ended. The theme of nature and
nurture, important for the Book's whole meaning, treats of the
savage man or 'salvage man', degenerate as cannibal and brigand
or, as innocent and untutored child of the woods, speaking in an
incomprehensible murmur and with knowledge of simples. The
terrain of the Book is, at one level, Eden after the Fall. In landscape
the Book is pastoral—and not in the literary sense only. Pasture with
flocks and herds borders the deep forest where evil forces lurk. A
hawk hovers over all, bird of wild nature that can be trained and a
natural product Ireland was famed for. A menace.

In the last Book as we have it, of Constancie (perseverance,
consistency) the landscape is expressly Ireland, indeed it is Aherlow/
Arlo in sight of Spenser's Kilcolman. In that forest Cynthia/Diana
delighted to hunt, but she has abandoned it forever and made it a

Spenser's 'Mulla mine', the Awbeg river.

63

place accursed. In an inset fable Spenser has woven together the classical legend of Diana and Actaeon and a tale of Irish river names, of place lore, in his own domain in Munster. The stream Molanna (sister of the Mulla whose story had been told in *Colin Clout*) loves another stream Fanchin and longs to wed him. Molanna, as Cynthia's handmaid, figures the Irish people; Fanchin may reflect 'ourselves alone' of *sinn fein*. In return for a promise to further the match, Molanna agrees to help Faunus, a savage wood-god, who is plotting to 'see Cynthia naked'—Elizabeth stripped of her Irish provinces. Faunus bribes Molanna with gifts symbolic of independence and the Catholic eucharist, 'Queene-apples and cherries of the Trie'. In Faunus we perceive Tyrone, by nature 'wild Irish' but nurtured in England, perfidious and malicious, conspirator and rebel. As was Tyrone, Faunus is hunted into outlawry (for which the term was 'put to the horn').

The great scene of Book VII canto vii shows Nature confronted by the Titaness Mutabilitie, child of chaos, force of rebellion and violent change; she argues her place in the cosmic scheme. She is arraigned before a council of the gods, not on Olympus but on Arlo Hill. It is not by chance but by grand design that the argument of the whole heroic poem has drawn ever nearer home. (The Virtues of the Books descend earthwards in linked sequence from God's throne, as we shall see.) In Aherlow/Arlo, 'a nest of robbers and outlaws', the issue of mutability was fought out in bloody actuality.

As the argument of his great poem developed Spenser was writing in Ireland, aware both with brain and nerves of its condition. This affected the angle from which he came to view the Queen and her rule, his conception of order and chaos, his feelings about the varieties of the family of man. What is more, the language he heard about him every day was the English of the Pale, antiquated in usage and affected by Celtic idiom. The way a word sounded and the spread of its possible meanings must often have diverged markedly from English as spoken in courtly circles in London. A poet's ear would not be deaf to this 'Doric' speech. Celtic names of river or hill he must have had translated for him, as his poetry betrays such knowledge. Topographical legends he wove into his fabling. Yet there have been critical discussions of *The Faerie Queene* and presentation of Spenser's poetry and use of language that virtually ignore the impact of Ireland. This imbalance I have here tried to redress.

3 Philosophical and Scientific Background

Space and place

For men of Edmund Spenser's day the universe was mysterious but explicable. It had been created by God to a grand design, harmoniously ordered. The earth was the centre of the great cosmos (macrocosm) and man, in whom God's creation had culminated, was made to a pattern that corresponded to the greater one; he was a microcosm, a cosmos in little. Man's nature was explicable first in terms of his place in universal order, in nearness to or distance from God.

The form of the universe was a sphere, the figure of perfection, 'a great round frame hung on two immoveable hooks' (the Poles) containing eleven heavens and spheres, each with its character and 'intelligence' or activating spirit. From the centre outwards the spheres were ranged in order thus: earth, the moon, Mercury, Venus, the sun, Mars, Jupiter, Saturn. The eighth sphere was of the fixed stars, 'fixed' because their distance from one another did not change; this was the firmament of Genesis. The ninth was the crystal heaven, the 'second moveable' when you counted from the outside in; the tenth was the 'first moveable' or *primum mobile* and the eleventh was the imperial heaven where God and his angels are said to dwell.

The ethereal region, the higher and upper part, enclosed the elementary region, the part below the moon's sphere (sublunary), 'in which are all corruptible bodies and things harmed by diverse alterations—*except the mind of man*'. As a creature of the sublunary region man was chief of the order of creation there; below him in order ranked bird, beast, fish, tree or plant and stones. Each rank had its peculiar excellence; the plant in growth, the beast in the senses, man in reason, which only he in that region possessed. The soul of man had three powers: vegetable life shared with plants, the life of the senses shared with beasts, and the reasonable soul in which he was akin to the angels above him.

As man was the culmination of creation, everything created was for his use and pleasure. It was for him by his reason to divine that use and put it into action. Everything created had its property (or virtue) and implanted in creatures were clues to their property which indicated their 'use to man'. (The shape of the walnut, resembling the brain, indicated a use as medicine for disorders of the brain.)

65

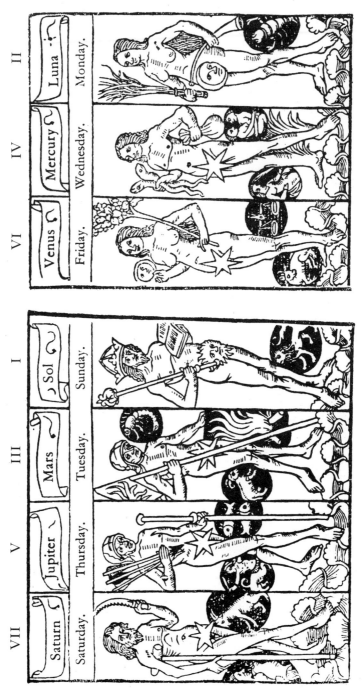

The planets with symbols of their nature and their zodiac signs. (Their order in the week is indicated by roman numerals)

All in the 'elementary' region was compounded of the four elements: fire, water, earth and air; these were in continual motion, fire and air tending upwards, earth and water downwards. The elements were expressed in the frame of man as choler, phlegm, blood and melancholy; they were present in proportions differing from individual to individual, each man's 'complexion' or temperament being determined by the disposition of power in the heavenly bodies at the moment of his birth. He was therefore 'inclined' by the stars at his birth towards one course or another of temperamental behaviour. But he being a creature of reason (his part of the divine), the responsibility for his behaviour lay with him in his governance of his temperamental inclination. The stars could not make a man sin.

This disposition of power in the heavenly bodies was reckoned in terms of the days of the week, each day of the seven belonging to and having as guardian a different planet in its moving sphere. The assigning of planet to day has left its record in the naming of the days, which is clearer in French than in English, where some retain kinship with Germanic gods. The days named in order of the planetary week are these

1	2	3	4	5	6	7
the sun	the moon	Mars	Mercury	Jove	Venus	Saturn
Sunday	Monday	Tuesday	Wednesday	Thursday	Friday	Saturday
dimanche	*lundi*	*mardi*	*mercredi*	*jeudi*	*vendredi*	*samedi*
(the Lord's day)						

Planetary influence extended to the hours of day and night. The same order obtained, the first hour of daylight belonging to the planet of the day, the next to the next, the sequence being resumed and repeated in order. Whatever the season, the day from sunrise to sunset was divided equally into twelve hours as was the night, in contrast to 'clock hours' of time numerically measured.

The guardianship and influence of each planet was exercised according to its nature, and here the derivation of the planet characters from the gods of antiquity becomes evident. Saturn and Mars were malignant, Jupiter and Venus benignant, Sol and Luna half good and half evil of will: 'the part towards the good planet is good, that towards the evil not so.' Mercury (who occupied a middle position) is good 'conjoined' with a good planet and *vice versa*.

The influence of a planet on one of his 'people' (born under his guardianship) went beyond a conditioning of complexion or physiognomy to communicating to them its own affinity with phenomena of nature, say an element; this inclined them to certain activities, callings or professions. Each planet had, moreover, a special relation-

67

ship with one or two signs of the zodiac; this association derived from astronomy and number but was 'confirmed' in an aptness to the planet's character. Each planet had also its apt weapon, insignia, emblem or instrument that could be seen to belong to some aspect of its nature; the authority for the association varied from astronomical fact or classical legend to folklore.

The accompanying illustration of the planetary week and of the planets' characters was current in Spenser's England. It is taken from a compendium of knowledge made in France in 1493 by a theologian who was also a printer. This was one of the earliest books designed for the common man, to provide him with an almanack and a guide to all he needed to know for his health of body, mind and spirit—*Le Compost et kalendrier des bergiers* by Guy Marchand. It was widely translated, and printed in England several times in the sixteenth century as *The Kalendar and Compost of Shepherds*. This was 'the old book' to which Spenser 'gave a new name' with *The Shepheardes Calender*, as we shall see. It is acceptable, then, as indicating what plain people knew and how that knowledge was felt to affect the conduct of their lives. It is a safe 'way in' to these matters as they appear in the poetry of Spenser because it brings to our mind what was taken for granted at that time. But Spenser was a scholar of classical languages, literature and philosophy, and an expert in 'the art mathematical', and his knowledge was at a far more sophisticated level. This summary is only a first exercise in approaching his whole meaning; it takes us as far as 'the understanding of the many', far short of the 'judgment of the learned'.

The woodcut shows the planets in their astronomical order from the earth. The character of each can to some extent be read by a modern eye. Saturn, for instance, is aged, using a crutch and bearing a sickle, as Father Time bears a scythe. His character is of old age, infirmity, change, the passage of time. Sol has the crown and sceptre of his kingship and a book for Phoebus' association with poetry. His sign is Leo, the lion of royalty. Venus has a looking-glass, emblem of love-lady and courtesan; she bears a fruiting branch for procreation and plenty. Taurus is for spring and growing plants and the Scales is for harvest-time, though it could be construed as indicating instability or 'variance'. (A cut from the same book giving Luna and her people will be found with the critical commentary on a passage from Book II of *The Faerie Queene* at p. 153.)

But was not the old picture of an earth-centred cosmos and God-centred universe affected by the findings of Copernicus? These were made known first in 1536 and published in 1543. To men of Spenser's generation the nature of his hypothesis—that the cosmos was sun-centred—was certainly accessible in various texts in print. But here is an intelligent man's reaction in the decade of Spenser's death—Thomas Blundevile in his *Exercises* (1594):

Some also deny that the Earth is in the middest of the world and some affirm that it is moveable, as also Copernicus by way of supposition and not for that he thought so indeed—who affirmeth that the Earth turneth about and that the sun standeth still in the midst of the Heavens; by help of which false supposition he hath made truer demonstrations of the motions and revolutions of the celestial spheres than ever were made before, as plainly appeareth by his book *De revolutionibus* dedicated to Pope Paul....But Ptolemy, Aristotle and all other old writers affirm the Earth to be in the middest and to remain unmoveable...proving the same truth with many strong reasons not needful here to be rehearsed, because I think few or none do doubt thereof, and especially the Holy Scripture affirming the foundations of the Earth to be laid so sure that it never should be moved at any time.

Men's minds were not yet ready to relinquish 'the old philosophy'. And here on the matter of stellar influence is Spenser's friend Sir Walter Raleigh, courtier, voyager, colonizer, student of science, writer of political treatise, poet and favourite of the Queen, writing, from imprisonment under her successor, his *Historie of the World*:

Certainly it cannot be doubted but the stars are instruments of far greater use than to give an obscure light and for men to gaze on after sunset, it being manifest that the diversity of seasons, the winters and summers more hot and cold are not so uncertained by the Sun and Moon alone who always keep one and the same course, but that the stars have also their working therein.

And if we cannot deny but that God hath given virtues to springs and fountains, to cold earth, to plants and stones, minerals and to the excremental parts of the basest living creatures, why should we rob the beautiful stars of their working powers? For seeing they are many in number and of eminent beauty and magnitude we may not think that in the treasury of His wisdom, who is infinite, there can be wanting even for every star a peculiar virtue and operation as every herb, plant, fruit and flower adorning the face of the earth hath the like. For as these were not created to beautify the earth alone and to cover and shadow her dusty face, but otherwise for the use of man and beast to feed them and cure them, so were not these uncountable glorious bodies set in the Firmament to no other end, than to adorn it, but for instruments and organs of His divine providence, so far as it hath pleased His just will to determine.

Origen [an early Father of the Church], upon this place of Genesis 'Let there be light in the Firmament' affirmeth that the stars are not causes (meaning perchance binding causes) but are as open books wherein are contained and set down all things

Sir Walter Raleigh, 1588.

70

whatsoever to come but not to be read by the eyes of human wisdom: *which latter part I believe well*. In this question of Fate, the middle course is to be followed, that as, with the heathen, we do not bend God to his creatures in this supposed necessity of destiny, so, on the contrary, we do not rob these beautiful creatures of their powers and offices.

However we are by the stars inclined at our birth, yet there are many things both in nature and art that encounter the same and weaken their operation. There is nothing after God's reserved power that so much setteth this art of influence out of square and rule as education doth; for there are none in the world so wickedly inclined but that a religious instruction and bringing up may fashion anew and reform them, nor any so well disposed whom, the reins being let loose, the continued fellowship and familiarity and the examples of dissolute men may not corrupt and deform.

This passage is a sensitive pointer to the sense of space and place, man's place in the cosmic scheme. It registers the relation of religion to science, the use of reason's middle course in judgment and the importance of human influence and education.

Since the Middle Ages the sense of space and place on the surface of the earth had changed vastly. The old *mappa mundi* had shown an inhabited world in the northern hemisphere only, whose centre was Jerusalem. Now the southern hemisphere was penetrated and shown to be habitable. 'The new map with the augmentation of the Indies' provided in its complication of lines a witty comparison for Malvolio's smile-wrinkled face. Space had expanded beyond all imagination. Drake in 1578 sailed round the world, 'and rich he is returned' added Philip Sidney. The intellectual stimulus was enormous but attended by the urge for gain. There was vigorous interest in mathematics as an aid to navigation, in geometry as an aid to cartography.

Territories enormous in their promise were glimpsed, inhabited by 'the salvage man'. The concept of man's place being hierarchic, the 'place' of the savage man was a point of debate. For Spenser the expansion of world space over the oceans made only a light impact, but his great pageant of rivers in Book IV of his epic scans the known world from Ganges to 'rich Oranochy, though but knowen late'. Elizabeth as *primum mobile* in our illustration of 1588 is Queen of England, France and Ireland. When Spenser dedicates his heroic poem to her in 1596 she is Queen of Virginia also.

Time

In the 'old philosophy' not only space and place but time itself was God-created and God-given. Time for an Elizabethan was a dimension still in the old manner, but this was now being affected and redirected by new pressures and emphases. In this gradual coming about of conceptual change advances in computation played their part as did developments in social pattern and activity.

In the dynamics of the sacral universe time had two aspects. First, it was *cyclic*, in the pattern laid down at the Creation, when the universe was set in motion: day and night, the lunar week, the solar year with its months and zodiac signs. The sure return of these was a manifestation of God's law and on their sure return depended man's survival, as keeper of beasts and tiller of the soil in season. Over the ages a rich lore had accrued to the course of the food year. Each season and each month had its character, which was compounded of its complexion in proportion of elements, its place in sequence, its zodiac ties and its use to man. The spring months of April, May and June were moist and hot, those of summer hot and dry, and so on. February, cold and wet, was aptly under Aquarius and Pisces. Each month had its work. That for February was wood-cutting for fuel. As February was the year's end according to one way of reckoning, the character of February would be rendered as an old man, warming himself at the fire. The character of the month was felt as it passed, in the labours and pastimes that belonged to it. Man was in touch with cosmic rhythm and visualized his life-span as of four seasons with the year, seven ages with the planets or twelve phases corresponding to the months.

The course of the year belonged also to the Christian Church, which had (and has) its seasons such as Advent, its great days of Christmas and Easter, and its many festivals of occasion or saint's day. In February fell the old pre-Christian feast of the returning sun; February opened with the due date for the Purification of the Blessed Virgin, which gave the Feast of Candlemas, in which the fire motif of the month's labour was confirmed. This way of thinking in parallel, of finding confirmation in one sequence by reference to another, because both testified to a grand universal plan, was deeply engrained as a habit of mind. It is present when a poet creates.

Both the substance and the habit of mind are present in Spenser's *The Shepheardes Calender* as we shall see. (Woodcuts from it showing some of the months are reproduced on pp. 100–101). In Book VII of *The Faerie Queene* the argument of change and mutability features cyclic time as a pageant of the course of the year in the seasons, the planets and the months in order. The character of each month is personified to render its pastime or labour, while its movement onwards is figured by a link with the zodiac sign as steed or walking companion. The process of poetry has further enriched this pageant by linking the month's figuring with apt myth of antiquity: for April the zodiac steed is the bull of Jove's love for Europa.

Cyclic time was measured by the calendar. The year as reckoned by the old Julian calendar was too long—365$\frac{2}{5}$ days. The discrepancy accumulated over centuries. By 1572 the vernal equinox had moved ten days from its proper date. This affected the timing of Easter. Pope Gregory, elected in that year, supported moves for reform. But general disquiet was felt at the prospect of 'losing' ten days in order to right matters. Spenser, shaping his pastoral as a *Calender* in 1579, touched a live interest in the issue of computation of time.

Time in its second sacral aspect moved *on* from Creation to Doomsday, again on a grand plan. Here it belonged manifestly to God, for in earlier times 'history' was the story of God's dealing with man on earth. Cosmic time began at the Creation but Eden was timeless and in a special sense time on earth began for man with his fall from grace. Thence it moved down through the dark period of the Old Testament to the Flood, with a second chance for man in Noah and the promise given; then onwards and downwards through the ancient world of the Old Law, but with voices of prophets foretelling the coming of Christ and with His earthly pedigree traced through chosen figures to culminate in His earthly mother, Mary.

Time began anew with Christ's birth, *Anno Domini*, and the epoch of the New Law it initiated. The thirty years of his life on earth had special significance and events in his life were envisaged as 'prefigured' in earlier time: the imperfect pattern of Abraham's sacrifice of Isaac was fulfilled in God's sacrifice of his son at the Crucifixion. This was the true type; the near-sacrifice of Isaac the 'antetype', the forerunner. From Crucifixion onwards the new pattern of redemption promised to the sinner held good for all Christians, and saints and martyrs bore witness to that.

Thinking in parallel between the Old Testament and the New was a familiar habit in church service; type and antetype were often featured in church windows. Spenser could count on his readers associating the Mount and its Sermon with Moses bringing the tablets of the Old Law from his mountain-top.

In accordance with this time scheme man in Elizabethan Christendom was still fallen man, his 'will infected' by the Fall but his 'wit erected', his reason still his portion of the divine, and able to operate. He had the ability to know good, to discern virtue—God's purpose for him—but lacked the will to perform it. His life-span was 'given', granted him to use for amendment of life, as the prayer says. The day of his death was appointed, but not revealed. His course onward through his time on earth should be a progress on his way to salvation, a battle against sin with the virtues on his side and the vice against him. Salvation he might hope to attain, in part through his works but ultimately through his acceptance of the gift of God's grace. The value of time and the evaluation of man and his conduct lay in the hereafter.

This scheme is operant in Spenser's poetry. *The Faerie Queene* in its first Book shows the progress of George (a man of earth as the name betokens, and so the ploughman who is everyman) learning through encounter and adventure, mistakes and failures and visitations of grace, to earn the armour of God as St George, the patron saint of England. Time is the onward-moving time of man's life on earth. He is learning the nature of Holiness and of himself as a wouldbe champion of that virtue; as such he loves Una, the one true faith, and his activity is conceived under Sol, the Sun of Righteousness, planet of the first day and governing power of Book I. So time for the Knight in his Book is some part of his imagined life-span on earth, onward-moving but in a live context of cosmic rhythm, a day of an enormous week of celestial motion. And as the grand pattern of the whole allegory unfolds, this life-span of George is related to the life of Christ's Church on earth, the whole story of man from Eden to the Apocalypse.

New and changing concepts of time also impinge on Spenser as man and poet. Only a bare summary statement can be made here of the conceptual development. Time in the old way was God-given for the amendment of life; usury was a sin because it exploited for worldly gain a God-given time factor. But in the renaissance world and its developing urban civilization commerce was assuming great importance; the parable of the talents was read with a new urgency. A world where accounts had to be balanced could envisage the Day of Judgment, of the weighing of souls, as a Day of Accounting. Time was a precious commodity in its short supply. Advice to seize time, *carpe diem*, was found in the writings of classical antiquity. Perhaps the shock of the plague, the death within hours of old and young alike, acted now not only as a *memento mori* but also as a warning that time was short. Improved measurement and computation in the invention of the mechanical clock and its wide dissemination affected the consciousness of time passing. Petrarch, in a sense the father of the renaissance of classical learning, would have nothing to do with astrology but was obsessed with the passage of time. He had a vivid sense of turning-point in a man's life. So had Spenser. *The Shepheardes Calender* celebrates the twenty-first year of Elizabeth's reign. I believe it was marriage in the forty-second year of his own life that Spenser celebrated so splendidly in *Epithalamion*.

In *The Faerie Queene* we are not urgently conscious of pressure of time passing. The projected scheme of each knight due to return to Gloriana's court, his quest completed, does not press on the action of the poem as we have it. Knights may be turned away from their quest to some other urgent task: 'not yet'. They may be within sight of arriving at an ultimate goal when the accomplishment is barred, or allowed to be achieved in part or for a period only. Within the single encounter we may feel strong anxiety: will Despair's persuasions prevail, will Guyon succumb to Mammon? The insidious enemy of active virtue—sloth, sleep or inaction—is ever there to sap energy, to delay, to whelm activity in oblivion. But in the interweaving of story lines, though there is a pattern of chance encounters in space, though dangers may lurk, the time factor as urgency of time passing is not in operation. (Only the rescue of Irena, the issue of Ireland, is attended by anxiety of time!) At the close of Book VI the poet maintains:

> For all that hetherto hath long delayd
> This gentle knight from sewing his first quest
> Though out of course, yet hath not bene missayd
> To shew the courtesie by him profest...
>
> VI. xii, 2

The displaying of virtue in action, the progress in understanding that virtue, by the Knight and by the reader who follows his course, takes precedence. *Carpe diem* is the counsel of the song in the villainess Acrasia's Bowre, and time is marked there by sundials, which record only sunshine hours. At the heart of Book III, in the Garden of Adonis, the enemy of cosmic love is Time; but time is shown overcome through procreation—love creating. Adonis is 'eterne in mutabilitie'. In a totally Christian imagining time may well be an enemy, time may be 'not yet', it may for one issue be dangerously urgent, but in the spirit of the action it is never 'too late'.

The 'fervent discovery of time' by renaissance man manifested itself in other responses that are present in Spenser's poetry. These responses may fitly be listed here with some indication of the way they interacted to form an 'argument of time'. They centre in the Renaissance emphasis on the dignity of man, his value declared and enhanced in this world, not in the hereafter. Time was a threat to man, his dignity, his works, the civilization he had achieved. Time's power to wreak destruction and work decay, to sink past achievement in oblivion, was everywhere to be seen, to be lamented and to be learned from. 'The triumphs of time', 'the ruins of Rome', 'the ruins of time' are important themes of renaissance thought and are causes of Renaissance poetry. Spenser translated from Petrarch and du Bellay poems on this issue in the *Theatre* and in his volume of *Complaints*. (We recall the picture of Rome on p. 13.) He learned and used in *The Faerie Queene* the symbol of the city as a token of civilization's achievement—of building, flourishing and then decay unless persisting in intellectual fruits. Such is the earthly city of Troynovant/London, set against the everlasting splendour of the City of God.

The response to time's threat of decay and oblivion was the achievement of continuance in this world in the flesh or in the spirit, by the begetting of children, building of a line, a succession, a name, or by winning the 'deathless name' of fame. Creation of a line, a great house, would make a contribution to civilization and a mark on history. In spirit, the threat of time was a spur to heroic endeavour, adventuring, voyaging, colonizing, notable service to monarch and commonweal. The historian and the scholar could play an important part by rescuing and restoring the valuable achievement of the past in action and great writings; these would serve as models of excellence and so be an inspiration to fresh endeavour.

The philosopher also had his place. A poignant aspect of time's devouring power was the perishable nature of human beauty and loveliness. (Consciousness of the body and its beauty as a good in itself was a 'discovery' of Renaissance man.) Beauty could be seized and enjoyed as a rose is plucked in an immediate response to the menace of fleeting time. But to respond to beauty with love in the ways of highest excellence, to discern in the perishable beauty of the beloved the ideal that was out of time, to desire that and attain union with it was sovran against time's power. This way of thinking was called Neoplatonism, of which we shall have more to say. It was fundamental to a Renaissance poet's writing.

In all this the poet held a key position, for poetry could itself transcend time and confer 'deathless name'. It could celebrate heroic endeavour in the heroic poem, the most important kind of poetry at the Renaissance. It could celebrate the noble line, as Spenser did the line of Dudley, Earl of Leicester. Celebration of the prince was a central concern. The poet as lover could show the way of love's excellence and render immortal the beauty of the beloved. Poetry could satisfy the 'need to feel the present moment in relation to time', which has been claimed as a key characteristic of Renaissance man: Spenser gave 'durance perpetuall' to the year 1579 in his *Calender*, to the day of his own wedding in *Epithalamion*.

Number

Men of the sixteenth century thought and felt about number in a way that has all but vanished from our modern world, unless it survive as a superstitious regard for, say, 13 as unlucky as a house number or the 7th of the month as a lucky date. In those days a feeling that each number had its character or property was current in simple form among plain people, for everything in the world had its property or use to man. But in learned and sophisticated minds the science of numerology was vastly complex and numbers were 'mystic', being a revelation of divine truth.

Deriving from the wisdom of the antique world—Greek, Egyptian, Jewish and Arabic—and developed and elaborated through the Dark and the Middle Ages, numerology had become imbued with Christian doctrine. The nature of mystic numbers was set out by St Augustine in his *Treatise of Christian Doctrine* (ch. II). At the Renaissance contact was renewed with ancient lore, and mystic and symbolic values of number underwent further penetration and elaboration by the minds of thinking men. The doctrine of number or the science of numerology was one aspect of the 'art mathematical', in which Edmund Spenser was said to excel. And Gabriel Harvey noted that poets of the highest order were astronomical poets.

Number had two main aspects, the first philosophical or 'Pythagorean', the second astronomical: one was found to confirm the other. In both number was God-created and fundamental to universal order. All numbers flow from Unity which is God and mind.

Unity or (number) 1 is associated with truth, the light, the guiding principle of the cosmic mind and of the individual mind. ('If the eye be single the body is full of light.') From unity or 1, which is single, proceeds diversity or more-than-oneness, which can be doubleness or duplicity or multiplicity of falsehood. 1 is not number and of no sex. In the planetary week 1 is of the sun.

2 is female. It is body rather than mind. It belongs to the order of nature, of earthly existence and values rather than transcendental or heavenly values and stands in contrast to its celestial predecessor and counterpart. 2 is of the moon and sublunary regions.

With 3 unity and diversity, which could war with one another, are restored to harmony. 3 had ancient magic properties and had strong association with the Christian Trinity. 3 was the first male (odd) number and had generative power. The threeness 'of the triad' is widely used by Spenser as a pattern of composition, both in the form of his heroic poem and within its narrative—as a pattern of 1 unfolding into three aspects, for instance the three sons of Night, Sans Foy, Sans Loy and Sans Joy. The planet is Mars.

4 is 2 + 2 and 2 × 2 and is a cosmic number of concord. World order was created out of 4 elements. There were 4 quarters of the world, 4 rivers of Paradise, and so on. 4 stood for stability, as in our 'foursquare'. The planet is Mercury.

5 is 3 + 2, male plus female, a summing of like and unlike. The human sum of male plus female is wedlock, a just relation of man to woman in which the male is the higher number. The summing of like and unlike figured Justice and so 5 carried a sovereign power. The Old Testament had the Pentateuch—the Five Books of the Old Law. The planet is Jupiter, his day Thursday.

6 is 2 × 3 and is linked with sexual love and procreation. It belongs to the planet Venus in the astronomical scheme, as producer of love, of procreative power, of peace and plenty. The day, Friday.

7 had the character of 'unbegotten, unbegetting', being a prime number and the only one that does not yield as a multiple any number up to ten. It was 'the key to the universe' in ancient lore. It was the number of days in the lunar week and belonged to the world of change. In Christendom it was the number of the days of Creation preceding 8, the day of completion and rest. It was a figure of change, but being 'unbegetting, unbegotten' it had the virtue also of immunity

from change. The planet is Saturn, power of old age and change, the power of time.

8 is the number of regeneration and of resurrection, of eternity. It has its place as the eighth day of Creation and the eighth day of Holy Week, when Christ rose again. (Baptismal fonts are traditionally octagonal in form.)

9 was a principal figure of virtue, the perfect form of the perfect 3, the number of the spheres (according to one system) and of the sphere of the angelic hierarchy, which the virtuous human mind resembled.

10 was a round number of completion; in the body of the fingers and toes, in Scripture of the Ten Commandments.

11 was a number of sin as it 'transgressed' the ten of the Decalogue, and Judas was the sinner among the twelve.

12 again was a number of completion, order and stability. It is a multiple of 2, 3, 4, and 6. There were 12 cardinal virtues according to Aristotle—and the apostles were twelve.

In this oversimplified vocabulary of number meanings a first step, and a first step only, is taken towards cultivation in the reader of a live reaction to number as a factor in earlier poetry. Number may be relevant to poetry at a very simple level or at a very sophisticated one. The important thing is for the reader to be alert to its possible presence and aware of the modes of its operation.

Number and poetry

'Numbers' is a word for metrical composition—the usual word in Elizabethan English. The idea of metre (measuring) entailed enumeration of what was 'measured', whether by counting feet or syllables. Measure implied proportion and harmony. Composition in verse, then, was understood to consist in a bringing of words into order, into a scheme of proportion and harmony that was conceived in terms of number. (The metaphorical force of other words used in describing poetry will be discussed in a later section.)

Poetry mirrored 'nature' (universal order), as will later be explained Number belonged to what was mirrored and so to the poetry that mirrored it, as a factor in harmony and proportion, as an ordering and activating principle, indeed as a mediator of the pulse of cosmic rhythm. (These three are not easily separable but as far as possible they will be considered in order.)

First, number was an aspect of the poem's form and as such could contribute towards the poem's total meaning. To take a simple instance, the central line of a poem numerically calculated could embody that centrality and mark its crucial point. The central line of *Colin Clout's Come Home Againe*, line 478, is a voicing of the heart of the poem's meaning; the neighbouring lines pivot on it as does the whole piece, which has a finely devised symmetry.

And I hers ever only, ever one
One ever I all vowed hers to bee
One ever I, and others never none.

By the same token the central line of the central Book in Chaucer's *Troilus and Criseyde* shows an identification of Criseyde with Fortune, in the verb used so often of Fortune's wheel:
'For with o word ye may his herte stere' (III 910).
The central line of Milton's *Paradise Lost* shows 'Son of Man'. (Such examples from different poets have a consistency that cannot be accidental.)

Because in Renaissance art part belongs to whole and whole to part, the number of stanzas in a poem and of lines in its stanza belong to the poem's subject and purpose. *Prothalamion*, as we shall see, with its ten stanzas of eighteen lines is an example of this. The stanza of *The Faerie Queene* is of nine lines. Why is that apt for a heroic poem? Ordering and activating *The Faerie Queene* as we have it, in seven Books, is the cosmic scheme of the planetary week; of this the diagram on page 118 gives a visual impression. What is more, the character of the 12 numbered cantos of each Book can be shown to be extensively related to number-meaning, witness the regular entry at canto viii of Arthur and God's grace into the poem's action, bringing regeneration. Look also at the sixth canto of each Book and consider the link with 6, Venus, the power of sex for good or ill. Aptness of number can, at salient points, extend to the stanza, as the reader can learn to mark and inwardly digest. In Book III of Chastity, of love and of generating power, the third stanza of canto iii relates the heroine specifically to love's generating power, looking forward to her engendering, through marriage with her beloved the great line that will bring eternal fame. The established code of number can be used by the poet at any point to confirm or underline his meaning. Further examples, cited with number of Book, canto and stanza, will emerge as the argument of this book develops. On these the reader can try his growing skill.

Number as an ordering principle frequently made a 'set'. Examples emerge from the list given above. From the world of antiquity were inherited certain famous sets—the three Graces, the nine Muses, the twelve labours of Hercules, the 'three days' spent by Aeneas in the underworld. From early Christendom came the seven capital sins and the seven virtues that opposed them, or the three days spent by Christ in Hell before the resurrection. Parallels were discerned between phenomena of these different regions of the mind and a shared number confirmed the parallel. The poet could extend the process. Spenser's Guyon spends three days underground in Mammon's cave, which brings both the classical and the Christian set of three into powerful operation in the reader's mind.

A number set, then, was an item of response that could be counted on in the reader. This is true today, only the sets we respond to are different. Recently a trio of photographs was published in the daily press, showing the aged Archbishop of Canterbury, wearying at a meeting, and with his hands covering first his eyes, then his ears, then his mouth. No caption was needed; the laughter was immediate. A Renaissance audience would react as quickly to the five senses or the seven sins. What is more, were the set presented as incomplete, that point would be taken too. Imagine the third photograph showing the mouth speaking: the inference would be libellous!

The number set, then, was a pattern that might simply be fulfilled, might show variation within itself, or might be presented with one item lacking; but once embarked on, it was in play and affected both form and meaning. For instance in *The Faerie Queene* the five senses enter into Book II, overtly and formally named in canto xi, at stanzas 9 to 13. They come again in canto xii, not formally listed, subtly and tacitly presented, in the enticements of the Bowre of Blisse. The reader, like Guyon, has been warned, and must be 'wary and wise'. The presence of a number set which might show variation within its pattern or sequence is an instrument of communication between poet and reader. Through its silent operation the reader is involved in the poem's meaning and in the moral issues presented. He has to notice and judge. Learning to be aware of number and its subtle and pervasive working is an important skill in learning to read Spenser's poetry.

Secondly, the Renaissance use of number as an ordering and activating principle in poetry reaches a zenith in Spenser's *Epithalamion*. In a study of this poem, *Short Time's Endless Monument*, A. Kent Hieatt first revealed the complexity, profundity and sophistication in poetic art attained by a learned and 'astronomical' poet. Spenser, we recall, married in southern Ireland at St Barnabas tide, June 11, midsummer in the old Julian calendar. He celebrates in poetry his own wedding, making for his bride a song 'in lieu of many ornaments'. It is not only a lovely and moving account of the wedding-day and night that made the marriage timeless in poetry. It is also 'the thing that may *the* mind delight'. The ceremony, the 'doing' of the day is, through the poet's devising, keyed into the rhythms of the universe.

The course of *Epithalamion* corresponds symbolically in one way to the passage of a day and in another to that of a year; beyond that it is made to belong to the greater motions and conformations of the cosmos, though we cannot in this brief account trace the whole complex argument. The poem has twenty-four stanzas for the hours of a day and night; but the hours, attendant on the bride, are also the hours of classical myth, the 'sidereal' hours as the term is still used in modern astronomy. Each stanza is an arrangement of long lines and short and the long lines number 365 for the year's days;

the short lines, Hieatt suggests, are of a number and distribution to render time's divisions.

In the course of the poem the hours run from sunrise onwards. The change from day to night is marked at a key point by a change in the refrain from positive to negative. 'The woods shall to me answer and my Eccho ring' becomes at stanza 17 'The woods shall no more answere nor your echo ring'. This division at the proportion of 16 + /7 + corresponds to the actual proportion of daylight hours to hours of darkness obtaining on midsummerday at the latitude of southern Ireland. Date and place have been rendered in universal terms through the form and the wording of the poetry; the mediating power is number.

The last point of our three is not developed by Hieatt. This act and ceremony, of love and marriage looking to procreation, was performed at the midsummer solstice, which is the zenith of the sun's power of transmitting cosmic energy. The summer solstice was understood to mark in man, the microcosm, the *optimum maximum* of sexual potency (witness other midsummer pieces, such as *Midsummer Night's Dream*). The poem made to celebrate the act and ceremony is itself an energy system of 'numbers' (poetry) in which number of the cosmos is an activating principle. Act, date and place of actuality are through the operation of 'numbers' and number in active communion with cosmic rhythm. What was individual and personal, unique and transitory, is now organically related to 'endless time, and is *auspiciously in touch with cosmic power*.

The dignity of man

The part played by man himself took on a new dignity at the Renaissance. He was still body, soul and spirit, but the body was no longer held to be only the 'gross tenement of clay', the domain of the senses that had to be subjected, the flesh that was corruptible, of little value in itself and a constant source of temptation to sin. Man was created in the image of God. The beauty of man the microcosm, the wonder of his proportions, had been revealed in the world of art through contact with the values of classical sculpture. Admiration for physical beauty as a good in itself brought nudity into a new perspective. A symbol of this new sensibility is seen in the David of Donatello, 'the first free-standing bronze statue since antiquity and the first life-size free-standing nude'.

Contact with the values revealed in the writings of classical antiquity, where concern was focused on conduct and quality of being in this life, enhanced in men's eyes the potential of the individual during his short span of living in the world. The new weight on human values was known as humanism and was linked with scholarship of classical languages, literature and philosophy, 'the humanities' as they are still called. Man's realizing of his highest potential was *virtù*, virtue, the quality of *vir*, a man; it was now articulated in such worldly terms as servant of the prince and commonweal, soldier, statesman, 'adventurer' on sea or land, scholar, orator, lover and poet, or a sum of conduct embracing all these. (There is variation in the spelling of virtue or vertue; in the second a link seems to be felt with *veritas*, truth, vertue being the 'true' quality or propensity belonging to a creature in the order of being.)

The ideal of the man of active virtue had been encouraged by the reading of the ethics of Aristotle, whose values are dominant in Book II of *The Faerie Queene*—the ruling power of reason, the value of self-discipline, the golden mean of moderation. Contact with the works of Plato stimulated thought and affected ways of feeling and behaving in another direction. Renaissance Italy had seen the formation of academies for the study and discussion of classical learning, and reconciliation of its values with tenets of Christian doctrine was sought. The most important of these groups of scholars was that at Florence under Marsilio Ficino and from it flowed the main stream of Neoplatonic doctrine.

They learned from Plato to view the phenomena of this life as imperfect versions only, of which the 'ideas' or 'forms' alone had reality, existed in heaven and were divine. They saw in the universe as created by God His imposing of divine ideas on formless chaos. Man as created in the image of God was now more important than man fallen and to be redeemed.

The universe, produced by the conjunction of form and first matter, was by its very nature full of the beauty and the 'loveliness' that the spiritual imparts to the corporeal. God created out of love and all-embracing love provided the dynamic of the universe: matter struggled upwards in its desire to attain ever purer form. Man aspired towards union with the divine. Such aspiration was met by divine love, which by perpetually seeking anew incarnation in matter completed the cyclic movement of power. This is the background against which should be read Spenser's Book III of *The Faerie Queene*, the Legend of Chastity, or of love as a creating power, especially the heart of the Book in canto vi, the Garden of Adonis:

> All be he subject to mortalitie
> Yet is eterne in mutabilitie,
> And by succession made perpetuall,
> Transformed oft, and changed diverslie:
> For him the Father of all formes they call;
> Therefore needs mote he live, that living gives to all.

This doctrine of love as a dynamic of the sacral universe affected love as a principle of conduct in human life. The medieval code of love, 'courtly love', had sought to transcend the limits of flesh; but obsessive love for a being of flesh and blood, however idealized in its intensity, had been prone to fail as its object was frail (witness Chaucer's *Troilus and Criseyde*). Such concentration of love was rightly directed to God alone. Now physical love, response to the beauty of the senses, was seen as a possible first step in aspiration to love of the highest. Beauty was the divine Idea in the material object; and love was the perception of that Idea. Love for the fair human beloved was for the lover 'a stayre (as it were) to climbe up to another farre higher than it.... And thus shall he beholde no more the particular beautie of one woman, but an universall, that decketh out all bodies' (Castiglione).

That love was a power that could render the lover more noble had been understood in the medieval code; but there it had been only uncomfortably accommodated to man's exercise of reason. And courtly love had been too often directed towards the lady who was unattainable because already married. There had been a dangerous proximity to sin. Marriage and procreation had been the way recommended to man as the best allowable channel of satisfaction of fleshly desire. Now the doctrine of love creating ranged these matters in a different perspective. God had looked on his own beauty and reproduced it in the universe. A lover could look on his beloved, and in love and desire for her beauty beget fair children. And this was a first rung of the ladder—matter tending upwards purer form. Where Neoplatonism merged with Christian doctrine, as in the poetry of Spenser, the end of loving was union with the beloved in Christian marriage and procreation of children—beauty's print of form on matter.

The course of true love as an ascent towards perception of ideal beauty is the pattern of experience informing many a sonnet sequence in Renaissance Europe. The name or title can bear witness to this: *l'Idée*, *Delia*, or Lydia being renderings of the concept 'ideal' in other literation. Spenser's is the only love-sonnet sequence to culminate in an Epithalamium. Shakespeare's sonnets, which are 'out of sequence', show love in two aspects. Love for the 'fair friend' pertains to the ideal: he is encouraged to wed and create fair children in whom his beauty may be perpetuated. Love for the 'dark lady' is destructive.

Varieties of love and ways of loving are explored in Spenser's pastoral, *Colin Clout's Come Home Againe*. At the centre is the avowal of utter devotion to the beloved, as we saw. Ranged on either side in rank or in contrast are such as these: love as conceived by rustic shepherd or by courtier poet; love-service to the monarch and her gracious response, her countenance reflecting the gracious light of heaven; but false love also found at court with jealousy, lies and selfish ambition; foul lust and incest that are punished by oblivion; but true love though unrequited yet celebrated by the poet-lover whose verses confer endless fame. A myth of love's birth and love creating lies at the poem's heart. Varieties of love and ways of loving are the substance of Books III and IV of *The Faerie Queene*. Spenser at the close of his life traced the path upwards in ways of loving in his *Fowre Hymnes* of love and beauty, earthly and heavenly.

At the Renaissance what was learned from Plato came together with what was learned from Aristotle. The way of loving as a discipline for man played a prominent part in the ideal of the man of active virtue. As society was hierarchical, with the Prince as 'the first' and God's representative, the ideal of service to the prince was visualized in the perfect courtier; and in the formulation of that sum of virtuous conduct the lover could have an honourable place. Love-service of the monarch was of the same kind as love-service of the beloved: where the monarch was female this was pronouncedly so, as we saw in discussing the queen-figure of Elizabeth. (In poem after poem Spenser with a poet's courtesy begs his sovereign lady's leave to celebrate his own beloved.)

The education of man towards the ideal of active virtue became a topic of major interest and important treatises were written. The forum was Europe-wide and continental works were translated into English. Machiavelli's *Il Principe* (1513) expounded the art of government and the dynamics of power in the Italian citystate. His work was widely translated and to some extent read mistakenly; but the way up to power and riches which he described with no illusions had little to do with the ascent of the soul through love of beauty to contemplation of the divine. For Spenser it belonged with Philotime in the Cave of Mammon, whose way of ambition led down to hell.

A more idealistic approach was that of Castiglione's *Il Libro del Cortegiano* (1528) translated by Sir Thomas Hoby as *The Book of the Courtyer* (1561), to which reference has already been made. (The work can be read also in modern translation in Penguin editions.) To study this delightful Renaissance dialogue is still the best way to understand how philosophic concepts of Neoplatonism affected the art, and the art of living, of Renaissance man. Its chapter 4 shows the ascent of love and desire of human beauty, through stages, to a vision of heavenly beauty and union with it through love.

When Spenser said of *The Faerie Queene* (in his 'Letter to Raleigh') that 'the general end of all this booke is to fashion a gentleman or noble person in vertuous and gentle discipline', he was setting out to do in the medium of heroic poetry what had been undertaken by Castiglione. The Books trace a sequence displaying the dignity of man, a progression of learning for the reader. Holiness treating of the spiritual on earth, Temperance of Aristotelian discipline and reason in conduct on earth, ways of loving conceived in heaven and practised in earthly friendship, the public virtue of Justice on earth and its counterpart in Courtesy, or the 'vertue' of a courtier.

Calidore, the Knight of the Legend of Courtesy, was felt to embody the 'lovely gift' of that quality, of which an exemplar in life had been seen in Sir Philip Sidney. Sidney was wellborn, handsome in person, loved and admired by his fellows, his opinion sought in counsel. He had been soldier and statesman, scholar and critic, lover and poet, and writer of an Arcadian romance wherein were displayed patterns of worth and dignity in human conduct and speech. Spenser's Book of Courtesy explores all aspects of such a courtier, though for the space of the Book he is presented in pastoral guise. But the high moment of cosmic vision belongs to the poet. It comes in canto x in the great figure of the graces and the 'general dance' of love and concord. The myth of classical antiquity and the medieval image of the dance of love, both earthly and heavenly, show a living cycle of love and grace given, enjoyed and returning. All this to the music of Colin's piping.

Certain great metaphors embody the way of thinking and of feeling we have attempted to outline; they declare themselves both in the form and the content of Renaissance poetry. The most notable is the Great Chain of Being by which the plenitude of God's love was transmitted through all creation in the 'vertue' of each order. The 'vertue' of man, as primate among creatures on earth, was visualized as sevenfold—a linked chain of vertues descending from the throne of God. (Spenser's sequence we now see expressing another movement.) First was Holiness, then Temperance where reason, man's special attribute, is in action—then Love as Chastity or as Friendship, then Justice wherein man learning from heaven seeks to enact justice on earth, then Courtesy where love and grace are planted in earth, a lowly flower growing upward. Then in Book VII Constancy, where time and change are outfaced and the poetry issues in a vision of eternity.

What is apparent in the form comes explicitly in the matter: in Book I (of Holinesse), canto ix (figure of egregious virtue), stanza 1:

> O goodly golden chaine wherewith yfere
> The vertues linked are in lovely wize:
> And noble minds of yore allyed were
> In brave poursuit of chevalrous emprize,
> That none did others safety despize ...

The context is chivalry, the code of the knight who is precursor of the courtier. Arthur has just intervened to help Redcrosse, extending help to his fellow knight in trouble with hands that transmit grace and favour. This, an example of the true chain of love transmitted, has its contrary, a 'false' form, in the chain of Philotime or worldly ambition (II. vii. 44); it stretches from earth to hell and man envies and treads down his fellow man in his effort to mount by it.

The great movement of love in the cosmos was 'the general dance',

Sir Philip Sidney

and dance could be in chain form or ring. The Great Chain of Being linking all creatures in order, the linked chain of vertues, the ladder by which the soul may ascend to union with the divine, the descent of grace through princely magnanimity or dignity of great doing, the round dance of the graces and the cosmic ring-dance of concord and love are the great metaphors that express for man of the Renaissance the involvement of man and God in a living current of being and bestowing, aspiration and incarnation, desire for beauty, and love.

4 Poetic Background

> The poet's eye in a fine frenzy rolling
> Doth glance from heaven to earth, from earth to heaven
> And as imagination bodies forth
> The forms of things unknown, the poet's pen
> Turns them to shapes and gives to airy nothing
> A local habitation and a name.
>
> Shakespeare, *A Midsummer Night's Dream*

A new poetry for Elizabeth's England

Certain regions of belief and attitude in Elizabethan times have been explored because they differed from ours today and acquaintance with them would help us to draw near to Spenser's poetry. We are now confronted with that poetry—again different in so many ways from ours today. We must find out how it works. We need to discern what the poet believed himself to be doing, what he aimed to achieve and by what means, and the reasons why he did so. In this project two things are difficult. First, there are voices enough from the sixteenth century of poet and of theorist, foreign or native, to inform us on those matters, but the terms they use are unfamiliar coinage to our minds, or, worse, they are oldfashioned and misleading as to the values they represent. Then there are certain important issues wherein poet and writer about poetry were *at that time* so completely agreed that these issues are not mentioned, far less debated.

The well-known verses quoted above come from Duke Theseus, a notable sceptic as to poetry or enchantment; but his words show what was taken for granted about the process of imaginative composition, though he speaks to discountenance it. A poet was inspired: his vision could be seen as a coming and going between earth and heaven, whence proceeded forms that shaped and ordered his purpose and matter, thus rendering the 'ideal' accessible in earthly terms. Certainly a general agreement existed on the nature of poetry and the special status of the poet. It was the fruit of more than a century of discussion and experiment, development and achievement, since the revival of learning had brought the poetry and philosophy of antiquity powerfully into the current of new thought and writing in western Europe, and since poetry in 'the sweet new style' had arisen in Italy, blossomed with Petrarch and spread to France with the work of du Bellay and Ronsard, to take firm root in England with the writing of Philip Sidney. At this point Spenser enters the story.

With this new poetry in the Renaissance style 'the theory and practice...form such a coherent unity that any poem written in what is called the Italianate tradition is a concrete embodiment of the theory that lies behind it, and even a slight working knowledge of this can add unsuspected dimensions to the poetry'. To begin then with the theory, and in the simplest terms possible. The view of the universe and of the nature of reality in which a poet was operating was still the hierarchical cosmos, in which the universal and the particular were bound together in a complex system of correspondences. If earth is a microcosmos, everything on earth is an earthly, finite, imperfect, perishable version of its ideal, perfect archetype existing in heaven. If the archetype is the true, the real, the ideal, then man should concern himself with that rather than with the imperfect manifestations he is in contact with in his everyday life. For if he comes to understand the real, the essential, he will understand fully and evaluate justly the imperfect manifestations of 'actual' experience.

A poet is a 'seer'—one who perceives the true, the real; his aim in his poetry is to express what he has perceived and convey it to those who hear or read his poems. The experience of hearing or reading the poems means for the receiver access to the true, the real, via the poet's vision—a process that brings the reader enlightenment. Poetry is didactic, not in the sense of finger-wagging precept but in that the poem well understood widens and deepens human experience. The effect to which contemporary readers of Spenser's poetry testify is, again and again, a 'fulness of joy', 'As who therein can ever joy their fill', or

> but let one dwell upon them [the works] and he shall feel a strange fullness and roundness in all he saith.... The most generous wines tickle the palate least but they are no sooner in the stomach but by their warmth and strength there, they discover what they are.

In the reading of poetry the enlarging of scope in perception and knowledge, the enriching of consciousness brings joy, or pleasure or delight. All three words are used and are sometimes interchangeable. When 'pleasure' is used, the argument recognizes the sensuous appeal of the verse medium—delectable pictures, rhythm, harmony proportion, sweet sound—and the fact that such appeal may make a moral lesson palatable, as with a 'medicine of cherries'. But 'delight' was intended also to convey that moment of excitement and achievement with which one nowadays exclaims 'I *see*'. It registers the moment of shared vision, of discovery of correspondence revealed by the poet, of access to the 'truth', of contact with the real.

That poetry should give 'profit and delight' was confirmed in classical theory; Horace had said it in his *Art of Poetry*. When the use of poetry to man was called in question this was apt to be the reply.

And so the function of poetry came to be defined as the discovery of truth (uncovering or revealing of the real, the ideal) and the giving of profit and delight. The function of poetry was extended farther along the line of discovery and imparting of truth to an inculcating of fresh insights spiritual, moral or (as we should say) psychological. Poetry had for centuries been regarded as a kind of rhetoric, belonging, that is, to the art of persuasion. Poetry in discovering the true, the real, should display virtues in their true brave colours and expose vices in their essential hatefulness, and so win men to love virtue and wish to cleave to it and hate, avoid and cast out vice. Poetry presented a picture of true kingship or heroism or loyalty, or the very essence of envy or malice; but it could go farther. By bodying forth the virtue to be attained only with effort, the easy and alluring vice, the evil seeming good, the moral dilemma, it could so involve the receiving mind that a mental act of choice and of will took place. 'Poetry' says George Puttenham 'invegleth the judgement of man, and carrieth his opinion this way and that' (*The Arte of English Poesie*, I, iv, p. 8). For instance, as we follow with our reason the argument between Despair and Redcrosse (see pp. 146–9) we, not being weary and spent as the Knight is, perceive the dangerous traps and will him to avoid them and to prevail. We have undergone the moral discipline of resisting despair through participating in the knight's adventure, reading the allegory from the inside.

A poet is also a maker. He was called so in earlier English and the Greek word *poesis* means 'making'. As he belongs to the microcosm and was himself created in God's image, his act of making is a repetition in little, an imitation, of God's great act of creation. It follows that what he makes will of necessity be created on the model of the ordered universe: of its very nature it should have order, harmony, proportion, hierarchy. Every aspect of it should be in keeping. Every contributory part of it should be 'in place', as everything has its appointed place in a sacral universe. Every part should have a vital relationship with other parts and with the whole. A poem thus conceived and executed had *decorum*. A poet observed decorum when he manifested the sense of what belongs to what, of what is fitting in context.

Decorum as a concept operates over the whole range of poetic theory and practice. As hierarchy was manifest in the cosmos and manifest in the pattern of man's living on earth from monarch downwards rank on rank, there belonged to each level a mode of converse that conveyed the part they played in the whole: royal, heroic, courtly, scholarly ... and so down to rustic and simple. So in poetry a treating of kings or heroes should be done in high and splendid terms, courtly matters should be couched in the speech of courts, and at the other end of the scale country matters and rustic manners should use simple, rough words and even rustic, regional turns of speech. The writing of a poem, then, is not only a matter of perceiving a vista of truth, reality, the ideal, and of communicating the perception but also of rendering it in the form, style and language that will best express it and present it to best advantage. (Clothes must fit perfectly and should be chosen to meet the occasion.) Hierarchy and rank in the universe made it natural that there should be different ranks in creative writing. Here the example of classical literature helped with its developed system of 'kinds'. Epic and tragedy are noble—to them a high style belongs. Pastoral treats of country matters and allows a satiric vein, so its style is low, simple and rough; being simple it was held to be well suited for a poet's first flight. A 'mean' or middle style of writing best suits the elegiac complaint and many varieties of poetry of love.

'Decorum' in large means literary 'kind' chosen according to the poet's purpose and subject-matter. In small it governs the choice of single words in their sentence or line of verse. An adjective is chosen not primarily in order to extend by an individual added detail the scope of the noun it qualifies; far less is it chosen to evince the author's powers of observation; it belongs to the whole stanza, indeed to the whole poem. For instance in *Prothalamion* stanza 3 (see p. 166) the waters are bidden not to wet the 'silken feathers' of the two swans who are most fair and white and pure. 'Silken' is precise and vivid as conveying delicacy and vulnerable finery and as reflecting on plumage of swans; but it is also there as the first hint of the major metaphor of the poem, for the swans will later be revealed as human brides on their way by river-barge to their betrothal ceremony. The silk belongs to the bridal gowns to come. Epithets that did not 'work' in this energetic way were condemned by Ronsard as lazy, *oisifs*.

Decorum is a much-embracing virtue of Spenser's poetry. In *The Shepheardes Calender* the new poet is praised in the introductory Epistle for

his complaints of love so lovely, his discourses of pleasure so pleasantly, his pastorall rudenesse, his moral wisenesse, his dewe observing of Decorum everyewhere, in personages, in seasons, in matter, in speach, and generally in al seemely simplicitie of handeling his matter and framing his words.

As to 'framing his words' we have seen it in the example of 'silken' above. The word is *in place*. Being in place and energetically contributing to the whole, it helps bind part to part and part to whole. So decorum is a dynamic principle in making a poem. And for the reader the perception of decorum at work is an experience both artistic and moral. 'What is in place' for renaissance poetry will not separate from the greater issue in the ordered universe—where 'nothing is there by chance'.

IMITATION OF NATURE. From the idea of poet as maker, we recall, derived the concept of imaginative composition fashioned on the model of the created universe. Such a process of creative composition went by the name of *imitation of nature*. Nature is divinely ordered, not formless but the source of form. The famous lines from Shakespeare given above express this process. The poet, inspired with vision from heaven, casts his eye up to heaven for form with which to express it; 'things unknown' in Theseus' phrase, are the ideal, the real, the true; the poet's pen then embodies them in earthly terms. The 'shaping spirit of imagination' derives from celestial pattern the order, harmony and proportion with which it endows its artefact, the poem.

How did an 'imitation of nature' show itself as successfully achieved, in a poem? In a total coherence. Metaphor, simile or personification that enters the poem must contribute to its value as an artistic construction; those of the 'April ode', (see p. 132) will serve as example. If number or set is introduced in any way into the substance or ordering of the poem it will be meaningful. (The concept of 'completeness could not enter into a poem through a treatment of *three* of the four elements). In so contributing to the whole of the poem either in content or in form, imagery, set or number take part in conveying the 'truth', which is the poem's purpose.

The use of poetic imagery, then, is not primarily decorative, though it may make for beauty, variety and enrichment of the whole effect. (Nor is it there because revelatory of the personal experience or subconscious trains of association in the mind of the poet.) But it is chosen and used of set purpose to direct the receiving mind to the *value* of what is being expressed. Again and again in *The Faerie Queene* an epithet, a simile or metaphor delivers the tacit message '*Think* what values are entailed!' The use of the epithet 'golden' in Book II, in the name of Guyon's horse Brigador (Bridle of Gold) and in many other places, directs the mind to the golden mean of temperance, a vital expression of the Book's Legend. The character in an adventure may be oblivious for the moment, or plain mistaken, as to what he is confronted with; but the reader can receive the poet's message if he is 'wary and wise'. The mythological simile that ends the description of Belphoebe/Gloriana is a good example of energetic poetic imagery: it 'dilates' the meaning, carrying it into new regions, enriching by the parallel and at the same time aiding the precise delineation of the poet's intention.

'Imitation of the model' had a further meaning, deriving from the first somewhat in this fashion: if poetry is an imitation of nature and excellent poets of antiquity had imitated nature excellently well, poets of the present age could learn how it was done from study of their poems. Such examples in Latin or Greek became intermediary models, as it were. Examples of excellence in description, in debate, in depiction of character through speech, in celebration of the ruler were studied, translated, analysed, discussed and reproduced in modern languages and used as models in fresh composition. The Gloss in *The Shepheardes Calender* draws attention to many points where the new poet has learned from makers of classical antiquity, or from earlier French or English poetry. The scale of the model used ranges from a turn of phrase, a figure of rhetoric, an inset fable or song, to the whole eclogue' for 'September' as imitated from Mantuan and 'December' from Marot. If we remember that the aim of such imitation was to 'learn how to do it well' and the outcome was an enormous widening and enriching of the scope of English poetry, we will not misjudge it. The mind receiving the poetry, if not lettered in Latin, French or Greek, enjoyed what it otherwise would not have reached: both the matter and something of the manner. The reader who knew the original had a pleasure like that of one listening to variations on a theme in music, the delighted recognition of points made in the implied parallel.

A poet learned his art through imitation of a model. Once master of his craft he could by a similar gesture pit his skill against that of a fellow poet in literary contest, as shepherd poets did in a singing match. Spenser calls this 'overgoing'. He set out to 'overgo' Ariosto in certain parts of *The Faerie Queene*—indeed in the passage studied from Book II in the critical analyses (see p. 160). He overgoes the French poet Marot in the lament for Dido, 'some mayden of greate bloud' in *The Shepheardes Calender*. Marot had written an elegy in pastoral mode for the Queen Mother of France, recently dead: 'De Madame Loyse de Savoye, mère du Roy'. In a single-standing eclogue of two shepherds Colin and Thenot, Colin the poet is requested to sing a mourning song in honour of the royal lady; he complies in a piece of 'ten times ten verses' (200 lines) and is then thanked and praised. The verse pattern is uniform throughout, continuous quatrains interlinked by rhyme, *abab, bcbc* and so on. Colin expresses the sense of loss felt for the well-loved royal lady and nature mourns in sympathy assuming mourning colours. Then the mood changes and he bids his verses cease to plain, for she is in the Elysian fields of the blessed. It is a beautiful and elegant poem in a mode that was perhaps 'old-fashioned' to poets of Spenser's day.

Spenser takes the theme, the persons of the shepherds and the verse form, and devises afresh an elegy for the unknown 'Dido'. He 'dilates' the theme by making it part of a greater coherence, his *Calender*. It now belongs to the season of dying in nature, to November. The lament is now *in place* in cosmic rhythm, and under the deadly archer Sagittarius, as the wood-cut shows. He distinguishes the lament from the speeches of Thenot and Colin by giving it a distinctive stanza. The stanza has a refrain element that marks by a change in its wording the change in mood from sorrow to joy: 'O heavie herse ... O carefull verse' becomes 'O happy herse ... O ioyfull verse'. The meaning is now articulate in the form. The whole is well trussed up together—in the phrase of the 'Epistle' that precedes *The Calender*. And form and meaning are at one in the reiterated refrain word 'herse'.

This is an excellent example of Spenser's 'wittinesse in devising, his pithinesse in uttering', again to quote the Epistle. This Renaissance pun is worth expounding. A modern reader knows 'hearse' and 'rehearse' but probably does not connect them; in fact 'rehearsal' probably *sounds* as if it were connected with hearing, 'a hearing of music in practice'. But all these words are in fact derived from the French word for harrow: to rehearse is to go over the ground again in preparation. From 'herse' as harrow the word came to designate the funeral bier which it resembled, and so to mean 'funeral ceremony' in Spenser's day. For him too the *sound* of the word embraced 'hearing' as well as recital. All these senses are made to reverberate in his poem as 'herse' echoes 'verse' throughout the elegy, voicing the quick of the poem's meaning.

> But now sike happy cheere is turnd to heavie chaunce
> Such pleasaunce now displast by dolors dint:
> All Musick sleepes, where death doth leade the daunce
> And shepherds wonted solace is extinct.
> The blue in black, the greene in gray is tinct.
>   The gaudie girlonds deck her grave,
> The faded flowres her corse embrave
>   O heauie herse
> Morne nowe my Muse, now morne with teares besprint
>   O carefull verse.

Spenser's ideas on the poet and on poetry were to have been expounded in his 'The English Poet', a work mentioned in *The Calender* as ready for print, but never published. Into the October Eclogue, however, he has poured as much as he could of his beliefs and intuition on this matter, his learning and his faith in his vocation: why the poet should be honoured by great men, the poet as seer and maker wielding extraordinary powers, the poet's inspiration, and his art bordering on that of magic.

The theme of poetry and inspiration belongs to October, month of the wine harvest in the old tradition of 'works and days', for 'Bacchus fruite is frend to Phoebus wise'. It belongs under Scorpio, sign of intellect and genius. The woodcut shows in the background a 'Florentine academy' with gentlemen grouped in discussion. From them advances into the shepherd scene a pastoral poet, bearing crook and pan-pipes and crowned with leaves—Bacchus' ivy or laurel for acclaim? The new Renaissance poetry is honoured in *The Calender*, its potentialities explored, its nature exemplified and expounded; and it is portrayed enjoying its due place in the cosmic scheme.

94

Pastoral and allegory

Allegory is metaphor sustained and explored. In pastoral the metaphor is of the shepherd living in a shepherd-land, who is everyman in his realm and in Christendom. By the same token in Spenser's heroic poem the metaphor is of the knight of chivalric virtue who is 'on his way' of endeavour in Faerieland, committed to be champion of a virtue and ready to challenge powers that oppose it, whether in the world or within himself.

In his pastoral poetry—*The Calender, Colin Clout* or Book VI of *The Faerie Queene*—Spenser shows that he is deeply versed in the long tradition of poetic pastoral, from the Greeks through Vergil and Mantuan to Skelton or Marot. The nature of that pastoral tradition and Spenser's contribution to it has been wisely expounded by Professor Kermode in his volume *English Pastoral Poetry*. It will serve our purpose here rather to show how Spenser went to the root of the shepherd metaphor as understood by plain people and how he then did something completely new in making his first pastoral a *Calender* of shepherds.

The metaphor of the shepherd in earlier pastoral had established a relation of shepherd-land to actual life: action there was 'ideal' in that it was human action reduced to simpler terms and 'removed' from more sophisticated civilization, which nonetheless it cast light on. In that 'ideal' landscape could be presented the essentials of the human lot.

In poetic pastoral certain patterns of activity, certain roles and themes, had become favourites: the good shepherd and the bad, the young and the old, at work with their flocks, the singing and piping of the shepherd in his hours of pastime and his simple joys and sorrows in love, a country commonwealth at peace with praise of the ruler. The relationship of shepherd-land to sophisticated society was rendered specifically in one of the themes: the shepherd's journey, from countryside to town and back again, with a telling of what he had learned.

The metaphor of the pastoral shepherd was familiar to every schoolboy who learned Latin, as the eclogues of Mantuan, Latin poet of fifteenth-century Italy, were an elementary textbook in common use. These were imitations of Vergil's eclogues and they made, more pronouncedly that he had done, satiric comment on contemporary society. In Tudor England classical eclogues had been printed in translation and eclogues had been composed in English in imitation, for instance by Barclay. 'Eclogues' means 'select pieces' and such eclogues were separate poems, 'episodes of shepherd life' rendered in dialogue, sometimes with narrative introduction and conclusion, presented alone or in a series.

Pastoral was regarded as the easiest and least ambitious of poetic kinds, 'in which a young poet could fittingly take his first flight'. The style was simple, 'low', even harsh where satire had hard things to say. Spenser in his first poetic endeavour aptly chose pastoral. But he took the pastoral of poetic tradition into a region it had not known. His pastoral work was to be Renaissance poetry in its fullest power. First, as to 'the part and the whole'. Spenser says in his preface that 'eclogues' does not mean 'select pieces'; the Greek word means 'goat-songs'. His book of verses will be no miscellany. His pastoral volume is a whole, a cycle not a series, with each part related to each other part in parallel and contrast, the sequence providing a pleasing variety of pieces moral, recreative or satirical; what is more, each single eclogue is now related to each other and to the whole through cosmic perspective.

Number comes into it. Vergil's eclogues had been ten, a good round number such as Romans liked. Spenser makes his eclogues twelve, 'proportionable to the twelve moneths', as his title announces. He has taken the pastoral's programme of scenes in shepherd-land that showed man's works and pastimes at various seasons and has related that work and pastime to the great medieval scheme of 'the labours of the months'. The activity or topic of each eclogue is related to its seasonable time in the solar cycle of the year, the course of the months in character under their zodiac signs, and there is tacit

The planet Sol/Phoebus, the sun, with zodiac Leo: his people – a king with sceptre and book (royalty, religion, poetry), a harper for kingly music, a hypocrite for false devotion.

'*August*' *from* The Kalendar and Compost of Shepherds, *with Leo and Virgo, pictured as Our Lady of the Assumption (August 15).*

reference to the year of the Church. Thus poetic 'truth', in the sense of how any phenomenon belonged to the sacral universe, is perceived, and imitation of nature is achieved for pastoral in a new way. In this new dimension decorum is observed throughout, both in form and content.

Secondly, Spenser enriched and extended the pastoral genre by combining it with another. (*Combinatio* was a skill of the rhetorician.) He laid Vergil's eclogues beside another very different book, but one also treating of the shepherd as everyman. This was 'an old book', familiar to men of Renaissance Europe in print in many languages, in English *The Kalendar and compost of Shepherds, Le compost et kalendrier des bons bergiers*. It was as we saw, a handbook for everyman 'the shepherd', bringing together all he needed to know for his physical moral and spiritual wellbeing. It gave a régime of diet for the season, a tree of the virtues and vices (with penalties), the main sacraments and prayers of the Church; it taught him to find his way by the stars and showed in diagrams how his body was constituted and conditioned by celestial powers of planet or zodiac sign. It was illustrated by many woodcuts which included pages giving the character of each month, its labours or pastimes, its zodiac sign and its religious festivals. Some of these woodcuts are reproduced on pages 66, 96–7.

Thirdly, Spenser, learning from earlier theological writing in French on the 'shepherd' theme, now explored the metaphor of the shepherd in terms of the sacral universe. (In a way he was providing a Christian gloss for Vergil's pastoral, as Renaissance scholars did for a classical text.) The shepherd of traditional pastoral poetry was everyman; but scripture showed 'the shepherd' as a far richer metaphor. The shepherd was Christ himself in his own words of parable, the good shepherd, keeper of the Christian flock. His antetype in the Old Testament was Abel, a good shepherd as Spenser points out—and his forerunner was David, shepherd-boy who became king, ancestor on earth of Christ, singer of 'the Psalms'. God in the twenty-third psalm led the human soul as a shepherd by quiet waters, as is seen in the picture for the December eclogue. Shepherd as *episcopus* was the bishop of the Christian Church, who carried a crook as emblem of his office. At several points the two uses of the metaphor confirmed one another. The pastoral shepherd sang of love, David of love of God. By thinking in parallel God could be figured as Pan, God of shepherds all. As the head of the Christian Church on earth was, in England since Henry VIII's reign, the monarch, Eliza is Queen of shepherds all; her pastoral genealogy shows her as daughter of Pan and Syrinx.

Exploration of the metaphor of the shepherd enriched the character of shepherd-land. The shepherd's journey in 'September' shows an eclogue of Mantuan done in reverse; Diggon Davie has journeyed not to the city or court but to a wilder land far in the west where 'all is of misery' and his curious dialect, echoing Celtic-English, brings news which can only be from Ireland. The May eclogue in a fable extends the view to Scotland—the court a goat-pen and the kid the boy king seduced by a wily Catholic. Universals of pastoral are linked by hint or name-conceit to particular living instances. The friend is Hobbinol/Harvey, critic of the poet-shepherd's singing. Two bishop-shepherds suggest the Bishop of Rochester (Roffy) and Grindal (Algrind). And Spenser (of the Merchant Taylors' School) is, aptly, Colin Clout: '*Colin*' had been the French poet Marot's pastoral name for himself and Colin Clout was that of the English poet Skelton under King Henry VIII. (Spenser's devising draws all these into one name-idea.) Historical pertinence gave particular examples of the general 'truth', as it was to do in *The Faerie Queene*. The delight of the reader in following the poet's invention was spiced with an element of 'delicious you-know-who'. The poet-shepherd emerges as chief among shepherd rôles. And Colin Clout we shall hear sing again in a later pastoral eclogue, play again in the apt Book of *The Faerie Queene*.

Spenser's reader, opening the pages of this work by an unknown poet, would see eclogues like Vergil's but with a title and pictures that strongly recalled those of the familiar handbook (indeed the month pictures were designed, like those in that volume, on the pattern of a Book of Hours). His imagination was challenged to relate the metaphor of the shepherd in one and in the other, to discern wherein lay the aptness of each woodcut to its eclogue's meaning. As in a Book of Hours the scene might be located by a significant building in the background. And the matter and manner of the shepherds' discourse would be deepened by its timing in season on earth and in the heavens.

For instance January, cold and wet under Aquarius the Water-carrier, shows the shepherd Colin Clout in a wintry landscape tending a dejected flock by a sheepcote. On the horizon is a strange group of buildings—the Coliseum for Rome, the bridge at Avignon for Petrarch, the twin towers of Rochester Cathedral, and a church; thus Colin is 'placed' as young Spenser, secretary at Rochester, pastoral poet of Christendom in a poetic tradition of Vergil, Mantuan and Petrarch. In the foreground lie his shepherd's bagpipes, broken. Colin's discourse is a plaint of love's pain and dejection in tune with the barren wintry season with its icy tears; unloved by Rosalind he has broken his pipe. And the 'broken pipe' glances by metaphor at the Circumcision, the feast of the Christian year with which January opens, when Christ suffered his first pain on earth for love of mankind. (The diagram on pp.102–3 will enable the modern reader to follow the poet's meaning in woodcut (pp. 100–1) and verses and discern the imaginative reverberation of the shepherd metaphor.)

The woodcuts from Spenser's The Shepheardes Calendar.

January. *Egloga prima.*

Februarie. *Egloga Secunda.*

March. *Egloga Tertia.*

Aprill. *Egloga Quarta.*

Maye. *Egloga Quinta.*

Iune. *Egloga sexta.*

September.

Ægloga Nona.

December.

Ægloga Duodecima.

August.

Ægloga octaua.

Nouember.

Ægloga vndecima.

Iulye.

Ægloga septima.

October.

Ægloga decima.

The Shepheardes Calender

	Characters	type of verse & language	'kind' of subject	Inset Fable or song	Woodcut building, work or festival of month	Zodiac Sign Church feast	Forebears
January 1	Colin	Stanzas—6 line smooth, iambic ababcc	plaint of love	eclogue is a (song)	Coliseum, cathedral great house	Aquarius	Skelton Mantuan Vergil
		stately				water, rain	
	(Rosalind)				winter, flocks distempered 'broken pipes'		
						Festival of Circumcision	
February 2	Thenot old shepherd	couplets nine syllable line stressed clownish	moral & general reverence to age	Fable oak & brier	shepherd cote sheep, cattle	Pisces	Chaucer
3	Cuddie young neatherd	Fable—running tetrameter couplets	religion & state	(Burleigh?)	boy chops tree down (wood cutting)	(last month of old year)	
March 4	Willye	romance stanzas aab ccb 443 443	pastime	Fable stone throwing at the bird 'Cupid'	none! bird-scaring by stone throwing boys	Aries lust	Theocritus Propertius Moschus
5	Thomalin shepherd boys	'a pretty round verse running currently together ...youthful talk' middle style	a love adventure	(Leicester)	stone throwing boys		
April 6	Thenot Hobbinol	nine/ten syllable line stressed clownish	Queen of Spring honoured	Song April Ode	shepherd cote church	Taurus trees & plants	Vergil
	(Elisa, Queen of shepherds)	song, noble—ode stately	Muses attendant state		regina avrillosa tribute of flowers		dance song & ode
May 7	Palinode Catholic	nine syllable line stressed couplets clownish	religious controversy over rites	Fable fox & kid	two churches (one ruined?)	Gemini	cf. Marot
8	Piers Protestant	Fable—same	state: religion		may cart and 'king & queen of May dancing country folk	clergy & doubleness	
June	Hobbinol	stanzas 8 line	rejection of love	e is	hills & dales	Cancer	cf. Marot

Month	Characters	Metre / Form	Theme	Setting	Genre	Calendar / Zodiac	Source
July 9	Thomalin Morrell (proud pastor) (Algrind)	pairs of divided fourteeners abab ballad measure uncouth & rusticall	good & bad pastors 'high & low' aims religion	hill cutting corn	Fable—eagle & shell fish (Grindal)	Leo pride 'the flying eagle'	Theocritus Vergil
August 10	Willye Perigot Cuddye (Colin)	nine/ten stressed line syllables uncouth rustical roundelay/ballad rustic stanza sestina-italianate stately	singing match love & poetry (Bonnibell Cynthia)	barn corn in stocks harvest home holiday lady of the harvest field	songs roundelay & sestina	Virgo virginity Lammas Feast of Assumption	3 & 1 folksong
September 11	Hobbinol Diggon Davie (Roffy)	couplets 4 stress lines uncouth (fable same) rusticall Irish dialect	dissolute pastors disorder, injustice in state	sheep cote wild weather vines round fruit-tree (biblical) good shepherd	Fable wolf & sheep	Scales good husbandry (wild weather of equinox)	Mantuan reversed
October	Pierce Cuddye (Colin)	stanzas 6 line pentameter iambic abbaba stately	poetry & lack of patronage new poetry for England	Florentine academy 'great house'	Eclogue 'is' a stately song for 2 voices	Scorpio 'genius & falseness'	Theocritus
November	Thenot Colin crowned (Dido, Lobbin)	variation on ababcbc . . . pentameters, iambic lament—a further variation stately, refrain, French words	lament for 'Dido' (Ambrosia Sidney?) Queen X Leicester	Church funeral procession	song/lament	Sagittarius (The Queens month) a man full of ingenuity & wise All Souls (death) St. Martins (death)	Marot Vergil moralised (Dido—desire to reign)
December	Colin	stanzas 6 line smooth iambic ababcc stately	plaint to God Pan recapitulation & close 4 ages of man	sheep cote mountain flocks by quiet waters (David) well of life good shepherd	eclogue "is" a song	Capricorn Advent A man of good life Christmas	Marot Chaucer

The eclogues for April and May are treated in the critical analysis of the 'April ode'.

The book was, moreover, a calendar that took the particular year 1579 and reflected life in the realm and Christendom in that year, showing issues and personalities of import in it. The year was the twenty-first of Elizabeth's reign, in number a 'turning-point' of life, as Petrarch expounded. The calendar was itself a focus of interest and anxiety at the time, as we have seen. Spenser made this one of poetry, the particular thus achieving universality. He endowed this year of his sovereign's reign with 'durance perpetual'.

> Loe I have made a Calender for every yeare
> That steele in strength and time in durance shall outweare
> And if I marked well the starres revolution
> It shall continewe till the world's dissolution.

In the great gesture of Renaissance creative writing, poetry should be seen to conquer time, in terms of time's own instrument. It was a project brilliant in conception and of dazzling ambition. Spenser the poet by it established himself as an accomplished Renaissance poet in English; but as a young man green in judgment he o'er-reached himself in vaulting ambition, and 'fell on the other'. The *Calender* indeed bodied forth the year 1579 in its essence, showing its place in the pattern of history unfolding; but the poet as 'seer' had seen more and spoken more 'truly' than certain great ones could tolerate.

One final feature of *The Shepheardes Calender* was remarkable. Each Eclogue had a Gloss, as scholarly texts did. Here unusual or difficult words were explained, figures of rhetoric noted, classical references explained and any use of literary 'model' noted. That is to say the new poetic work was presented as for serious study. But a teasing note can be detected here and there. The maker of the Gloss is one 'E. K.', who may be Spenser's friend Edward Kirke but is as likely to stand for Edmundus Kalendarius—Spenser the *Calender*-maker. This is a clever young man's production. For instance some of the woodcuts feature bird flight and in the Gloss augury by bird flight is recommended as worth a young man's study! No one has cracked the code here, but something momentous in the events of the year 1579 may be registered. The Renaissance poet's delight in the arcane, that was to lead Spenser to use Egyptian symbol in Britomart's dream in his heroic poem, is already here. In his first work Spenser's poetry may indeed be 'perceived of the leaste, understoode of the mooste, but judged only by the learned'.

New language for the new poetry

> Some blame deep Spenser for his grandam words
> Others protest that in them he records
> His masterpiece of cunning, giving praise
> And gravity to his profound-pricked lays.

Everard Guilpin, *Skialetheia* 1598

The Shepheardes Calender was meant to make an impact by its newness and it did so, especially in the choice of language the unknown poet used for his poetry. 'Of many thinges which in him be straunge, I know will seeme the straungest, the words them selves being so auncient...' Thus the prefatory Epistle, anticipating surprise and objection, hastens to justify the new writer's bringing into the language of his verses words that were not to be found in poetry of the day: they are those that best suit the poet's purpose and therefore are acceptable. In a word, they are apt. But the new verbal repertory of the *Calender* was not only a breakaway from tradition in England, it was a lively move in an argument that dated from the revival of learning and was still agitating pens throughout western Europe.

The issues were these. Were the modern tongues of Europe capable of expressing profound and sophisticated meaning such as was admired in Vergil or Cicero? If not, what could be done to strengthen and enrich them? Should words be brought in from Greek and Latin where no word for the concept existed in the vernaculars—'Italian', French, 'Dutch' or English? (The issue became urgent with the extensive programme of translation that was to fore.) Should contemporary foreign languages be drawn on when, say, English vocabulary failed? Or should the modern writer keep proudly to 'native language' and go about to render the idea in simpler words? And what *was* 'the native language' to be so employed? The best 'language men do use' in contemporary converse at court or in discourse or argument in court of law? And if the poet found such language was for his purpose thin and bare should he look farther afield to supply his need, and where should he look? To his experience of varieties of English speech in regional dialects or to his reading of older poets of English stock—where were many good words now gone out of use and 'clean disinherited'?

It was into a battleground of theory and practice that the new poet of England rode with rhetorical colours flying. He offered a challenge on major issues. His choice of the pastoral kind in which to do so was exceedingly shrewd, as well as being most decorous for a young poet's first flight. Language befitting a pastoral would account for all that he wished to do in widening the field of language for poetry. According to the tenets of the new poetry, language should be apt to the literary kind, to the speaker, to the matter and to the occasion.

Language for pastoral was to be 'low', using simple even rough phrases; as apt in decorum of speech it was 'shepherd-talk' and could appropriately imitate the speech of country-folk, which is notably retentive of old style and of regional forms and idioms. But by classical precedent pastoral could not only descend to satire, it could—'where good occasion offered of higher vein and more Heroicall argument'—rise to eulogy of the ruler, treat of affairs of Church or state, express the aspirations of love, or embrace a song or a story. And so the words best suited to serve the poet's purpose would fitly explore at many levels the resources of the English tongue and would go beyond it where need was felt. Spenser in *The Calender* goes to French poetry for 'iouisaunce' or 'sovenance', 'ouverture' or 'paunce', to Chaucer for 'chevisaunce' and a host of others.

Decorum of speech is qualified by decorum of subject-matter and of purpose; the use of 'grandam words', rustic turns of speech or words 'northernely spoken with *a* for *o*', furnishes a shepherd-talk that belongs to the pastoral guise. But in *The Calender* this shepherd-talk is not evenly thick all through. 'October', whose purpose is to treat of the poet, his nature and his fortunes, shows this clearly. In its eclogue Cuddie, a shepherd-poet, has written pastoral and ditties (with little reward) and speaks with a touch of anciency and rusticity; but Piers, arguing to persuade him to aspire now to heroic poetry, bids him 'abandon then the base and viler clowne', and the language rises to heroic and royal. (The Gloss, under the word 'Display', draws attention to the fact.) When Cuddie's verse mounts to celebrate poetry as inspired, his language mounts in sympathy. Yet with the Eclogue's closing couplet, spoken by Piers, a return is made to shepherd level with a 'northernely spoken' vowel and an idiom from country matters:

And when my Gates shall han their bellies layd: [i.e. given birth]
Cuddie shall have a Kidde to store his farme.

This low-style couplet resolves a range of the Eclogue's concerns—poetry as 'bringing forth', emptiness and fullness, due reward for the poet whether by noble or goat-herd patron. The *placing* of the grandam word or of the rustic coloured line is part of the art of its use: it makes us think why, and invites judgment. So we may allow Guilpin's pair of contrary opinions (quoted above) to go to the heart of Spenser's choice of language for his poetry. They may be roughly rendered thus: 'Some blame a poet as profound as Spenser for using archaic and dialect words, while others protest that this shows his consummate art, his use of them being an important contributory factor in the rendering of a meaning that is both profound and complex, as polyphonic music is.'

Spenser, then, uses 'grandam words' from regional speech or earlier usage of poets and dialect variants of sound or syntax as best serves his poetical purpose over all. The Epistle introducing *The Calender* makes these further points: the new poet uses archaic words because he is so deeply read in older English poetry that now they come naturally; he also does it of set purpose—their roughness, apt for shepherds, apt for satire, serves as a foil to 'brave and glorious words'; these 'aunciente solemne wordes are moreover an eternall image of antiquitie and meet for discoursing matters of gravity and importaunce'. The outcome of Spenser's choice—the vast extension and enrichment of the English tongue in use for poetry—is also indicated by the Epistle as having being envisaged and intended.

In the view of the Pléiade poets of France there was a second practice to be encouraged for the enrichment of the language for poetry. They called it *provignement*, applying to words the metaphor from the vineyard: by 'layering', a shoot of the parent stem is slit and rooted, to become a separate plant. Spenser is certainly doing this in his poetry, first in *The Calender* and then extensively throughout *The Faerie Queene*. If in current usage a verb exists but no noun from the same root, the verb can be used as a noun or a noun can be formed by the addition of a suffix or prefix. An adverb may be formed from an adjective, or vice versa, and so with other parts of speech. The 'new' word might indeed have existed in the past and have fallen from use; in any case it is 'reasonable' that it should exist now.

'Layering' is a discovery of a process of language, an imitation of nature's ways, a doing likewise. For example 'upbraid' existed as a verb and had existed as a noun also: Spenser uses both and forms the verb 'upbray' (to bring reproach on) and the noun 'upbrayes' (reproaches). From 'unruly' he forms 'unruliment' and on the same principle 'dreriment', 'hardiment', 'wariment'. The use of prefix or suffix is done advisedly, from precedent; different force is felt in '—ment', in '—head' as in 'beastlyhead', 'goodlihead', or in '—nesse'. Wariment, for instance, is from the root 'ware', wary or aware which is akin to 'ward', to fend off or guard. Wariment is not the same as awareness or wariness: it is, so to speak, awareness and wariness in perfective aspect, a positive state with outcome in action, even achievement.

> Full many strokes, that mortally were ment
>   The whiles were enterchaunged twixt them two;
> Yet they were all with so good wariment
>   Or warded, or auoyded and let goe
>   That still the life stood fearelesse of her foe.

> (*F.Q.* IV. iii, 17)

Near the new word stand 'warded' and 'ment' giving confirmation by context of components of its meaning.

A third aspect of language, and one that is linked with both the preceding, entails consideration of Spenser's spelling. (We recall that he was at hand in England while his major works were printing; his spelling is conscious and deliberate and there is system in it if not absolute consistency.) The adding of new members to a word family bore witness to consciousness of the root and its meaning. In the employment of words from old poets Spenser shows that he realized such archaic words had a nucleus of meanings—witness in 'Maye' the Gloss on Chevisaunce 'sometime of Chaucer used for game: sometime of other for spoile or bootie or enterprise and sometime for chiefdome'. (His use of this word in context is discussed on p. 138.) In both circumstances the presence of a root meaning perceived by him might be indicated by spelling. We must recall also that Spenser's poetry was published at a time when poetry, still frequently read aloud, met the medium of print: the sound of the word, which was often a clue to its root-meaning, must be indicated for those who would come to it far from the presence of the author or his personal acquaintance, and in a poem unglossed, as was *The Faerie Queene*. Spelling could do this. (Confirmation could also come through rhyme, as we shall see.)

Consider these. For 'cowardice' Spenser uses 'cowardree' in *Mother Hubberd's Tale* (line 986); but in Book VI of *The Faerie Queene* (canto x. 37) he has 'cowherdize', and 'cowheard' as adjective or adverb has the force of 'cowardly' at several points in Books V and VI. In the usage of these later Books he is displaying through spelling an identification of cowardice and the nature of the cowherd. He may have believed both words to derive from the noun 'cow' and 'its' verb with the sense 'intimidate'. (That later scholars derive 'cowardice', via French *couardise*, from '*cou*' or '*queue*' a tail, is beside the point.) He certainly wished to display the identity of sound, in which lay an identity of meaning; in the Books of Justice and of Courtesy the terrain at times has an Irish colour and cowhearding had the stigma of the pursuit characteristic of the 'other' way of life. 'Neatherd' has no such strong pejorative force though it indicates an ignoble activity, fit pursuit for the rejected Coridon.

A last instance shows a Celtic word subjected to the same process. Colin Clout has a list of terrors in Irish life that are unknown in England—'no nightly bodrags, nor no hue and cries'. 'Bodrag' is *buaidhreadh*, which now means 'affliction, or the act of afflicting' and is linked with *buaidh*, triumph or victory. But in Book II of *The Faerie Queene* the chronicles of British kings in canto x has 'sundry bordragings of neighbour Scots'; the spelling shows what Spenser *heard*, rendered as a concept 'border-raging' (the word 'neighbour' confirms 'border'). In both instances what matters is the sound of the word in the context of poetry. The thought process is the same that bred the serious pun and the name conceit; it is one that lies at the heart of the practice and theory of Renaissance poetry. And the modern reader of James Joyce's *Ulysses* can learn to delight in it.

The pun had been a serious vehicle of meaning in medieval poetry —witness the famous lyric on the Blessed Virgin 'I sing of a maiden that is makeles', where the word 'makeles' is a nucleus of significances at the heart of the poem: matchless (unmated and also peerless) along with 'immaculate', without spot. The last has, for us, no philological connection with the other, but for them the sound made the identification. The word was of God; meaning in it was to be discovered and expounded as was meaning in scripture (the pun was drawn on in expounding Holy Writ). On the same principle the pun is widely used by Spenser as a point where a range of indwelling senses can be drawn from a word, or, conversely, as a gathering point of ideas. We saw his use of 'herse' in the November lament. A notable example is the birds/brides of *Prothalamion* discussed at p. 174.

In *The Faerie Queene*, as Book VI moves towards the contest with the Blatant Beast, that creature of slander and calumny is painted full of tongues of beast or man (canto xii, st. 27); with these he fights through infamy and lies when his teeth and claws have not availed. The approach to this contest has kept in play the idea of evil speech as the final enemy of courtesy, whose voice is fair speech.

> For all that hetherto hath long delayd
> This gentle knight from sewing his first quest
> Though out of course, yet hath not bene missayd
> To shew the courtesie by him profest ...   xii. 2

Missayd is mis-assayed and mis-said. And the weapon with which Calidore is armed is 'a sword of better say'—both composition and tempered quality of metal—and fair and effective speech. (And the idea of tempering of metal was already on the reader's mind since it belongs to the Legend of *Temperaunce*.)

By the same token, the name-conceit is central to Spenser's devising. 'Somersheat' in *Prothalamion* is an extraction of sound-meanings from an actual name, Somerset. Every name in *The Faerie Queene* is full of sense and many show Spenser's 'secret wit'. Again Spenser is heir to medieval practice: witness the morality plays from *Everyman* to Skelton's *Magnificence* or instances in Chaucer's *Canterbury Tales*—'Constance', 'January and May' or 'Dorigen' who had generosity as an 'inborn gift'. Skelton and Chaucer were named by Spenser as his masters. Many examples could be cited also from literature of antiquity, where the pun served an equally serious purpose. The name-conceit has been discussed in masterly fashion by Martha Craig in her article 'The secret wit of Spenser's language', and other critics have contributed to the mining of this rich seam of meaning. To aid the reader fresh to *The Faerie Queene* I have complied a glossary of names with their inlaid significance expounded (see p. 126), for many depend on an understanding of Greek or Latin, or an acquaintance with regions of knowledge which are no longer common ground for author and reader.

Verse form, rhythms and rhyme

The stock of English poetry was refreshed and enriched as much in versification as in language by the new poet's printed *Calender*. Published verse for a generation had been predominantly in the plain style and in regular iambic tread. Now here in one volume were some seventeen different patterns or combinations of rhythm and verse form, some old and native, some newly brought in from France or Italy, some from courtly and sophisticated poetry and one or two smacking of popular ballad or folk-song. All were delightful in their aptness to the matter they treated of, the *genre* they were written in, or the shepherd who spoke them or sang them. The introductory epistle does not include versification in its catalogue of happy decorum. It did not need to.

First, to match the shepherd-talk there were rhythms that savoured of 'ancientry', and there the poet made return to the old stressed line of alliterative verse as he understood it to run in, say, Langland's *Piers Plowman*. He did not fully understand the principles of the alliterative long line nor did he the metre of Chaucer's poetry: Elizabethans reading medieval verse were unsure of the extent to which the final 'e' had been sounded in earlier English so much had the language changed in the meanwhile. But Spenser caught enough of the spirit and art of stressed verse to write couplets like this:

> The kene cold blowes through my beaten hyde
> All as I were through the body gryde
> My ragged rontes all shiver and shake
> As doen high Towers in an earthquake
> They wont in the wind wagge their wrigle tailes
> Perke as peacock: but now it avales ...

or
> So loytring live you little herdgroomes
> Keeping your beastes in the budded broomes

This is 'clownish' and in keeping with the speakers Cuddie and Thenot, with their conversation of sheep-keeping and with the rough winter season of February.

This must have been the 'most straunge' of the verse forms now falling unexpected on the Elizabethan ear: lines with four stresses, the stresses in a majority of the lines marked by alliteration either in pairs by the half-line or with three to the line. (He does not seem to have realized that alliteration could also be on any *vowel* with any other vowels, so some lines lack binding alliteration on stress, as some in his models may have seemed to do.) The lines are in couplets, bound also by end-rhyme. He could have found lines of alliterative verse bound by end-rhyme in a number of old romances —or in prologues to Gavin Douglas's *Eneados* (London, *c.* 1553), a translation of Vergil's *Aeneid* which he certainly knew.

In March the shepherds' talk and their fable are in 'a pretty round verse, running currently together [that] expresseth notably light and youthful talk'. Webbe, in his *Discourse of English Poetrie* (1586) is delighted as much by the sound as by the aptness. He there enumerates and appreciates the range of versification in *The Calender*.

January had opened in accomplished stanzas of rhyme royal. Colin Clout, poet and shepherd, is singing his 'complaint of love so lovely'. The style is eloquent and dignified, the verse smoothly flowing, the argument rhetorically patterned, the love Petrarchan. 'Ancientry' or rusticity is judiciously touched in. Alliteration is a binding force, guiding the mind to connect word and word in sense; but the accent it marks is here metrical and regular.

So in the first three eclogues great variety was displayed, and consummate decorum. With the aid of the diagram the reader can trace the way the verse form follows as the changes are rung on satirical bitterness, recreative merriment or moral gravity, with inset of tale or song. He can note too how modulation in verse-form corresponds to modulation in language.

How sophisticated are the pleasures offered by the poet's skill in versification can be gauged in the singing match in August. Perigot and Willye sing a rustic roundelay with a refrain that shows the words went to the tune of 'Heigh ho holiday', a popular tune of the time that has survived. The shepherds sing line about. Perigot's lines carry the narrative onwards; Willye's lines repeat a phrase with 'hey ho', or comment on the story. The lines fall into fours, as in a ballad of tradition with alternating refrain. The pattern resembles that of the old carol dance-song with its onward movement and stepping-on-the-spot. The element of improvization is there, as in ancient work-song. And recapitulation belonged to the courtly *rondeau*, of which this is, in a way, a rusticated version. It matches in tone the matter, which is a celebration of a rustic lass, Bonnibel, 'good and fair', and Bessy-Eliza-Isabel, as we saw.

The reply in the singing contest is, in every way but one, a contrast. Cuddie's piece, made by Colin Clout, is courtly, Italianate, in long lines of smoothly running eloquent rhetoric, not rhymed in the usual sense but with a change-ringing on six words in the end-rhyme position. Six lines make a stanza; the next stanza presents the same 'rhyme words' in order, but with recapitulation of one. A coda gathers all of them together. The grave and mournful plaint emphasises by contrast the bouncing ballad that went before, as rough words show up bright and splendid terms. Yet both are love songs. The wit of the contest lies in the fact that though one is ancient native folk-song and the other courtly continental complaint, the 'form', the principle of recapitulation with forward-moving change, is the same in both.

> PERIGOT It fell upon a holly eve,
> WILLYE hey ho hollidaye,
> PERIGOT When holly fathers wont to shrieve;
> WILLYE now gynneth this roundelay.
> PERIGOT Sitting upon a hill so hye
> WILLYE hey ho the high hyll,
> PERIGOT The while my flocke did feede thereby,
> WILLYE the while the shepheard selfe did spill:
> PERIGOT I saw the bouncing Bellibone,
> WILLYE hey ho Bonibell . . .

against Cuddie:

> Ye wastefull woodes beare witnesse of my woe,
> Wherein my plaints did oftentimes resound:
> Ye carelesse byrds are privie to my cryes,
> Which in your songs were wont to make a part:
> Thou pleasaunt spring hast luld me oft a sleepe,
> Whose streames my tricklinge teares did ofte augment.

> Resort of people doth my greefs augment,
> The walled townes do worke me greater woe:
> The forest wide is fitter to resound
> The hollow Echo of my carefull cryes,
> I hate the house, since thence my love did part,
> Whose waylefull want debarres myne eyes from sleepe.'

There may be more in the contest. Had Spenser seen Philip Sidney's 'Ye Gote-heard Gods, that love the grassie mountaines'? Is *Immerito* 'overgoing' the nobleman pastoral poet?

Versification, as much as the substance of the verses and the shaping of the thought, was an 'imitation of nature', not only an imitation of a model, native or foreign, and at times an 'overgoing', but also a doing as nature does. A common term for the rhythm of verse at the time was 'flowing'; King James of Scotland uses it in his *Schort Treatise* of 1584, *Essayes of a Prentise in the Divine Arte of Poesy*. Verse flowed as water does. Time and again Spenser uses the figure 'to tune his verses to the waters fall'. Poetry rose like water from a spring—Helicon, the Castalian spring where the muses haunted. In a good poet it proceeded from Bonfont, in an evil from Malfont as in *The Faerie Queene* V. ix. 26. Spenser's farewell poem, *Prothalamion*, bids time and the river run softly till he end his song. The movement of verse was in accord with a movement of nature, in harmony with the cosmos.

Rhyme was a binding principle in verse, one of the ways in which, to quote the Epistle, matter was 'finely framed and strongly trussed up together'. Rhyme in Spenser is *energetic*, as is the epithet or the classical simile: it serves the whole coherence. I suggested earlier that rhyme contributes to the purveyance of sense. Rhyme can even serve to denote the selection that the poet intends from a word's nucleus of meaning, by prescribing one sound out of a choice of two or more. A singularly happy example has been pointed out to me by Miss Deborah Johnson, at present writing on Spenser's vocabulary: knowing feast, *fête* and *fiesta*, festal and festive, Spenser can rhyme 'feast' with 'beast' when he intends the eating aspect of the concept (belonging to the lower order of nature); but for the festal or festive he sounds and spells it 'fest', in rhyme with 'guest'. Rhyme acts as does neighbourhood confirmation by the cognate word. Many of the puns are placed in position as rhyme words, where the sound is dwelt on and interaction of association invited with the meaning (as well as the sound) of the other rhymes. Away with those critics who would always see Spenser reaching for an archaism or varying his spelling to help him to a rhyme in a demanding stanza pattern!

As with language so with versification Spenser moves from experiment to mastery. Where the *Calender* explored and displayed a vast variety of language and of rhythms, metres and verse forms, so in *The Faerie Queene* the master-poet fashioned from his great resources in both a single instrument in style and form wonderfully suited to his noble purpose, to the terrain of 'far away and long ago' of a romance of Faerieland, and to the dignity of his heroic poem.

To conclude, consider this tribute from a contemporary poet, who has perceived the spirit and the art of Spenser's making and offers him the compliment of imitation of his model. The sonnet prefaces the *Amoretti* and is believed to be by Geoffrey Whitney, author of an emblem book:

> Ah Colin, whether on the lowly plaine,
>> pyping to shepherds thy sweet roundelaies:
> or whether singing in some lofty vaine,
>> heroick deedes, of past, or present daies,
> Or whether in thy louely mistris praise
>> thou list to exercise thy learned quill,
>> thy muse hath got such grace, and power to please,
>> with rare invention bewtified by skill
> As who therein can ever ioy their fill!
>> O therefore let that happy muse proceede
>> to clime the height of vertues sacred hill,
>> where endles honor shall be made thy meede.
> Because no malice of succeeding daies
>> can rase those records of thy lasting praise.

Geoffrey Whitney

This tribute sums up and exemplifies the nature of the new poet, the practice of the new poetry. It names the three kinds of poetry and their degrees of style. Alliteration is seen as a binding force, '*l*', on *lowly*, *lofty* and *lovely* (a sequence) then throws emphasis on *learned*, the particular attribute of Spenser's love sonnets informed as they were by neoplatonism; lovely is bound to learned, as the learning concerned the love. There is a pun (not a weak repetition of the same word) in *praise*. This is in the rhyme position and shows praise as appraisal, prizing, of value of the lovely (beautiful and deserving of love that discerns beauty) and it is also praise, honouring by tribute of words. It shows the poet as seer and maker, having received and now transmitting grace and power through his art and by virtuous action ascending to be himself honoured and graced, for poetry brings everlasting fame.

The heroic poem

> Lyft up thy selfe out of the lowly dust
> And sing of bloody Mars, of wars, of giusts,
> Turne thee to those, that weld the awful crowne
> To doubted Knights, whose woundlesse armour rusts
> And helmes unbruzed wexen dayly browne.

October Eclogue

Spenser's heroic endeavour in poetry was to compose for England a great poem—the heroic poem that each nation of Europe hoped for at that time as an expression of the youthful patriotism of a Renaissance state, the glory of its prince.

Long before in western Europe there had been heroic poetry, first of oral recitation then committed to writing, expressing warrior values—valour, physical prowess, loyalty to the chief: in Old English *Beowulf*'s endeavour against hero-rival or threatening monster, Christ himself celebrated as a heroic warrior figure in the Old Saxon *Heliand*. From the people of romance tongues (those derived from Latin) there was the French *Chanson de Roland*, of combat between a prince of Christendom and the forces of Antichrist, the conquering Moors in Spain. And for 'Britayne' emerged the hero figure of Arthur.

Throughout the Middle Ages heroic endeavour had been expressed in chivalric adventure. The story of Thebes and of Troy had been retold in these terms. King Arthur, whose beginnings are in shadowy legend of a war-leader defending Celtic Britain after the Romans left—had gathered knights around him from various regions of legend to sit at the Table Round as champions of chivalric virtue or go forth on adventures that put to the test those virtues and the fortitude with which they were maintained. A spiritual orientation for endeavour came in with the theme developed as the Quest for the Holy Grail.

Arthur's fame and the wealth of story associated with him spread widely from Celtic lands through Europe. Through a derivation of 'Britayne' from Brutus its legendary founder, Arthur's chivalry was deemed heir to heroic action at Troy and thence, via Aeneas, to the founding of Rome. For 'Britayne' Arthur could be claimed as both champion of chivalry and forerunner of the spirit of the land and the nation. Indeed chroniclers of the Tudor dynasty exploited the Welsh roots of that family to foster this legendary descent. Its prince and heir as the sixteenth century opened bore the name of Arthur.

Medieval romances of chivalry had come to concern themselves also with adventure in love. In a quest of adventure to prove worth, values of 'love-service' (love in a code of devotion to the beloved) intertwined with achievements in arms and with a knight's journey towards a spiritual goal, to make the romance an exploration of spiritual and moral values. In English Malory's *Morte Arthur* was the culmination. (The pearl of medieval romances in English, *Sir Gawayne and the Grene Knight* was lying unknown, though there are hints that Spenser knew something of it.)

By the time Spenser began to picture in his mind a heroic poem for Elizabeth's 'Britayne', heroic poems of a new kind had been composed in several European tongues. With the renaissance of classical learning the *Aeneid*, the *Iliad* and the *Odyssey* entered the minds of scholars and poets directly from the texts in Latin or Greek or through fresh translation. These furnished examples of excellence in heroic conduct and provided magnificent models in imaginative composition. (These poems were read 'with moral gloss'—as typifying in their heroes and trials the efforts of man towards goodness.) Now in Italy Boiardo's *Orlando Innamorata* of 1495 and Ariosto's *Orlando Furioso* of 1510 to 1548 were heroic poems of the new kind: they had roots in older romance but their authors were educated in the classics and were writing in a spirit that had left the Middle Ages behind.

Fresh contact with classical antiquity took other forms. With the translation of Aristotle's *Poetics* into Italian in 1548 the idea of heroic poetry or epic became a subject of excited discussion. It raised a whole range of questions, what was poetry for, in what way was poetry 'like life' and how should it convey this 'verisimilitude'? If the aim of poetry was to convey 'universal' truth, how could it embody the universal in the particular? If poetry had a moral purpose how could it bring this into force, how best instruct the reader by presenting an example of virtue in action and how win him to wish to emulate such example, to wish to act as he had seen and felt through poetry that it was admirable to act? In all this heroic poetry was held as the noblest form, as epic had been for classical antiquity. Classical epic was now the model, but the rich inheritance from the Middle Ages was still cherished to the advantage of the new writing.

It is important to see Spenser's *The Faerie Queene* in this European

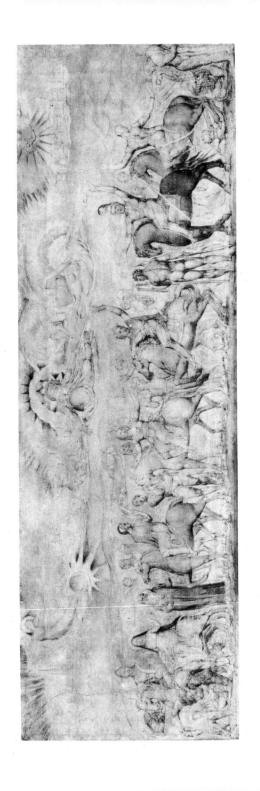

When William Blake illustrated his own lyrics or the work of another poet he did far more than render in a new medium the design, the matter and the inner sense of the verses. He penetrated to the core of the poem's meaning and then, as it were, melted it down and forged it anew. Blake's illustrations for Spenser, therefore, make us more deeply and sharply aware of moral and spiritual values implicit in Spenser's poetry as we perceive these understood, challenged and recreated in visual art. Blake draws on his own repertory of imagery and gesture, of landscape earthly or supernatural, which is to be found in his own poetry and painting. In Blake's rendering of Spenser's themes irony is often present and sharpens up our reaction to Spenser.

Blake painted in watercolour 'The Characters of The Faerie Queene' showing them as a procession or cavalcade. It is a companion piece to his 'Chaucer's Canterbury Pilgrims'. Chaucer's pilgrims move forward over an imagined England of their time. But Blake is aware that Spenser's poem is an allegoria (the means by which, for events in this world, higher ranges are intimated, wider perspectives of meaning revealed). Blake was alone in his time to appreciate Spenser as an 'astronomicall poet', to feel the planetary forces at work in the design and matter of Spenser's romance.

Blake's 'visionary conception' of The Faerie Queene was of a progress led by the main figures of Book I, followed by key characters from the ensuing Books in order. They are moving forward is a cosmic landscape that shows in the heavens powers raining influence on those below them and regions there above that are significant of stages in the progress of the cavalcade—and of mankind.

The whole procession is led by a little child-Eros (Book 1 3). Above Redcrosse and Una we glimpse the Celestial City. A sun-and-moon together, from which issues a haloed Mercy, shine over them and over the Palmer and Guyon of Book II. Guyon, mounted, is looking behind him at a lady from Books III and IV. But between them stands a lascivious and churlish male figure leering at Guyon and pointing at the Lady—the lecherous boatman? Above Guyon's raised sword-point is the Bowre of Blisse as a city showing the dome-and-spire of the Venus symbol. The Lady is mounted, not in armour but dressed in lovely clothes and wearing a girdle. Her arms are outspread in all-loving welcome. Florimell—but not fugitive: Florimell/Amoret with a wiser woman's face appearing behind her in affectionate concern. This summing Lady of the Ladies of Books III and IV is on her other hand touching fingers with Prince Arthur, crowned. These two are central to Blake's whole composition: above

them he has drawn a version of his God-of-this-world, whose right hand extends 'creative fingers' downwards towards the Lady's head. God's left hand holds a sword or wand whose tip touches Prince Arthur's hand, raised in noble gesture. ('Virtue' is seen to pass from God down to earth through Love and to return through magnanimity in action.)

From the tip of God's instrument issues Astraea/Justice, starred and holding her Balance. Below her Talus and Artegall. Behind him rides Calidore, his horse trampling a defeated foe. His hand is outstretched in benediction to a couple bowing humbly and bound (Serena and Calepine). At their feet the Blatant Beast, muzzled in chains. Above Calidore in the celestial landscape is seen the sun eclipsed and a dreadful city of Moloch with the tower of Babel. Thus by a wonderful visionary pun Blake has devised that the Beast, the power of speech for evil, the foe of courtesy and grace, shall appear directly below Babel, prime source of confusion of tongues. The four graces of the dance-vision in Book VI haunt about the subdued pair of lovers—and balance the Eros who led the cavalcade. (In Spenser's Book VI the planet Venus reigned.)

Blake has perceived a two-way 'progress': I to VI and VI to I. He makes us re-think the poem.

The Faerie Queene

Number, Book, Virtue	Knight, Quest	Opponents, Contraries	Queen Image, historical pertinence
Unity, God I Holinesse conscience grace the individual, the Christian church	George becoming K. of Redcrosse, patron saint Quest for Una	Error Archimago Orgoglio Duessa Despair Dragon	Gloriana Una The Pope Philip of Spain Mary, Q. of Scots
female doubleness II Temperaunce tempering self-control middle way of reason	Sir Guyon (palmer) to destroy Acrasia's Bowre	Acrasia Furor/Occasion Phedon Pyrochles/Cymochles Phaedra Mammon Philotime Maleger	Cynthia/moon Diana Gloriana/Belphoebe Medina French match?
procreation III. Chastitie true love and the individual	Britomartis Belphoebe/Amoret seek true love Artegall rescue Amoret	Duessa Malecasta False Florimell witch Malbecco/Hellenore Satyrs Busirane	Britomart Belphoebe/Amoret The Queen, Ralei
Concord IV Friendship amity	Cambel and Telamond Amoret/Belphoebe Canacee/Cambina Florimell Marinell win concord	Duessa Corflambo Placidas, Paridell False Florimell	(Gloriana) Belpho the Queen, Raleig
just sum of male and female V Justice distributive retributive sanctity of contract equity	Artegall (Talus) ... and Britomart rescue Irena	Giant Munera, Pollente Gerioneo Grantorto Radigund Guile Blatant Beast Envie, Detraction	Astraea, Mercilla Radigund Britomart Lord Grey Philip of Spain Pope, Henry of N Mary, Q. of Scots
VI Courtesie by nature and nurture grace	Sir Calidore capture the Blatant Beast rescue Pastorella	Blatant Beast Turpine Crudor Mirabella Maleffort Disdaine savages	None (nominal referenc Cynthia's Cour Sidney? Irish affairs 'savage man'
change changelessness VII Constancie (Mutabilitie) perseverance	? Arthur	Mutabilitie Titaness (defies Jove, Nature)	Cynthia in eclipse the Irish people Tyrone rebellion

This chart is not exhaustive either in categories or entries (Arthur, for example, is omitted). This is deliberate. It is for the reader to extend the analysis and engross further detail for himself.

Pageants, visions	Terrain and Houses	Planet, its attributes and its folk	Forebears
Sins Holy City	transcendental, air forest, wandering wood. House of Pride Prison Den of Despair House of Holinesse Mount of Contemplation	Sun of righteouness, light v. darkness lion 'hypocrisy in religion'	Bible Apocalypse saint's life folk-play
Gloriana to Arthur Belphoebe/Gloriana to Braggadocchio and Trompart chronicles (read)	Sublunary, earth 2 springs of water Ydle Lake House of Alma Cave of Mammon Voyage Bowre of Blisse	Moon horn (Diana) power over growth and waters 'goers on foot'	pilgrimage books Aeneid Circe legend Italian romance Chronicles
mirror vision Merlin's of Artegall roynovant tapestries Maske of Cupid	Castle Joyeous Wales Belphoebe's Bowre Garden of Adonis House of Busirane	Mars and Venus strife in love armed contest by man or woman Bellona Minerva	Italian romance Arthurian legend chronicles
tournaments Marriage of Thames and Medway	watery element House of Care Temple of Venus Proteus Hall	Mercury and Venus commerce travel by water 'many friends'	Italian romance Chaucer
Spousals of Florimell Britomart's dream	Europe, high seas, Ireland, Netherlands Court of Mercilla Isis Church	Jupiter sovereign rule 'righteous men'	Astraea legend law books Omphale legend Egyptian myth
court of Cupid dance of graces and shepherds penitential procession	pastoral world forest Ireland Briana's castle House of Meliboe lair of brigands	Venus innate grace music, poetry 'fair and gentle folk'	Courtesy books pastoral poetry poems of courtly love Chaucer disc. of 'the savage man'
everlable trial of Mutabilitie cosmic cycle 'eternity'	Ireland, Munster Arlo Hill, Mount Olympus	Saturn change old age 'given to revenge and litigation'	War of Titans Actaeon myth Alanus Irish placelore

perspective. A panoramic view of heroic poems in Renaissance Europe shows that they fall into two phases, before Tasso and after. There were poems that were national in spirit and straight imitations of classical models in form and verse: Ronsard's *Franciade*, a learned work based on legend of early Gaul, or Trissino's *Italia Liberata dai Goti* (Italy liberated from the Goths), again a theme from the distant past. The greatest triumph in living poetry was that of Camões of Portugal, who wrote splendidly of Vasco da Gama, his adventures (within living memory) into the wonders of uncharted oceans and the magic of new continents: *Os Lusiádos*, 1572. A Spanish-Basque poet, Ercilla, who had soldiered in the New World, wrote of the conquest of Chile in *La Araucana*, published in parts from 1569 onwards. There tribute is paid to heroism in battle both in the Spaniards and in their opponents, the 'savage Indians', the Araucanians, noble warriors outside Christendom. (In Spenser's consciousness of the savage oppugnancy of the Irish there is no tribute to heroic quality.)

In the second phase, as Renaissance moves to Reformation, the mainspring of feeling and action in Europe came to draw on religious concern. Poetry was called on to serve the Church militant, alarmed by the Reformation. In 1581 Tasso composed *Gerusalomme Liberata*, reflecting the liberation of Jerusalem from the Turk. He aimed to write a poem both religious and national in force. Other poets followed him, taking heroes from the scriptures or the lives of saints: this line descended to the Catholic Vondel in the Netherlands, to the Protestant Milton in England. One branch of the religious epic took the whole universe and all time as its scope and waxed cosmological with *La Sepmaine* (the Week of Creation and of Christian Time) from the French Protestant poet Salluste du Bartas in 1579, and *Il Mondo Creato* from Tasso in 1600. This summary view shows cross currents of national-political concern and religious enthusiasm running strong in Western Europe, and the response in poetic energy. From these we can justly view the heroic poem of Edmund Spenser.

Mulcaster's nourishing of gifted pupils with 'whole arguments of whole poetic works ancient and modern' as well as Spenser's wider reading at Cambridge encourage us to think that he was aware of poetic activities in Europe on a very wide scale. French and Italian studies we know he pursued. Ariosto and Tasso he drew on directly, 'overgoing' Ariosto in *The Faerie Queene* (for example in the episode studied in the critical survey, p. 153). Du Bartas was soon translated into English by Sylvester and became favourite reading in England. The astronomical and mathematical poet in Spenser must have found nourishment and encouragement there, though his cosmological *Calender* was *La Sepmaine*'s exact contemporary.

For Spenser the national-religious issue was England's Protestantism *versus* the Church of Rome and its champions. In timing it joined issue with the Counter-Reformation. Only timidly or vicariously through the admired Raleigh, did his mind brave uncharted seas. But in Ireland, where he was present in campaigns, he found himself in action where patriotism of the Tudor Renaissance state confronted the 'disorder' and inimical energy of the savage man—the fierce resistance of a people, if not yet of a nation. The warriors were not outside Christendom, like Araucanian or Turk, but they were outside 'the true Church'—and were, moreover, supported by the 'alarm spiritual' of the Counter-Reformation in the form of Jesuit priests active in Ireland, or soldiers from the Pope or from Spain.

How does Spenser's heroic poem accord with contemporary tenets of what a modern epic should be? And what other influences are at work? Let us pass over discussion of Spenser's scheme as originally mooted and discussed with friends—twelve Books as in classical epic, portraying the twelve virtues as conceived by Aristotle . . . perhaps another twelve! Let us consider *The Faerie Queene* as we have it; the first three Books printed in 1590, then Books I to VI in 1596, plus the Two Cantos of Mutabilitie with 'the VIII Canto unperfite' that 'appear to be part of Book VII under the Legend of Constancie'. (These last survived apparently in manuscript and were included in the Folio of 1609.) This seems to be all that time and health permitted the poet to complete, or fortune suffered to survive.

First, the verse medium Spenser chose for *The Faerie Queen* was not the long line, related to classical hexameter or neoclassical Alexandrine. Nor was it the *terza rima*, the three-line stanza, of Italian poetry. He fashioned for himself a long rhymed stanza, eight iambic pentameters interlaced in end-rhyme *ababbcbc* as in his sonnets, then a ninth line, a hexameter confirming the rhyme in *c*. Following classical precedent in epic he begins in the middle of the action. Book I opens as a knight is riding on his quest, which, we learn later, is one of many quests undertaken in service of Gloriana, Queen of Faerieland. (Fairyland and the Queen of Fairies or the fairy mistress had played a part in medieval romance.) At some point the knights are to return from quest to her court. The pattern of knight, journey of endeavour and tested virtue came through from earlier romance narrative to romance epic of the Renaissance poets.

According to recommended epic practice the heroic poem should have a hero who was historical, but of legendary history. Arthur had already been moulded by legend, chronicle and poetic narrative to a figure 'ideal' rather than factual. As a sum of chivalric virtue and a forebear of national dynasty he was a perfect choice, malleable to fresh devising. Here he is Prince Arthur, 'before he became king'. He is charged with exemplifying the sum of virtue in action, the princely quality of Magnificence, which is at one and the same time 'great doing' and, as we should say, magnanimity, greatness of soul. He is in love with Gloriana, whom he has encountered only in dream. (The love of the faraway lady, yet unknown was an inheritance from romance.) Gloriana, like Petrarch's Laura is beloved and desired as lady and also as *gloire*, fame ('Laura' meant both). She is the instigation of all heroic endeavour—Gloriana/Elizabeth wherein is figured in ideal terms the monarch of England, Tudor lady and head of the true Church. (The spiritual orientation has been diverted from the quest for the Holy Grail.) The religious issue is treated first, in the Legend of Holinesse, Book I.

Should epic have a single hero, a single action, as in the *Aeneid* or the *Odyssey*, or multiple hero and action as had, for example, Malory's *Morte Arthur*? The point was keenly debated. Spenser's chosen scheme shows him aware of the advantages of both. His scheme is polyphonic, like the many-voiced music of the sixteenth century: but the 'ground' to which the several voice parts of such music relate throughout, is the action of the principal hero, Arthur. The poem is conceived on the main principle of Renaissance art, the vital relationship of whole to part, and part to part of the whole. The sum of virtues in Arthur is unfolded into six virtues, perhaps seven: one for each Book, each with chivalric championing in knightly person. The virtues are 'linked in lovely wize' in a chain extending from Holiness at God's throne down to courtesy on earth.

The principle of aptness or decorum is operating also—aptness of champion to the virtue of the Book and to its cosmic guardian, the planetary force in operation. The sequence of Book succeeding Book, moreover, is a sequence showing development and progress, as do some sequences in mathematics: what happens next is building on what has gone before—because we, the reader, are learning as we read and our minds are being exercised in the perception of virtue and affected by a desire to seek it.

Let us look then at the whole from the point of view of the sum of virtues unfolded into parts, remembering other principles involved. Book I is of Holiness under the Sun; the hero is 'a man of earth' a ploughman (like Piers, ploughman and pilgrim, in the medieval dream poem). He is wearing old armour, that of St George, patron saint of England, whose name itself means 'earth'. But he does not 'win' that armour by proved worth until near the Book's close. The relationship of Sun (the 'sun of justice' of monarch and of sovereign planet) to earth informs the terrain of the Book. Light and its opponent darkness are all-important as the action moves into and out of one or the other. The quest is for Una, beautiful and beloved, the one-ness of light and of true religion. She is also the 'great lady' of the Book, who embodies an aspect of Gloriana—an ideal aspect of the monarch. (We recall that for English Protestantism Queen Elizabeth was head of the Church.) The image of the Queen is present in each book, as tribute to the 'prince' was an important function of the heroic poem; Elizabeth as female monarch was in some eyes especially in need of an imaginative 'build-up'—a service poetry could fulfil.

Book II 'runs like course' to Book I, as the text makes clear in canto i. 32. (The second element in a sequence declares the nature of that sequence.) The Book belongs to the Moon, as Book I did to the Sun. The Moon has power over water, hence water features largely in the narrative; it begins with one spring and ends with another. The champion is Guyon, whose name draws meaning from several sources: first the Gawain of Arthurian legend, 'light of life and light of love'; next one of the rivers of Eden, Gehon (for the moon-book is concerned with water); and finally an early British king, Guyonn. For Book II the 'great lady' is unfolded into two. Belphoebe appears, moon-goddess and aspect of Gloriana/Elizabeth, virgin and inspiring force. (Her exhortation to heroic endeavour is studied on p. 163.) And there is also Medina, showing in name, person and behaviour the middle way of reason, middle sister of three between extremes of temperament, composer of quarrels, kind foster-nurse of a lost babe. The Virtue also has two main aspects. Temperance is the middle way of reason and it is self-control, reason ruling the animal passions (the word is explored more fully later). Guyon has to learn the nature of both and achieve virtuous conduct in terms of one reinforcing the other. All is devised aptly for a Book of the Moon: we find waxing and waning, forward and froward natures, control of extremes of excess and defect, the right mean to be found for such vital rhythms. These declare themselves in characters, encounters and terrain. Idle Lake has no tides. The Bowre of Blisse is also a bower of inaction, sloth. The villainess of the Book is Acrasia, whose names means 'bad mixture'—disproportion, and bad mixed with bad. As concupiscence, excess of vital energy in sex, ungoverned, she tests the self-control and 'golden mean' of the hero.

In the grand scheme Books III and IV are also a pair, as are V and VI. Book III of Chastity is a study in depth of the nature of 'true' love and of Britomart's learning its nature. It is followed in IV by love explored in its widest sense, amity or Friendship. What the Legend of Justice could not accomplish in V, the legend of Courtesy will attempt in another way in VI. It is possible that for VII Arthur himself would have been hero: 'Constancie' is Perseverance 'the summing virtue', as Magnificence is 'the virtues' princely sum'. The relation of Arthur to the Book's champion is constant in point of occurrence, though it changes in nature as the whole poem develops. Where the hero is failing or desperate Arthur enters the action to bring the succour of grace.

A diagram has been prepared to convey a panoramic view of the whole heroic and cosmic theme (see p. 118).

The Faerie Queene needs to be apprehended as a panorama, in its grand plan; there is no racing through it. Spenser's poetry needs to be read with alert mind yet with narrowed attention. The single word may reveal a 'through-meaning', a relevance over widely dispersed areas. The impact of a whole canto may reflect back on a canto that came much earlier; for example the spring with which Book II ends is vitally related to the spring in which it had begun. The impact of a whole canto may affect the way one took a stanza early in its unfolding. With Shakespeare's plays the live performance witnessed in the theatre yields us a version of a play's grand plan and often reveals fresh meaning in a soliloquy, an exchange of wit, or an exit: both leads can be pursued at leisure in the study. For Spenser there is no live performance of, say, Book II that one can listen to several times over, as one does to a symphony. But we can read Spenser aloud in company Book by Book, canto by canto, and discuss it afterwards as we, the listeners, move onwards with the unfolding meaning. That is the best way of all and it was the Elizabethan way—witness the scene conjured up at Bryskett's cottage near Dublin.

In this prefatory book the introductory discussion and the analysis of chosen passages are aimed at helping the modern reader to listen with mind alert and judgment ever ready—'wary and wise' as Guyon was advised to be. The diagram aims to supply some sense of the whole. For his own fuller understanding the reader should make himself a second diagram—Book above Book, canto by canto in order, thus rendering the meaning that lies in that order and tracing the course of the poem as it develops, marking the progress of 'learning'. The summary on number should be kept in mind.

Here are some pointers. In the cantos in numbered sequence canto i gives an important *prohemium* and (after Book I) may effect a linking with what has gone before, especially in story lines; ii gives prominence to a female figure, good or evil; v to a crisis of judgment or justice; vi has relevance to Venus for good or ill, love, sex or lust; vii makes severe trial of the virtue—change may be effected or withstood; viii usually brings intervention of Arthur, transmitting grace and effecting revival and regeneration; ix, a notable figuring of virtue in action; x, some large statement or gathering together, completeness, a period—in II, for example, the chronicles; xi, a great evil—except in IV, where (by natural magic of ceremony) concord prevails; xii, conclusion—but 'something ever more about to be'.

Alertness should extend to the numbering of canto stanzas, especially those in key positions such as the canto and stanza of the Book's number. Some have already been indicated. II. ii. 2 gives 'Such is the state of men' for the Book on earth; V. v. 5 names Fortune, relevant in that dark book and V. v. 25 the victory of female tyranny in the Amazon Queen; VI. vi. 6 the terrible nature of the Beast's bite inflicted for a love-fault.

Watch for paired contraries, false and true Florimell, Una and Duessa. Notice parallels from Book to Book: the Fradubio story in I, the Amavia story in II. Pay heed to genealogies and look up references to classical myth in an encyclopaedia. Be ever alert to sets and sequences, the order that items come in and whether one item is absent from a set or, in a sequence, whether one item is of a different kind. In Book II, the House of Alma, in the allegory of the parts of the human body what is missing? Why? Among the trees catalogued in I. i, whose 'use to man' is happily noted by the straying travellers, one is not a tree: myrrh, plant of sacrifice, a reminder that the Book shows the way of sacrifice and salvation. (The travellers do not pause to consider—but we should.)

It is impossible in an introductory study of this scope to demonstrate the working of the whole allegorical poem on the reader's mind. At most an indication of method and some elementary apparatus have been supplied. The reader having exercised his mind on panoramic diagram along with name conceit and number guide, being alerted to the nature of Spenser's new language, should be ready to profit from first one, then another, of several fine critical works that are companions to *The Faerie Queene* or analyses of its structure. These are named in the Bibliography.

Name-concept and name-conceit

> In that Faery Queene I meane glory in my general intention but in my particular I conceive the most excellent and glorious person of our soveraine the Queene and her kingdome in Faeryland. And yet in some places els, I doe otherwise shadow her. For considering she beareth two persons, the one of a most royall Queene or Empresse, the other of a most vertuous and beautifull Lady, this latter part in some places I doe expresse in Belphoebe, fashioning her name according to your owne excellent conceipt of Cynthia (Phoebe and Cynthia being both names of Diana).
>
> Letter to Raleigh.

It was understood that name should indicate nature. A name can simply be the abstract word for that 'nature', vice or virtue, temperament, 'complexion' or 'humour'. We have Despair, Error, Shamefastnesse or Praysdesire in plain English, in Latin Caelia (heavenly) in Greek Sophy (wisdom). A name concept may be a new combination of two elements; these may interact in more than one way, be active or passive in operation, be understood with ironic intent or may entail a pun. A name-concept may come as one of a pair, of likes or contraries, a two or three of family relationship, or in a set or series, with the set indicated by end-rhyme or head-rhyme or by sameness of ending: Diamond is a jewel of great hardness and value and Di- suggests 'two'. Diamond is second in a trio of brothers, with Priamond and Triamond, where the nature of Diamond extends to the other two.

Names indicating nature may be interlinked with names derived from story or legend (Cambalo and Canace, brother and sister, from Chaucer's *The Squire's Tale*), or reflecting or echoing classical references. Such information is provided in annotated texts of the work.

It is seldom that a name composed of elements in a foreign tongue comes without 'neighbourhood confirmation', as we found was the case with freshly coined words. A phrase will expound in English the name's content or overtones; the family tree of the person may be given or the person will act in character. A person may enter the story unnamed, as does Belphoebe/Gloriana in Book II (p. 153) her nature made known by other means.

Many of the important names have been interpreted in earlier pages and are not repeated here. But I give below a list of name-conceits that may not declare their nature to the modern reader as they would have done to an educated Elizabethan, schooled in Latin and probably taught 'Greek roots'.

Adicia L.   injustice
Aladine L.   nourish
Agape G.   love, 'charity' in the New Testament sense; complement
    to and contrasted with *eros, amor* sexual love, desire
Amavia L.   'I have loved' and 'way of love'; paired with
    Mordant L.   death-giver or given death
Amoret L. It.   cf. *Amoretti* little love
Amidas L.   *amor*
Amphisa G.   double nature (mortal and supernatural)
Anamnestes G.   the reminder, servant of Eumnestes, memory.
Argante G.   daughter of Titans, of chaos; begot in incest; prosti-
    tution of others.
Bacchante G.   wine-bibbing; Gardante It. observing
Basciante It.   kissing; cf. Noctante night revelry.
Calepine G.   beauty, paired with
    Turpine L. cowardice.
Chrysogone G.   golden-born
Cymochles G.   a wave or billow, tumescent; and disturb, power of
    movement (uncontrolled vital energy, of sex; cf. Pyrochles G.
    uncontrolled vital energy, of fire; self-consuming
Dolon G.   a trick
Druon G.   a solitary
Elissa G.   smaller; inhibition of vital energy.
Perissa G.   excessive; cf. Medina
Eumenias G.   kindly
Fidessa L.   faith, ironic pseudonym for Duessa
Florimell L.   flower and honey; sweet feminine power of sexual
    attraction: 'The same flower yields honey to the bee, poison to
    the spider'

Lucida L. light. Lucifera L. light-bearer, cf. Lucifer, the angel who fell through pride; morning star

Malecasta L. evil—chaste; unchaste

Malbecco L. It. 'evil beak', erotic sense, impotence or sexually diseased; 'the cuckold'

Marinell L. Sea, sea-born; cf. Paridell

Meliboe G. honey tone cf. Chaucer's *Tale of Melibee*

Melissa G. bee, honey; natural sweetness

Mirabella L. beautiful, admired

Mnemon G. the 'remembrancer'

Munera L. reward or favour, 'graft', bribery

Ollyphant, a giant: old word for elephant, also Fr. war-horn; G. to destroy; English 'oll': pour scorn, contempt, Giant in Chaucer's Tale of Sir Thopas'

Palladine G. L. cf. Pallas Athene, and paladin

Phaedria G. glittering, gay in pejorative sense, wild gaiety of youth: immodest mirth

Philemon G. Love (ironic)

Philotime G. love of honour, II. vii. 49 'she rightly hight' warns us of irony—cf. Chaucer's use of 'worthy': ambition

Philtera G. dearer, twice dear (in two love-stories); also cf. love-philtre

Phlegeton G. the fiery river of Hades; fire-raising

Placidas L. calm, making calm; cf. Bracidas

Poeana cf. L. punishment, expiation

Pollente L. compelling, extortion

Pyrochles G. fire, sweep, disturb; see Cymochles

Radegund G. reckless, woman ('women's lib.')

Ruddymane, red hand; cf. original sin; cf. blood feud (Ulster)

Satyrane, son of satyr (cf. Sir John Perrot, Lord Governor in Ireland, bastard son of Henry VIII)

Hellenore and Paridell: cf. Helen and Paris; *Hellen's Rape* an Elizabethan mock-epic. Hell, evil; Paridell, a rake

Access to Spenser's name-concepts is difficult for a modern reader in another way. We have lost the meaning many English words held in Spenser's day and often we are not conscious of that loss. Earlier spread of meanings can be recaptured by consulting the *New Oxford Dictionary*, looking always at verb and noun and at derivative forms, and paying attention to the date of the examples cited. Often the important aspect of meaning lies in senses now 'obsolete' or 'in dialect only'. A Shakespeare concordance or dictionary is also useful.

An example is Busyrane, Busirane, the enchanter of Book III. As was usual in romances, the adventuring knight or lady was at some point 'confronted by the imperfectly understood'—as a 'test'. The name and nature of an enchanter are to be pondered. (Acrasia is another example.) To approach by the sound in English the elements of Busyrane are 'busy', perhaps 'abuse'—and 'rane' sounding like 'reign'. 'Busy' had strong sexual connotation which it retains in dialect today: 'Thou hast been too busy with a man and art with child.' 'To busy' included 'to trouble the body or mind, to afflict, worry, disturb, perplex'. Also 'busy' of things means elaborate, intricate, 'curious': the charge made against courtly love elsewhere in Spenser. 'Rane' suggests power over subjects—and 'rane' in print in the sixteenth century meant 'a long string of words, a rigmarole', expression *empty* of meaning. For 'abuse' we find imposture, deceit, delusion (Hamlet, of the ghost); injury, wrong, ill-usage—and 'violation, defilement' (Sidney); improper use of words; 'abusion' is perversion of truth, deceit, deception (*F.Q.* II. xi).

Busiris was known in English poetry already as a symbol of tyranny and cruelty, and in Ovid's *Metamorphoses* he defiled his temples with strangers' blood. For Spenser the meaning dwelling in the sound of English words is confirmed in legend, revealing the 'truth' of the concept. The sound of English words, pondered in a conceit, would put the Elizabethan reader on the right lines.

Part Two
Critical Analyses

This choice from Spenser's poetry has been made in order to show as many aspects of his genius as is possible in a volume of small compass: amorous-philosophical sonnet, pastoral-political song of panegyric, heroic-tragic and heroic-comic of allegorical temper, and celebrative-symbolic ode. The Christian muse of *Fowre Hymnes* is not here represented nor is the elegiac of his *Complaints*; nor is there any sample of his masterly art in fable—from *Mother Hubberd's Tale* to those inset in the pastorals or *The Faerie Queene*. Nor is his prose represented. Each item chosen save one is part of a greater whole, which is borne in mind throughout. *Prothalamion* is presented complete, exemplar of the wholeness that Spenser and his contemporaries understood as significant and comprehensive celebration.

Amoretti (1595)

Sonnet LXXVIII

Lackyng my love I go from place to place,
    lyke a young fawne that late hath lost the hynd:
    and seeke each where, where last I sawe her face,
    whose ymage yet I carry fresh in mynd.
I seeke the fields with her late footing synd,   5
    I seeke her bowre with her late presence deckt,
    yet nor in field nor bowre I her can fynd:
    yet field and bowre are full of her aspect.
But when myne eyes I thereunto direct,
    they ydly back returne to me agayne,   10
    and when I hope to see theyr trew obiect,
    I fynd my selfe but fed with fancies vayne.
Ceasse then mynè eyes, to seeke her selfe to see,
    and let my thoughts behold her selfe in mee.

(1595)

This is Spenser at his simple best. The state of restless hungry seeking in the lover whose beloved is gone away is vividly rendered in the 'likening' to the fawn that has lost its mother: the image is of physical deprivation but the tone is tender. Bewildered seeking is felt in the line of 'each where, where . . .'. A hind is traced by footprints and has a 'bowre'; 'fynd' gathers force from the likening as it is the word in hunting for establishing contact with the quarry, a force it retains when it appears again in line 12. The likening operates delicately throughout the first eight lines and is still in play, with 'fynd' and 'fed', as the argument draws to a close.

The shape of the sonnet—three quatrains interlinked by the rhyme scheme which runs *on*, then a summing couplet—is Spenser's particular choice from among a number of possible sonnet patterns; he uses it throughout the *Amoretti*. The three quatrains here record three phases: a statement, a particularising and unfolding of it into two (fields/footing and bowre/presence, which are beautifully balanced), then confrontation with the negative result. The couplet then interprets the experience, summing, balancing and penetrating to the 'truth' of it. Alliteration is used lightly and subtly to link words that the author wishes us to think of together so that their meanings may intensify one another: lacking love, late lost last, field footing fynd—and there are others.

But is it so simple? Look at the spelling; 'synd' for signed may be so spelt to make clear its perfect rhyme with 'hynd' (as is the case in Sonnet LXXXIII), but 'ymage' is not the usual spelling and makes one pause to think about the word's whole range of meaning. So too with 'ydly': 'ydlesse' of Book VI, canto ii stanza 31 is not the same as the idleness of Idle Lake in Book II, canto vi stanza 10 of *The Faerie Queene*. And 'behold', key-word in the summing couplet? The form directs us to balance 'eyes ... see' against 'thoughts ... behold'. Behold is a powerful form of 'hold', and Spenser spells it 'be-hold' when he means it as 'retain, capture' as in the September Eclogue line 229. To behold is to regard with concentration of eyes and mind, capturing and retaining by a mental and spiritual process. It is done by thoughts.

In the phrase of the excellent complimentary sonnet Spenser is here exercising his learned quill in his poetry for his lovely mistress. For the sonnet marks a learning by the lover, a progress from blind seeking of the physical—the face recorded in memory—through the denial of satisfaction by the traces of her physical presence (aspect) moving on to the need to find 'the trew obiect' (the goal love's desire ought to be making for) and the revelation that the object of love is the 'idea', the very self of the beloved, which is within the lover's mind. The progress is upward, along the way defined by Neo-platonism, from actual/physical to ideal, which is reality. We, reading the sonnet, learn too.

In the sonnet itself can be found 'rare invention, bewtified by skill', unity of form and meaning, relation of part to part and to the whole, and aptness in likening and in language. As a part of a larger whole the sonnet comes in the wonderfully varied but always onward-moving sequence of the *Amoretti*. Before it ran two sonnets, couched in richer language, of sensuous delight in the beloved's physical presence and beauty. In LXXVI frail thoughts may be led astray to wanton in her lovely breast, a nearness of touch the lover is not allowed. In LXXVII the breasts of the beloved are a vision of glorying sensuous delight, echoing the scriptural 'apples of gold in dishes of silver', 'exceeding sweet, yet voyd of sinfull vice'—a table spread at which the thoughts are guests, and would fain have fed. After these the sonnet of sudden absence, with the fawn deprived of food and comforting presence, takes the stronger hold on the imagination. And the sonnet that follows after that is on true beauty, not perishable as is beauty of the body, but unfading because of the mind—'deriv'd from that fayre Spirit from whom al true/and perfect beauty did at first proceed'.

As a gloss, read 'The Song of Songs, which is Solomon's'. There are the hind and the lover, the loss and the seeking, and the banquet of sense.

The Shepheardes Calender (1579)

From Aprill Aegloga Quarta

Hobbinoll

Contented I: then will I singe his laye
Of fayre *Elisa*, Queene of shepheardes all:
Which once he made, as by a spring he laye,
And tuned it vnto the Waters fall.

A   Ye dayntye Nymphs, that in this blessed Brooke
       doe bathe your brest,
A¹ Forsake your watry bowres, and hether looke,
       at my request: 40
B   And eke you Virgins, that on *Parnasse* dwell,
B¹ Whence floweth *Helicon* the learned well,
C   Helpe me to blaze
C¹   Her worthy praise,
coda Which in her sexe doth all excell.

Of fayre *Elisa* be your siluer song,
       that blessed wight:
The flowre of Virgins, may shee florish long,
       In princely plight.
For shee is *Syrinx* daughter without spotte,   50
Which *Pan* the shepheards God of her begot:
       So sprong her grace
       Of heauenly race,
No mortall blemishe may her blotte.

See, where she sits vpon the grassie greene,
       (O seemely sight)
Yclad in Scarlot like a mayden Queene,
       And Ermines white.
Vpon her head a Cremosin coronet,
With Damaske roses and Daffadillies set: 60
       Bayleaues betweene,
       And Primroses greene
Embellish the sweete Violet.

Tell me, haue ye seene her angelick face,
     Like *Phœbe* fayre?
Her heauenly haueour, her princely grace
     can you well compare?
The Redde rose medled with the White yfere,
In either cheeke depeincten liuely chere.
     Her modest eye,   70
     Her Maiestie,
Where haue you seene the like, but there?

I sawe *Phœus* thrust out his golden hedde,
     vpon her to gaze:
But when he sawe, how broade her beames did spredde,
     it did him amaze.
He blusht to see another Sunne belowe,
No durst againe his fyrye face out Showe:
     Let him, if he dare,
     His brightnesse compare   80
With hers, to haue the ouerthrowe.

Shewe thy selfe *Cynthia* with thy siluer rayes,
     and be not abasht:
When shee the beames of her beauty displayes,
     O how art thou dasht?
But I will not match her with *Latonaes* seede,
Such follie great sorow to *Niobe* did breede.
     Now she is a stone,
     And makes dayly mone,
Warning all other to take heede.   90

Pan may be proud, that euer he begot
     such a Bellibone,
And *Syrinx* reioyse, that euer was her lot
     to beare such an one.
Soone as my younglings cryen for the dam,
To her will I offer a milkwhite Lamb:
     Shee is my goddesse plaine,
     And I her shepherds swayne,
Albee forswonck and forswatt I am.

I see *Calliope* speede her to the place,   100
   where my Goddesse shines:
And after her the other Muses trace,
   with their Violines.
Bene they not Bay braunches, which they doe beare,
All for *Elisa* in her hand to weare?
    So Sweetely they play,
    And sing all the way,
That it a heauen is to heare.

Lo how finely the graces can it foote
   to the Instrument: 110
They dauncen deffly, and singen soote,
   in their meriment.
Wants not a fourth grace, to make the daunce euen?
Let that rowme to my Lady be yeuen:
    She shalbe a grace,
    To fyll the fourth place,
And reigne with the rest in heauen.
And whither rennes this beuie of Ladies bright,
   raunged in a rowe?
They bene all Ladyes of the lake behight,   120
   that vnto her goe.
Chloris, that is the chiefest Nymph of al,
Of Oliue braunches beares a Coronall:
    Oliues bene for peace,
    When wars doe surcease:
Such for a Princesse bene principall.

Ye shepheards daughters, that dwell on the greene,
   hye you there apace:
Let none come there, but that Virgins bene,
   to adorne her grace.   130
And when you come, whereas shee is in place,
See, that your rudenesse doe not you disgrace:
    Binde your fillets faste,
    And gird in your waste,
For more finesse, with a tawdrie lace.

Bring hether the Pincke and purple Cullambine,
      With Gelliflowers:
Bring Coronations, and Sops in wine,
      worne of Paramoures.
Strowe me the ground with Daffadowndillies,   140
And Cowslips, and Kingcups, and loued Lillies:
      The pretie Pawnce,
      And the Cheuisaunce,
Shall match with the fayre flowre Delice.
Now ryse vp *Elisa*, decked as thou art,
      in royall aray:
And now ye daintie Damsells may depart
      echeone her way,
I feare, I haue troubled your troupes to longe:
Let dame *Eliza* thanke you for her song.   150
      And if you come hether,
      When Damsines I gether,
I will part them all you among.

This is Colin Clout's 'laye' sung by Hobbinol in the Eclogue for April. It celebrates Elizabeth of England in the land of pastoral at the propitious season of life renewed through all nature. She is 'imaged' as a 'mayden Queene'—a maiden and a queen of the may, *regina avrillosa*.

It was a time-honoured rite of spring, handed down from antiquity through the Roman *Floralia* or festival of Flora, and widespread throughout western Europe, that as April ended and May began each community—village or town, castle or royal court—should choose a beautiful unmarried girl, crown her with tribute of flowers, surround her with a train of attendant maidens and, in many regions, present her as 'bride' of the spirit of the young year, the 'may', vigour renewed, who had arrived in the region as summer king.

Often the rite was associated with a source of running water, as at Peschiéra del Garda in Italy to this day. Throughout France the may queen was *l'épousée*, la mariée. To this day the rite obtains in remote regions among children, a little girl with a bunch of flowers and a lace-curtain veil parades the streets while companions sing

The Shepheardes Calender

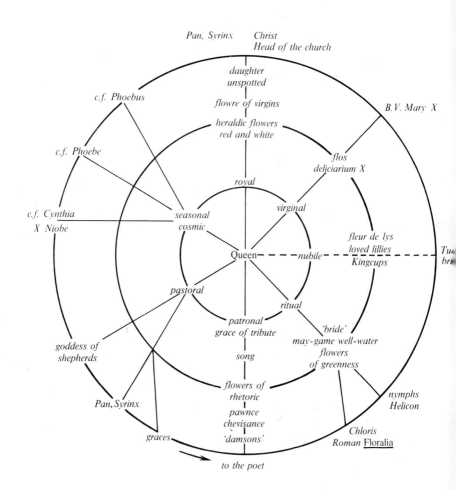

and gather pennies. The rite of the spring 'bride' was pictured in high seigneurial style in the fifteenth-century in the Book of Hours of the Duc de Berry (*Les très riches Heures*). This rite was a point of outset for hundreds of lyrics in medieval Europe, for rising 'corage' of spring makes birds and lovers seek their loves and makes birds and poets sing.

The 'cause' of Spenser's laye is his desire to honour the Queen within his pastoral and cosmic *Calender*. In conceiving her as queen of shepherds in their rustic queen-rite of April into May he is placing her in the great web of meaning and at the same time linking his imaginative act of creation with cosmic rhythm. He is not 'making it up'; it is all there to be discovered, revealed. From the central act of imagination, his 'invention' in the Elizabethan sense, all other meaning rays out.

The diagram on page 136 may serve to show this. The immediate poetic context, the dialogue of the Eclogue, is included as are the emblems and extensive Gloss or notes that follow in a complete text. The flower motif is seen as an integrating factor. The enlargement of meaning to embrace concepts of classical poetry, to the enrichment of the whole, is rendered visually by the outer circle. At several points possible reverberations of associated meanings have been muted by Spenser but not excised; these are marked by X.

The poem is an imitation of nature; it is moreover an imitation of an action, as Aristotle recommended. The pattern of the laye follows the pattern of spring rite. It begins with running water; it was made by a spring and is tuned 'unto the Waters fall'. There is a summoning of attendant virgins and we witness their coming—nymphs, celestial powers, muses, graces, then shepherd-girls. There is music and dancing, praise of the queen of spring, including a telling of her origin and virgin state, a bringing of green branches, a decking of her with flowers, then the departure of the company. There is also, as we shall see, a glance at the *quête*, or collecting of tribute.

Colin in his laye speaks as the master of ceremonies, who in the may play was called the foreman or crier of the play. Stanza by stanza, in invocation, exhortation, benediction, demonstration, interrogation, narration, exclamation Colin's words involve us in the action, varying the mode in which the matter is presented by having recourse to all these 'figures of rhetoric' but all in the natural and spontaneous manner of delighted and excited speech.

Different modes of likening, or indicating parallels in the web of meaning, vary from simile, 'like mayden Queen'; metaphor, 'the flowre of Virgins'; allegory, 'shee is Syrinx daughter'; synecdoche, 'the red rose and the white'; personification, 'Phoebus blushed, Cynthia was abashed', to the emblems and symbols of the flowers.

If we follow the idea of tribute gifts for a may queen we begin to appreciate the complexity of the poem and can delight in the integration, each part belonging to each other part and to the whole.

On the line of pastoral Colin as rustic shepherd offers a lamb to his 'goddess'. In cosmic rhythm, flowers of the spring season are given. To the Queen Elizabeth Tudor, in scarlet and white ermine, a flower coronet of heraldic roses and lilies has been presented. Bay and olive branches are fit for a sovereign and green branches are brought in may ceremony.

Some of the flowers to deck her or strew her way are virginal as well as vernal: green primroses and 'lilies' in one aspect; 'flowre Delice' is *flos deliciarum* eminent as a flower symbol of the Blessed Virgin; Elisa is 'flowre of Virgins' in stanza 2. (Elizabeth fell heir to the flower symbolism of the Blessed Virgin Mary.) As in polyphonic music, a 'ground' is present of sacred and Catholic devotion but the composition devised on it is new. Stanza 2 boldly redirects 'without spotte' (Immaculate) to assert the legitimacy of Elizabeth's birth and 'flowre of Virgins' with its scriptural overtones glances at supremacy. How the 'flowre Delice' is reoriented we shall see.

The Queen devised as ritual queen of spring was heir also to all the symbolic flower language of the may game, when lover planted 'the may' at his beloved's door with a flower token indicating his state of affection—from roses ('rule me') to nettle ('I break it off'). The flowers for Elisa are a sequence full of meaning: pinks, carnations and sops-in-wine are all true-love tokens to this day, 'worn of paramours' at weddings. But why spell it 'Coronations'? Purple Cullambine signified the humble devotion of the courtier and 'gelliflowres' are 'queen-flowers'. English flowers of springtime strew the ground: cowslips are 'keyflowers' and Kingcups, we note, are paired with 'loved Lilies'. The Pawnce is the pansy for thoughts; as such it was used for the arrangement of a posy of flowers emblems. And the Chevisaunce? The Gloss says 'all these be names of flowers'. Scholars have hunted the chevisaunce in herbals, to find only the 'cherisance', but that is the gillyflower or queen-flower. The word chevisaunce is used elsewhere in the *Calender* and also in *The Faerie Queene*. It is glossed for the May Eclogue as 'gaine, spoyle, bootie, enterprise and sometime for cheifdome'. All these senses emanate from 'chevisaunce' after 'pawnce' has guided our minds from floral to abstract:

> The pretie Pawnce
> And the Chevisaunce
> Shall match with the fayre flowre Delice.

Fleur-de-lys, flower of the Virgin, iris—but also manifestly plant-badge emblem of princely France. Surely the secret wit of Colin's laye glances at something delicately in the air at the time, a French match for the Queen?

The hint is confirmed elsewhere. The nymphs of the opening are glossed, under 'Ladyes of the lake'—as 'well-water and ... bride';

'bride' is a concept central to the spring-rite; stanza (2) wishes 'the flowre of Virgins may she flourish long/In princely plight', where plight is condition (of being prince, *princeps*); but from the verb, plight carries the sense of 'plighted, pledged'. The secret wish could be read either way, according as the year unfolded one outcome or another to the proposal for espousal: may Elisa flourish long in her state as Virgin Prince, pledged (to her people), or, if the royal match went forward, 'plighted in princely style'!

There is, I suggest, one more thread of meaning to trace, implicit rather than overtly expressed. The singers of songs for a may queen gathered pennies, or tribute in apt style. Flowers are also flowers of rhetoric. The laye by Colin may be graciously rewarded; the enterprise may bring gain? The request is indirect and tactful: 'Let dame Eliza thank the shepherdesses for the song'. And if any fruitful outcome reach the poet, he will share with them.

VERSE FORM Colin's laye is a song whose accompaniment of music and dancing is presented in the poetry. As far as is known it was not written for music or to match a current tune; but the verse form is 'lyric', being stanzaic. Spenser uses a version of the 'long stanza' with its arrangement of long lines interspersed with short, the stanza of Elizabethan dance-songs such as Clement Robinson gathered (mentioning their tunes) in his *A Handefull of Pleasant Delites* (1568 and reprinted). (By the way, the prefatory poem of this volume, not itself a dance-song, gives the language of flowers.)

The words of a dance-song were written to match a dance-tune and could be sung for dancing to. The pattern of a dance-song stanza was characteristically of three 'traces' or units of the dance; each trace was self-repeating (each step being performed twice) and the whole ended in a coda for the 'reverence', the bow and courtsy. The pattern of traces may be rendered as A A', B B', C C', coda. These rhythmic sections I have marked against Spenser's text. The rhyme scheme confirms the pattern: in rhyme, A matches A' and so on, while the coda harks back to B.

In Colin's laye stanza matches stanza in rhyme scheme as in pattern of traces with their stresses, as befits a dance-song. There is no reason why a scheme of exact metrical conformity should be demanded between stanza and stanza; in fact the character of dance-song stanza lies partly in a freedom to vary the metrical foot while preserving the stress pattern. Discussing Spenser's poem C.S.Lewis (*English Literature in the Sixteenth Century*, p. 360–1), has begged someone to explain the metre: he has striven in vain to establish a scheme of metrical regularity. I suggest that he was looking for what is not there. The poetry is stressed with the beats of dance rhythm, not strictly metrical. Devised in the *spirit* of older English stressed alliterative poetry, the long lines have four main stresses, the short lines two—as a half-line had—while the closing line of his stanza usually has three. As in alliterative stressed verse, the number of unstressed syllables can vary freely.

In old-style lines of alliterative stressed poetry the main stresses were marked by head-rhyme, three or more to the long-line. In some examples from about the year 1500 two would on occasion do, one in each half line. Spenser does not keep to the old scheme as we know it; he has, after all, 'married' it to the dance-song. But pairs of words in a line, alliterating and bearing stress, are integral to the poem's pattern and movement. No stanza has fewer than two examples and many have more. His intention is declared as the poem opens: 'this blessed Brooke, Doe bathe your breast'. A later example is 'With Damaske roses and Daffadillies set'. This is alliterative poetry in the spirit, if not to the last letter. It is something new on an old model, as are the stressed lines elsewhere in the *Calender*.

The form apt for high celebration in Renaissance poetry was the ode. Lewis calls this piece 'a Ronsardian ode'; this is truer than he knew. Ronsard brought the idea of the Pindaric ode of antiquity with its form of *strophe, antistrophe* and *epode* into touch with contemporary part-song in France, a *chanson* form that was based ultimately on the dance. (His ode in *Les Amours* of 1552 had matching part music printed with it.) Ben Jonson too recognized a kinship between antique ode form and pattern·of current court dance: in one ode he names its parts 'turn', 'counter-turn' and 'stand', which are terms used of the larger divisions of the dance. Spenser for his ode that is a dance-song observes this form: in his thirteen stanzas he makes a subtle change after six, gives an indication of close at the twelfth with a last stanza as epode or 'stand': 'Now ryse up Eliza ...' For the first six stanzas the first line ends in a prominent phrase of adjective and noun marked by stress and, at the opening, by alliteration too: 'this blessed Brooke'. This pattern of prominent phrase is dropped at 7 but resumed at 12 with 'purple Cullambine'. The ode form is present but is not emphasized. (By the same token the ode form is present but not emphasized in *Epithalamion*: it is made up of two sequences of stanzas 1 to 12 and 13 to 24, with 24 in a new form as coda and envoy. Hieatt showed the subtle matching of stanzas paired in sequence 1 with 13 and so on; but he sought for the reason for this in astronomical number, and was not satisfied that he had found it. I offer the simpler explanation that *Epithalamion* too is an ode/dance-song in form—the dance of the hours.)

The placing of significant phrases in a poem was important in Renaissance poetry, as we saw. The prominent phrases cited above, through which the change from 'turn' to 'counter-turn' is indicated, are key phrases in meaning also. They repay careful study. For instance the adjectives are notably energetic: with 'angelick face', of 4 the face of the 'mayden Queene' we are admiring is raised above mortal level to celestial Phœbe, expecting the 'heavenly haveour and princely grace' of the sovereign. 'Golden hedde' for Phœbus and 'silver rayes' for Cynthia are apt as generic, but the two in their similar siting interact with and enhance one another. And when this pattern is resumed in 12, 'purple Cullambine' underlines the royal aspect of the blue aquilegia, flower-token of may rite.

LANGUAGE Vocabulary is apt. It ranges from royal and celestial terms for her majesty through middle style for love matters to touches of clownish and old-fashioned speech where the concern is markedly rustic: 'Bellibone' and 'Albee forswonck and forswatt I am', or Colin's 'damsins', which is glossed as 'a base reward of a clownish giver'. Decorum of matter takes precedence over decorum of speech.

The superb aptness of the laye to its eclogue and month we have seen. On a larger scale the April Eclogue as part of the *Calender* as a whole is paired with that of May. They share the great festival of spring, rendering different aspects of it. April under Taurus 'for plants and flowers' then May under Gemini, a twin sign of doubleness, sometimes for sexual ardour of summer, sometimes for dissension. Here as in some continental calendars we have for May the theme of 'the quarrelling doctors', the shepherds Palinode and Piers.

Palinode loves the may game as joyous pastime, when country folk go

> To fetchen home May with their musicall:
> And home they bringen in a royall throne
> Crowned as king: and his Queene attone
> Was Lady Flora . . .

This is the may cart of English country tradition, 'played' also by King Henry VIII in royal pastime, as recorded by chroniclers. Piers is against the may game, as were the Puritans—against any rite as such, seasonal or religious, against vain and time-wasting 'merrimake' that led to lust, debauchery and fighting, drunkenness and foolish talk. The may rite of shepherds extends as symbol to the rite of pastors. The inset fable is of country beasts and their enemy the fox; it points, we recall, at the dangerous Catholic presence in the Scots court in later 1579, influencing the boy king. The woodcut shows the fable, the arguing shepherds and the may cart bearing king *and* queen, if I am not mistaken. It is drawn by Pegasus, winged steed for poetry and horse of honour for lords and princes. The matter of a spouse for the 'mayden Queene' is now viewed in the perspective of affairs of state and religious controversy. And before April stood March, in which Eclogue were teasingly inscribed the secret amours or marriage of Lord Leicester. 'April' with a royal song for a nubile queen is indeed in place, in significant sequence.

Book I, canto ix, stanzas 21–54

So as they traueild, lo they gan espy   21
    An armed knight towards them gallop fast,
    That seemed from some feared foe to fly,
    Or other griesly thing, that him agast.
    Still as he fled, his eye was backward cast,
    As if his feare still followed him behind;
    Als flew his steed, as he his bands had brast,
    And with his winged heeles did tread the wind,
As he had been a fole of *Pegasus* his kind.

Night as he drew, they might perceiue his head   22
    To be vnarmed, and curld vncombed heares
    Vpstaring stiffe, dismayd with vncouth dread;
    Nor drop of bloud in all his face appeares
    Nor life in limbe: and to increase his feares,
    In fowle reproch of knighthoods faire degree,
    About his neck an hempen rope he weares,
    That with his glistring armes does ill agree;
But he of rope or armes has now no memoree.

The *Redcrosse* knight toward him crossed fast,   23
    To weet, what mister wight was so dismayd:
    There him he finds all sencelesse and aghast,
    That of him selfe he seemd to be afrayd;
    Whom hardly he from flying forward stayd,
    Till he these wordes to him deliuer might;
    Sir knight, aread who hath ye thus arayd,
    And eke from whom make ye this hasty flight:
For neuer knight I saw in such misseeming plight.

He answerd nought at all, but adding new   24
    Feare to his first amazment, staring wide
    With stony eyes, and hartlesse hollow hew,
    Astonisht stood, as one that had aspide
    Infernall furies, with their chaines vntide.
    Him yet againe, and yet againe bespake
    The gentle knight; who nought to him replide,
    But trembling euery ioynt did inly quake,
And foltring tongue at last these words seemed forth to shake.

For Gods deare loue, Sir knight, do me not stay;   25
   For loe he comes, he comes fast after mee.
   Eft looking backe would faine haue runne away;
   But he him forst to stay, and tellen free
   The secret cause of his perplexitie:
   Yet nathemore by his bold hartie speach,
   Could his bloud-forsen hart emboldned bee,
   But through his boldnesse rather feare did reach,
Yet forst, at last he made through silence suddein breach.

And am I now in safetie sure (quoth he)   26
   From him, that would haue forced me to dye?
   And is the point of death now turned fro mee,
   That I may tell this haplesse history?
   Feare nought: (quoth he) no daunger now is nye.
   Then shall I you recount a ruefull cace,
   (Said he) the which with this vnlucky eye
   I late beheld, and had not greater grace
Me reft from it, had bene partaker of the place.

I lately chaunst (Would I had neuer chaunst)   27
   With a faire knight to keepen companee,
   Sir *Terwin* hight, that well himselfe aduaunst
   In all affaires, and was both bold and free,
   But not so happie as mote happie bee:
   He lou'd, as was his lot, a Ladie gent,
   That him againe lou'd in the least degree:
   For she was proud, and of too high intent,
And ioyd to see her louer languish and lament.

From whom returning sad and comfortlesse,   28
   As on the way together we did fare,
   We met that villen (God from him me blesse)
   That cursed wight, from whom I scapt whyleare,
   A man of hell, that cals himselfe *Despaire*:
   Who first vs greets, and after faire areedes
   Of tydings strange, and of aduentures rare:
   So creeping close, as Snake in hidden weedes,
Inquireth of our states, and of our knightly deedes.

Which when he knew, and felt our feeble harts   29
    Embost with bale, and bitter byting griefe,
    Which loue had launched with his deadly darts,
    With wounding words and terms of foule repriefe,
    He pluckt from vs all hope of due reliefe,
    That earst vs held in loue of lingring life;
    Then hopelesse hartlesse, gan the cunning thiefe
    Perswade vs die, to stin. .ll further strife:
To me he lent this rope, to him a rustie knife.

With which sad instrument of hastie death,   30
    That wofull louer, loathing lenger light,
    A wide way made to let forth liuing breath.
    But I more fearefull, or more luckie wight,
    Dismayd with that deformed dismall sight,
    Fled fast away, halfe dead with dying feare:
    Ne yet assur'd of life by you, Sir knight,
    Whose like infirmitie like chaunce may beare:
But God you neuer let his charmed speeches heare.

How may a man (said he) with idle speach   31
    Be wonne, to spoyle the Castle of his health?
    I wote (quoth he) whom triall late did teach,
    That like would not for all this worldes wealth:
    His subtill tongue, like dropping honny, mealt'h
    Into the hart, and searcheth euery vaine,
    That ere one be aware, by secret stealth
    His powre is reft, and weaknesse doth remaine.
O neuer Sir desire to try his guilefull traine.

Certes (said he) hence shall I neuer rest,   32
    Till I that treachours art haue heard and tride;
    And you Sir knight, whose name mote I request,
    Of grace do me vnto his cabin guide.
    I that hight *Treuisan* (quoth he) will ride
    Against my liking backe, to doe you grace:
    But nor for gold nor glee will I abide
    By you, when ye arriue in that same place;
For leuer had I die, then see his deadly face.

Ere long they come, where that same wicked wight   33
    His dwelling has, low in an hollow caue,
    Farre vnderneath a craggie clift ypight,
    Darke, dolefull, drearie, like a greedie graue,
    That still for carrion carcases doth craue:
    On top whereof aye dwelt the ghastly Owle,
    Shrieking his balefull note, which euer draue
    Farre from that haunt all other chearefull fowle;
And all about it wandring ghostes did waile and howle.

And all about old stockes and stubs of trees,   34
    Whereon nor fruit, nor leafe was euer seene,
    Did hang vpon the ragged rocky knees;
    On which had many wretches hanged beene,
    Whose carcases were scattered on the greene,
    And throwne about the cliffs. Arriued there,
    That bare-head knight for dread and dolefull teene,
    Would faine haue fled, ne drust approchen neare,
But th'other forst him stay, and comforted in feare.

That darkesome caue they enter, where they find   35
    That cursed man, low sitting on the ground,
    Musing full sadly in his sullein mind;
    His griesie lockes, long growen, and vnbound,
    Disordred hong about his shoulders round,
    And hid his face; through which his hollow eyne
    Lookt deadly dull, and stared as astound;
    His raw-bone cheekes through penurie and pine,
Were shronke into his iawes, as he did neuer dine.

His garment nought but many ragged clouts,   36
    With thornes together pind and patched was,
    The which his naked sides he wrapt abouts;
    And him beside there lay vpon the gras
    A drearie corse, whose life away did pas,
    All wallowd in his owne yet luke-warme blood,
    That from his wound yet welled fresh alas;
    In which a rustie knife fast fixed stood,
And made an open passage for the gushing flood.

Which piteous spectacle, approuing trew   37
    The wofull tale that *Treuisan* had told,
    When as the gentle *Redcrosse* knight did vew,
    With firie zeale he burnt in courage bold,
    Him to auenge, before his bloud were cold,
    And to the villein said, Thou damned wight,
    The author of this fact, we here behold,
    What iustice can but iudge against thee right,
With thine owne bloud to price his bloud, here shed in sight.

What franticke fit (quoth he) hath thus distraught   38
    Thee, foolish man, so rash a doome to giue?
    What iustice euer other iudgement taught,
    But he should die, who merites not to liue?
    None else to death this man despayring driue,
    But his owne guiltie mind deseruing death.
    Is then vniust to each his due to giue?
    Or let him die, that loatheth liuing breath?
Or let him die at ease, that liueth here vneath?

Who trauels by the wearie wandring way,   39
    To come vnto his wished home in haste,
    And meetes a flood, that doth his passage stay,
    Is not great grace to helpe him ouer past,
    Or free his feet, that in the myre sticke fast?
    Most enuious man, that grieues at neighbours good,
    And fond, that ioyest in the woe thou hast,
    Why wilt not let him passe, that long hath stood
Vpon the banke, yet wilt thy selfe not passe the flood?

He there does now enioy eternall rest   40
    And happie ease, which thou doest want and craue,
    And further from it daily wanderest:
    What if some litle paine the passage haue,
    That makes fraile flesh to feare the bitter waue?
    Is not short paine well borne, that brings long ease,
    And layes the soule to sleepe in quiet graue?
    Sleepe after toyle, port after stormie seas,
Ease after warre, death after life does greatly please.

The knight much wondred at his suddeine wit,   41
    And said, The terme of life is limited,
    Ne may a man prolong, nor shorten it;
    The souldier may not moue from watchfull sted,
    Nor leaue his stand, vntill his Captaine bed.
    Who life did limit by almightie doome,
    (Quoth he) knowes best the termes established;
    And he, that points the Centonell his roome,
Doth license him depart at sound of morning droome.

Is not his deed, what euer thing is donne,   42
    In heauen and earth? did not he all create
    To die againe? all ends that was begonne.
    Their times in his eternall booke of fate
    Are written sure, and haue their certaine date.
    Who then can striue with strong necessitie,
    That holds the world in his still chaunging state,
    Or shunne the death ordaynd by destinie?
When houre of death is come, let none aske whence, nor why.

The lenger life, I wote the greater sin,   43
    The greater sin, the greater punishment:
    All those great battels, which thou boasts to win,
    Through Strife, and bloud-shed, and auengement,
    Now praysd, hereafter deare thou shalt repent:
    For life must life, and bloud must bloud repay.
    Is not enough thy euill life forespent?
    For he, that once hath missed the right way,
The further he doth goe, the further he doth stray.

Then do no further goe, no further stray,   44
    But here lie downe, and to thy rest betake,
    Th'ill to preuent, that life ensewen may.
    For what hath life, that may it loued make,
    And giues not rather cause it to forsake?
    Feare, sicknesse, age, losse, labour, sorrow, strife,
    Paine, hunger, cold, that makes the hart to quake;
    And euer fickle fortune rageth rife,
All which, and thousands mo do make a loathsome life.

Thou wretched man, of death hast greatest need,   45
    If in true ballance thou wilt weigh thy state:
    For neuer knight, that dared warlike deede,
    More lucklesse disauentures did amate:
    Witnesse the dongeon deepe, wherein of late
    Thy life shut vp, for death so oft did call;
    And though good lucke prolonged hath thy date,
    Yet death then, would the like mishaps forestall,
Into the which hereafter thou maiest happen fall.

Why then doest thou, O man of sin, desire   46
    To draw thy dayes forth to their last degree?
    Is not the measure of thy sinfull hire
    High heaped vp with huge iniquitie,
    Against the day of wrath, to burden thee?
    Is not enough, that to this Ladie milde
    Thou falsed hast thy faith with periurie,
    And sold thy selfe to serue *Duessa* vilde,
With whom in all abuse thou hast thy selfe defilde?

Is not he iust, that all this doth behold   47
    From highest heauen, and beares an equall eye?
    Shall he thy sins vp in his knowledge fold,
    And guiltie be of thine impietie?
    Is not his law, Let euery sinner die:
    Die shall all flesh? what then must needs be donne,
    Is it not better to doe willinglie,
    Then linger, till the glasse be all out ronne?
Death is the end of woes: die soone, O faeries sonne.

The knight was much enmoued with his speach,   48
    That as a swords point through his hart did perse,
    And in his conscience made a secret breach,
    Well knowing true all, that he did reherse,
    And to his fresh remembrance did reuerse
    The vgly vew of his deformed crimes,
    That all his manly powres it did disperse,
    As he were charmed with inchaunted rimes,
That oftentimes he quakt, and fainted oftentimes.

In which amazement, when the Miscreant   49
    Perceiued him to wauer weake and fraile,
    Whiles trembling horror did his conscience dant,
    And hellish anguish did his soule assaile,
    To driue him to despaire, and quite to quaile,
    He shew'd him painted in a table plaine,
    The damned ghosts, that doe in torments waile,
    And thousand feends that doe them endlesse paine
With fire and brimstone, which for euer shall remaine.

The sight whereof so throughly him dismaid,   50
    That nought but death before his eyes he saw,
    And euer burning wrath before him laid,
    By righteous sentence of th'Almighties law:
    Then gan the villein him to ouercraw,
    And brought vnto him swords, ropes, poison, fire,
    And all that might him to perdition draw;
    And bad him choose, what death he would'desire:
For death was due to him, that had prouokt Gods ire.

But when as none of them he saw him take,   51
    He to him raught a dagger sharpe and keene,
    And gaue it him in hand: his hand did quake,
    And tremble like a leafe of Aspin greene,
    And troubled bloud through his pale face was seene
    To come, and goe with tydings from the hart,
    As it a running messenger had beene.
    At last resolu'd to worke his finall smart,
He lifted vp his hand, that backe againe did start.

Which when as *Vna* saw, through euery vaine   52
    The crudled cold ran to her well of life,
    As in a swowne: but soone reliu'd againe,
    Out of his hand she snatcht the cursed knife,
    And threw it to the ground, enraged rife,
    And to him said, Fie, fie, faint harted knight,
    What meanest thou by this reprochfull strife?
    Is this the battell, which thou vauntst to fight
With that fire-mouthed Dragon, horrible and bright?

Come, come away, fraile, feeble, fleshly wight,   53
   Ne let vaine words bewitch thy manly hart,
   Ne diuelish thoughts dismay thy constant spright.
   In heauenly mercies hast thou not a part?
   Why shouldst thou then despeire, that chosen art?
   Where iustice growes, there grows eke greater grace,
   The which doth quench the brond of hellish smart,
   And that accurst hand-writing doth deface.
Arise, Sir knight arise, and leaue this cursed place.

So vp he rose, and thence amounted streight.   54
   Which when the carle beheld, and saw his guest
   Would safe depart, for all his subtill sleight,
   He chose an halter from among the rest,
   And with it hung himselfe, vnbid vnblest.
   But death he could not worke himselfe thereby;
   For thousand times he so himselfe had drest,
   Yet nathelesse it could not doe him die,
Till he should die his last, that is eternally.

Book I is of Holinesse; 9 is a principal figure of virtue. The canto
opens with 'O goodly golden chaine . . . of vertues linked . . . in lovely
wize'. In the bond of chivalry each knight helps his fellow. The first
adventure is of high chivalric romance, and is narrated. Arthur tells
Una and Redcrosse how the Queen of the Faeries had appeared
to him in a love-dream, since when he has loved her face divine and
will seek till he finds her, having vowed himself to noble deeds in
her service. The knights exchange pledges and gifts, Redcrosse giving
the New Testament. Arthur departs on his chosen quest in high hope.
As often in mid-canto the mood changes to a 'contrary'. There is
affinity between Arthur and Redcrosse, but a deeper contrast. Redcrosse is in poor shape, weak and weary, not yet recovered from the
dire imprisonment from which Arthur had rescued him, and still
defiled from contact with Duessa.

Suddenly towards Redcrosse and his lady there gallops a knight
in deadly terror, a hempen rope about his neck that disgraces his
knighthood. His story is with difficulty drawn from him. He has
escaped from 'A man of hell that calls himself Despaire'. He and
a companion knight, in low spirits because of hopeless love, had been
seized on as likely victims and cunningly persuaded to suicide. He has
fled but his companion lies bleeding to death. He warns against the
fearful power of these 'charmed speeches', but Redcrosse 'must help
and confront the evil.

The encounter that ensues, Redcrosse versus Despair, is crucial for
the knight's understanding of himself and for his spiritual progress.
He is vulnerable because of recent experiences, but Una is with him.

The confrontation is timely: the adversary belongs to his state of body and soul and the terrain, the Den of Despair, is landscape of the mind.

The argument is opened by Redcrosse's own wrathful words at sight of the dying victim. 'Damned wight' he addresses Despair, 'Justice demands your blood in vengeance'. ('An eye for an eye' of the Old Testament has been invoked.) We follow Despair's argument, watching how true is everything he says, on his own limited terms, but how untrue when other, wider, issues are taken into consideration.

(38) The victim desired death, therefore by his own guilty mind deserved death. (It is just to 'render to each man his due' by classical definition, and justice is enough in the Old Testament. But what of Mercy?)

(39) He wanted to die—to go home, why grudge him help to reach home? (By implication of the metaphor 'to want to die' has become a natural and good desire)

(40) He is at peace, his weary suffering over. (The poetry lulls and lures to rest. But is he 'at peace' if he is facing judgment for self-slaughter? And is rest, ease, an end of exertion a 'good', or may it not be a sin, sloth, when duty demands unrelenting endeavour? The satisfaction of a craving is a 'pleasure'; but is the attainment of what we crave a 'good' if what we crave is evil'?)

(41) Redcrosse here objects: a man may neither prolong his life nor shorten it, as a soldier may not leave his post. Despair: He who appointed him his spell of duty will appoint an end to that spell.

(42) God ordained all. Whatever is done in heaven and earth is his deed. Death is appointed for each man, his death-date fixed. Therefore when that date comes who should question it? (Where is the fallacy in this argument?)

(43) The longer life, the greater scope for sinning and so the greater punishment in store. You, Redcrosse, have done bloody deeds which must be repaid in blood. You are on the wrong road and can only stray farther. (Despair works on Redcrosse's consciousness of past sin. But we pray for 'time for *amendment* of life'.)

(45) If you weigh your life in the balance (of worldly justice), Despair says, you have sinned and failed, witness your punishment in prison. (But Redcrosse had been rescued by the intervention of Grace through Arthur.)

(46) Why should you, O man of sin, desire to live longer? (But is that an argument for self-slaughter, a farther sin, to be committed *now*?)

(47) Is it not God's just law: let every sinner die?—But in the New Testament it is not. Why not die willingly?

Then the temptation to end suffering and weariness is renewed. 'O faeries sonne': Despair could not name Redcrosse in any other way without conjuring up an antidote to his poisoning persuasion.

(48) The shot goes home on Redcrosse's conscience: he sees himself as deformed by sin, and the simile suggests that the drugging of the poetry is taking effect.

(49) Despair seeing Redcrosse despairing of salvation, shows him the tortures of the damned. He has provoked the wrath of God. Here we, listening, are in terror of Despair's success. He is now named villain and his work as drawing the victim to perdition, death of the soul as well as of the body.

(51) He is on the brink. Redcrosse trembles like an aspen. Why? (The aspen trembles because Judas hanged himself on its branches.) Why green? 'Green with fear'? 'Green' because Redcrosse's reaction is immature? Or because the aspen flourishes, to be used, or misused by man, to be a warning, or to hang yourself on? (Wickedness flourisheth as the green bay tree?)

Redcrosse is saved by Una. Her speech counters point by point the dangerous persuasions of Despair. A knight should have fortitude, should strive against the Dragon not against himself with self-reproach; frailty and feebleness are acting as body only, without soul or spirit; he has lost hope and faith and forgotten heavenly mercy, forgotten that Justice's counterpart is grace, which can quench the pangs of guilt. As 'Sir Knight' he is summoned to depart from that place.

The ending is terrible. Despair (who in pictures and in early plays hangs himself, like Judas) chooses the halter now. He seeks death and cannot obtain it; his hour is not yet come and the decision is not his alone. (The hour is not yet come for Sin to leave the earth.) All his own pernicious arguments for self-slaughter are hereby annihilated. His 'guest' departs with his life. He himself 'unbid, unblest'— proverbial for the unwelcome guest—may not reach the 'home' of the earlier argument. The death-wish personified cannot win its desire, until in the end he shall win eternal damnation.

Throughout the fearful combat the reader has been tested with Redcrosse. Did he use his reason, his erected wit, against the evil of the rhetoric's power? Was he lulled by the incantation of stanza 40 —so often quoted in isolation as a triumph of *Spenser*'s power to persuade! Having shared the knight's adventures from the first the reader feels the weariness, weakness and guilt and is dangerously near to the point when the will is suborned. 'Poetry invegleth the judgment of men' said Puttenham. And of this there are few examples so fine. We can with profit and delight compare with it the confrontation of Christian with Giant Despair in *The Pilgrim's Progress*, and grant that Spenser's is the deeper imagining.

In the context of the Book, Redcrosse, now rescued for a second time, has to win his own way back to spiritual health. Canto x takes him for instruction to the House of Holinesse where the seven virtues are supplied to him that were wanting when he could not himself counter Despair's argument—faith, hope and charity, patience, humility, reverence and zeal. The reader looking back on the argument, finds it now met at every point. Redcrosse is now *able* to fight the Dragon in the great combat to come in canto xi. In the larger context again of the whole heroic poem, the battle against Despair has been won. No other character has to meet this terrible adversary.

Book II, canto iii, stanzas 19–46

... then dead through great affright
They both nigh were, and each bad other flie:
Both fled attonce, ne ever backe returned eie.

Till that they come vnto a forrest greene,   20
    In which they shrowd themselues from causelesse feare;
    Yet feare them followes still, where so they beene,
    Each trembling leafe, and whistling wind they heare,
    As ghastly bug their haire on end does reare:
    Yet both doe striue their fearfulnesse to faine.
    At last they heard a horne, that shrilled cleare
    Throughout the wood, that ecchoed againe,
And made the forrest ring, as it would riue in twaine.

Eft through the thicke they heard one rudely rush;   21
    With noyse whereof he from his loftie steed
    Downe fell to ground, and crept into a bush,
    To hide his coward head from dying dreed.
    But *Trompart* stoutly stayed to taken heed,
    Of what might hap. Eftsoone there stepped forth
    A goodly Ladie clad in hunters weed,
    That seemd to be a woman of great worth,
And by her stately portance, borne of heauenly birth.

Her face so faire as flesh it seemed not,   22
    But heauenly pourtraict of bright Angels hew,
    Cleare as the skie, withouten blame or blot,
    Through goodly mixture of complexions dew;
    And in her cheekes the vermeill red did shew
    Like roses in a bed of lillies shed,
    The which ambrosiall odours from them threw,
    And gazers sense with double pleasure fed,
Hable to heale the sicke, and to reuiue the ded.

In her faire eyes two liuing lamps did flame,   23
    Kindled aboue at th'heauenly makers light,
    And darted fyrie beames out of the same,
    So passing persant, and so wondrous bright,
    That quite bereau'd the rash beholders sight:
    In them the blinded god his lustfull fire
    To kindle oft assayd, but had no might;
    For with dredd Maiestie, and awfull ire,
She broke his wanton darts, and quenched base desire.

Her iuorie forhead, full of bountie braue,   24
    Like a broad table did it selfe dispred,
    For Loue his loftie triumphes to engraue,
    And write the battels of his great godhed:
    All good and honour might therein be red:
    For there their dwelling was. And when she spake,
    Sweet words, like dropping honny she did shed,
    And twixt the perles and rubins softly brake
A siluer sound, that heauenly musicke seemd to make.

Vpon her eyelids many Graces sate,   25
    Vnder the shadow of her euen browes,
    Working belgards, and amorous retrate,
    And euery one her with a grace endowes:
    And euery one with meekenesse to her bowes.
So glorious mirrhour of celestiall grace,
    And soueraine moniment of mortall vowes,
    How shall fraile pen descriue her heauenly face,
For feare through want of skill her beautie to disgrace?

So faire, and thousand thousand times more faire   26
    She seemd, when she presented was to sight,
    And was yclad, for heat of scorching aire,
    All in a silken Camus lylly whight,
    Purfled vpon with many a folded plight,
    Which all aboue besprinckled was throughout,
    With golden aygulets, that glistred bright,
    Like twinckling starres, and all the skirt about
Was hemd with golden fringe

Below her ham her weed did somewhat traine,   27
    And her streight legs most brauely were embayld
    In gilden buskins of costly Cordwaine,
    All bard with golden bendes, which were entayld
    With curious antickes, and full faire aumayld:
    Before they fastned were vnder her knee
    In a rich Iewell, and therein entrayld
    The ends of all their knots, that none might see, ·
How they within their fouldings close enwrapped bee.

Like two faire marble pillours they were seene,   28
    Which doe the temple of the Gods support,
    Whom all the people decke with girlands greene,
    And honour in their festiuall resort;
    Those same with stately grace, and princely port
    She taught to tread, when she her selfe would grace,
    But with the wooddie Nymphes when she did sport,
    Or when the flying Libbard she did chace,
She could them nimbly moue, and after fly apace.

And in her hand a sharpe bore-speare she held,   29
    And at her backe a bow and quiuer gay,
    Stuft with steele-headed darts, wherewith she queld
    The saluage beastes in her victorious play,
    Knit with a golden bauldricke, which forelay
    Athwart her snowy brest, and did diuide
    Her daintie paps; which like young fruit in May
    Now little gan to swell, and being tide,
Through her thin weed their places only signifide.

Her yellow lockes crisped, like golden wyre,   30
    About her shoulders weren loosely shed,
    And when the winde emongst them did inspyre,
    They waued like a penon wide dispred,
    And low behinde her backe were scattered:
    And whether art it were, or heedlesse hap,
    As through the flouring forrest rash she fled
    In her rude haires sweet flowres themselues did lap,
And flourishing fresh leaues and blossomes did enwrap.

Such as *Diana* by the sandie shore 31
    Of swift *Eurotas*, or on *Cyntbus* greene,
    Where all the Nymphes haue her vnwares forlore,
    Wandreth alone with bow and arrowes keene,
    To seeke her game: Or as that famous Queene
    Of *Amazons*, whom *Pyrrbus* did destroy,
    The day that first of *Priame* she was seene,
    Did shew her selfe in great triumphant joy,
To succour the weake state of sad afflicted *Troy*.

Such when as hartlesse *Trompart* her did vew, 32
    He was dismayed in his coward mind,
    And doubted, whether he himselfe should shew,
    Or fly away, or bide alone behind:
    Both feare and hope he in her face did find,
    When she at last him spying thus bespake;
    Hayle Groome; didst not thou see a bleeding Hind,
    Whose right haunch larst my stedfast arrow Strake?
If thou didst, tell me, that I may her ouertake.

Wherewith reviu'd, this answere forth he threw; 33
    O Goddesse, (for such I thee take to bee)
    For neither doth thy face terrestriall shew,
    Nor voyce sound mortall; I auow to thee,
    Such wounded beast, as that, I did not see,
    Sith earst into this forrest wild I came.
    But mote thy goodlyhed forgiue it mee,
    To weet, which of the Gods I shall thee name,
That vnto thee due worship I may rightly frame.

To whom she thus; but ere her words ensewed, 34
    Vnto the bush her eye did suddein glaunce,
    In which vaine *Braggadocchio* was mewed,
    And saw it stirre: she left her percing launce,
    And towards gan a deadly shaft aduaunce,
    In mind to marke the beast. At which sad stowre,
    Trompart forth stept, to stay the mortall chaunce,
    Out crying, O what euer heauenly powre,
Or earthly wight thou be, withhold this deadly howre.

O stay thy hand for yonder is no game   35
   For thy fierce arrowes, them to exercize,
   But loe my Lord, my liege, whose warlike name,
   Is farre renowmd through many bold emprize;
   And now in shade he shrowded yonder lies.
   She staid: with that he crauld out of his nest,
   Forth creeping on his caitiue hands and thies,
   And standing stoutly vp, his loftie crest
Did fiercely shake, and rowze, as comming late from rest.

As fearefull fowle, that long in secret caue   36
   For dread of soaring hauke her selfe hath hid,
   Not caring how, her silly life to saue,
   She her gay painted plumes disorderid,
   Seeing at last her selfe from daunger rid,
   Peepes foorth, and soone renewes her natiue pride;
   She gins her feathers foule disfigured
   Proudly to prune, and set on euery side,
So shakes off shame, ne thinks how erst she did her hide.

So when her goodly visage he beheld,   37
   He gan himselfe to vaunt: but when he vewed
   Those deadly tooles, which in her hand she held,
   Soone into other fits he was transmewed,
   Till she to him her gratious speach renewed;
   All haile, Sir knight, and well may thee befall,
   As all the like, which honour haue pursewed
   Through deedes of armes and prowesse martiall;
All vertue merits praise, but such the most of all.

To whom he thus; O fairest vnder skie,   38
   True be thy words, and worthy of thy praise,
   That warlike feats doest highest glorifie.
   Therein haue I spent all my youthly daies,
   And many battailes fought, and many fraies
   Throughout the world, wher so they might be found,
   Endeuouring my dreadded name to raise
   Aboue the Moone, that fame may it resound
In her eternall trompe, with laurell girland cround.

But what art thou, O Ladie, which doest raunge   39
  In this wilde forrest, where no pleasure is,
  And doest not it for ioyous court exchaunge,
  Emongst thine equall peres, where happie blis
  And all delight does raigne, much more then this?
  There thou maist loue, and dearely loued bee,
  And swim in pleasure, which thou here doest mis;
  There maist thou best be seene, and best maist see:
The wood is fit for beasts, the court is fit for thee.

Who so in pompe of proud estate (quoth she)   40
  Does swim, and bathes himselfe in courtly blis,
  Does waste his dayes in darke obscuritee,
  And in obliuion euer buried is:
  Where ease abounds, yt's eath to doe amis;
  But who his limbs with labours, and his mind
  Behaues with cares, cannot so easie mis.
  Abroad in armes, at home in studious kind
Who seekes with painfull toile, shall honor soonest find.

In woods, in waues, in warres she wonts to dwell,   41
  And will be found with perill and with paine;
  Ne can the man, that moulds in idle cell,
  Vnto her happie mansion attaine:
  Before her gate high God did Sweat ordaine,
  And wakefull watches euer to abide:
  But easie is the way, and passage plaine
  To pleasures pallace; it may soone be spide,
And day and night her dores to all stand open wide.

In Princes court, The rest she would haue said,   42
  But that the foolish man, fild with delight
  Of her sweet words, that all his sence dismaid,
  And with her wondrous beautie rauisht quight,
  Gan burne in filthy lust, and leaping light,
  Thought in his bastard armes her to embrace.
  With that she swaruing backe, her Iauelin bright
  Against him bent, and fiercely did menace:
So turned her about, and fled away apace.

Which when the Peasant saw, amazd he stood,　　　43
　　And grieued at her flight; yet durst he not
　　Pursew her steps, through wild vnknowen wood;
　　Besides he feard her wrath, and threatned shot
　　Whiles in the bush he lay, not yet forgot:
　　Ne car'd he greatly for her presence vaine,
　　But turning said to *Trompart*, What foule blot
　　Is this to knight, that Ladie should againe
Depart to woods vntoucht, and leaue so proud disdaine?

Perdie (said *Trompart*) let her passe at will,　　　44
　　Least by her presence daunger mote befall.
　　For who can tell (and sure I feare it ill)
　　But that she is some powre celestiall?
　　For whiles she spake, her great words did apall
　　My feeble courage, and my hart oppresse,
　　That yet I quake and tremble ouer all.
　　And I (said *Braggadocchio*) thought no lesse,
When first I heard her horne sound with such ghastlinesse.

For from my mothers wombe this grace I haue　　　45
　　Me giuen by eternall destinie,
　　That earthly thing may not my courage braue
　　Dismay with feare, or cause on foot to flie,
　　But either hellish feends, or powres on hie:
　　Which was the cause, when earst that horne I heard,
　　Weening it had beene thunder in the skie,
　　I hid my selfe from it, as one affeard;
But when I other knew, my selfe I boldly reard.

But now for feare of worse, that may betide,　　　46
　　Let vs soone hence depart. They soone agree;
　　So to his steed he got, and gan to ride,
　　As one vnfit therefore, that all might see
　　He had not trayned bene in cheualree.
　　Which well that valiant courser did discerne;
　　For he despysd to tread in dew degree,
　　But chaufd and fom'd, with courage fierce and sterne,
And to be easd of that base burden still did erne.

The planet Luna, the moon, bearing horn and thornbush: her people 'go slowly on foot' and work with water. Her zodiac sign Scorpio, for intellectual distinction.

In Book II we need to think of the moon, its waxing and waning, its crescent phase propitious 'for things requiring to be done', its control over ebb and flow of tides or of vital energy in creatures—all aspects of its functioning in cosmic rhythm. We need to bear in mind the moon's goddess aspect as Phœbe, Cynthia, Diana: virgin queen and huntress and a name-of-glory for Elizabeth; we recall the moon's emblem of crescent horn, hunting-horn and the moon-folk who are temperate and go much on foot. Her realm is 'all under the moon', man's life in the sublunary world, lived according to the order of nature.

Temperaunce is for Spenser a gathering together, a penetrating analysis of conceptions of that virtue in beliefs of antiquity and of his time. And a finding of a point of oneness in their diversity. Temperaunce is self-control, reason in man governing the animal passions as trained rider does his steed. And Temperaunce chooses the middle way, avoiding excess and extremes positive or negative. To temper is to bring metal to a desired degree of hardness by exposure to alternating excesses of heat and cold. Temperaunce tempers, mediates and reconciles. It affects vital energy whether of sex or of aggressive instinct, operating in conduct of love or combat of arms; it moderates vital energy in its ebb and flow, 'froward' or 'forward' temperament, whether seen in woman's behaviour in love matters or man's in cowardice or desperate fury; the middle way of temperaunce is seen in schooled knightly conduct, in behaviour 'wary and wise'. Contrary to and inimical to Temperaunce are extremes of vital energy, positive or negative, as also is disproportion. Chief enemy of the hero is the enchantress he encounters, Acrasia, 'bad mixture', whose temptation to sin can turn men to beasts. Akin to her is all that is ill-consorted, or bad combined with bad. The dynamics of Temperaunce and intemperaunce are displayed in context of good or of evil: 'love' can cause 'war' to cease even when that 'love' has been found in the empty-headed. Extremes intensify one another and are destructive of one another, as we shall see.

THE PASSAGE IN CONTEXT By Canto II Guyon has met misadventure. First, an episode broached earlier is completed with happy outcome for a victim. In that encounter a rash act, even if done on a generous impulse, had found the knight unwary and his horse and spear have been stolen. 'Patience perforce' he must proceed on foot (as moon-men do) and as a rider must if deprived of his steed. He is now on the same footing as the Palmer, his companion. The horse-thief, Braggadocchio is splendidly caricatured, a boaster and a coward at heart with no knightly virtues and unschooled in knightly skills. He lashes his mount and sets off for Gloriana's court, accompanied by our laughter. The eloquent figure of sham knighthood gains an admiring servitor in Trompart, flatterer and coward—'a well-consorted pair' (a mixture of bad, defect of virtue matched with its complement). To them enters Archimago, enchanter and arch-deceiver, reappearing from Book I. He is himself taken in by the sham knight and would fain employ him in evil machinations against the hero and Arthur. To this end he offers to supply Braggadocchio's lack of sword, but it is Arthur's flaming brand he offers, and this calls the boaster's bluff. His terror at the prospect is intensified when the enchanter takes wing and flies away.

The terrain so far has been lightly indicated: a 'green-wood side' for Guyon's rash rescue and 'a sunny bank' where the flatterer sat at ease. Now 'the forrest greene' is entered and the forest is to each according to his nature, as it is in *As You Like It* ('Let the forest judge'). The forest in Book I had been the wandering wood of Error where the light of the sun did not penetrate. Now it is cover for the coward.

The passage here chosen, the canto's second part, is complement and counterpart to the earlier half. First, the terrain: 'the forrest greene' is extended to greenwood chase for a huntress where trees give tribute of flowers to a swiftly-moving woodland goddess; it is a whispering threat to the craven, bushy cover for the coward; it is a close private retreat for paramours (to the lustful eye), and for wanderers it is a wild and '*unknowen* wood'. For the uninformed the forest is contrary to the court (again as in Shakespeare's play).

But the central speech by the great lady gathers woods together with waves and wars in alliterative concord as fit arena for vital energy exercised in virtuous activity, to win honour. Entry on our part to a significant terrain is an important step towards understanding.

The two-part canto bids us weigh adventure against adventure. In both a supernatural presence challenges the sham knight and his squire, revealing their true nature, by the impact of the sword in one, in the other of the horn and boar-spear. (Braggadocchio's plea at the close that only the supernatural scares him, underlines the balance, besides being a telling comic stroke!) The first apparition was as evil as the second is heavenly good. Archimago was not there described becuase he was already known. The second apparition does not vouchsafe her name in the text but is presented in full description, to be read and recognized by us but misread and misinterpreted by braggart coward and lecher and his companion, each according to his lights.

To us she reveals herself as the great lady of the Book of the Moon. Her presence is of majesty, patently a goddess even to the uninformed witness defective in reason and virtue. Her coming was announced by the sound of the horn, crescent horn of moon-planet and of huntress Diana/Cynthia. Her face reflects the light of heaven as does the moon's the sun's and as does the countenance of the sovereign, mirror of heavenly grace. We can trace the full import in metaphor and epithet, in detail of dress, of mien, of contact with her surroundings. We note her beauty, flawless and a 'goodly mixture' of complexions, red and white (as in moon-women) like lilies and roses, not amorous however but health-giving and life-restoring. Cupid is abashed. The nobility of her forehead, the silver sound and heavenly music of her voice; she is even-browed (as moon-people are); she is dressed as a huntress, richly, as if star-sprinkled, in short costume, firmly girt for active exercise and 'close enwrapped' for virgin discretion. In the delineation of her body erotic fantasy is discountenanced. Her boar-spear is for action against savage beasts, the boar (of lust) among them. She is young and virginal, her breasts still growing (crescent as in the moon's phase that is propitious for noble endeavour). Her tresses wave, but like a pennon; her hair is flower-decked, but not by herself for wantonness. A summary stanza, 31, delineates her nature through comparison with goddess and queen from antique legend: she is like Diana when hunting alone and she is like the Amazon Queen when she stood forth to encourage Priam and hearten an afflicted people (as did Elizabeth at Tilbury).

The impact on Trompart of this presence, of huntress in moon-majesty, causes vital energy to ebb and flow; he finds fear and hope in her face. 'O goddess' from him is flattery, but it is also a tribute to an image of virtue from one defective in honour and understanding, a tribute such as Una drew from the satyrs in Book I. The impact on Braggadocchio 'mewed' in the bushes is that of huntress on lurking game, and is conveyed in movement, gesture and mien. Purely comic is the emergence of the 'dischevelled fowle', his preening himself at sight of a lovely lady, then the filmic 'double take' as he spies her 'deadly toole'. To such a figure her 'Sir Knight' is gracious indeed, eliciting boasts from the boaster who understands her nature only as a lady of a very terrestrial court. Her retort, the great stanzas of exhortation to honour through strenuous virtue, resound in high heroic style—service abroad, devoted study at home, hunting, voyaging on the ocean or service in arms is the sweat ordained by God to Adam fallen. This path of noble endeavour is in eloquent contrast to the open door of pleasure and ease.

The great call to virtuous action fell on deaf ears; the scornful pointing to the easy path of pleasure is seized on as an immediate invitation to lust (the other vital energy, of sex). In Braggadocchio intemperance is unfolded and disgraced in laughter.

This canto as a whole has shown us two examples of the use of the supernatural, or of magic, in romance. 'Confrontation with the imperfectly understood' was a type of adventure important in the old chivalric romances, for instance that of Sir Gawain and the eldritch Green Knight. There as in Spenser's heroic romance the knight-hero clinches with the daunting unknown and learns from the experience, and we learn with him. The Knight of Book II will clinch with Mammon and with Acrasia. The chosen canto shows, twice, side characters confronted with a power which they are ill-equipped, or wrongly equipped, to come to terms with. In their failure to connect lies the experience for us, our delighted recognition and progress toward enlightenment. (It is from Gawain's failure to connect that we learn most in his romance, but Gawain ultimately 'sees'.) At the close Trompart is still quaking. For Braggadocchio the glorious lady was 'a presence vaine' (with adjective and noun in full intercommunion). His regret is that she got away unraped. His self-conceit excuses his disgrace: only the supernatural scares him! He mounts Guyon's steed and rides abominably, its noble vital energy not governable by his untrained hand, his manifest lack of reason. (Brigador—the 'bridle of the golden mean'—is no mount for him.)

Within the canto, the more we think about one episode in terms of the other the better we will understand both!

Consider the canto passage in the larger context of *The Faerie Queene*, first of Books I to III as it was first published. The Lady of the Book matches with the presence of Una in Book I as with the Ladies of Chastity in Book III, Britomart at their head. Each great lady illuminates an aspect of Gloriana/Elizabeth. The Book of the Sun and the way of grace showed Una, the one true faith, of which Elizabeth was Defender. The Book of the Moon sets out 'like course to run' and its great lady points the way of virtue in sublunary terms. In Book I the hero Red Crosse seeks Una as a Christian does the faith and as a lover does his beloved. The Lady is one. In Book II she is two: the vision in the forest is Queen, goddess and inspiration; there is also Medina, who expresses 'the middle way' of temperance, of the moon governing ebb and flow, of Elizabeth's policy. In Book III the great lady· who is aspect of Gloriana is unfolded into three: Belphœbe with her twin Amoret, and Britomart. Medina is the lady counterpart of Guyon's Legend, the serene, the mediator and reconciler in quarrels, receiver of an orphan babe for training, mid-sister of three, steadfast between extremes of temperament of shamefastness and forwardness, ebb and flow. The Book needs Medina's affinity with Guyon's virtue and it needs the impact of the Belphœbe incident and many other adventures for 'the goodly frame of Temperaunce fairly to rise', for the complete and complex conception of Temperaunce to be made in our minds. By the time the great combat comes in canto xii against Acrasia in the Bowre of Blisse, we perceive 'bad mixture', and mixture of evils, excess of vital energy in sensual pleasure and snare of love falsely conceived; against her on her terrain comes the final test of self-control. We are by then prepared to feel on our pulses the full range of the conflict, ready for the destruction of Acrasia and her Bowre.

The story line of the side characters will interweave with the fortunes of knights at later points in the whole fabric of the poem. Braggadocchio will be 'uncased' of his sham knighthood in tournament. Belphœbe will proudly repulse advances again, but her rejection of Timias will be shown as a 'misdeeming': Timias had served her in 'woods, in waves, in warres' abroad in arms and at home in poetry and political thought, for he is a rendering in ideal terms of Raleigh, Spenser's friend. We readers must store the impact of this canto in our minds; it will enrich our understanding of the rest of the poem.

There is one more reason why this passage was chosen. It shows Spenser 'overgoing Ariosto'. A translation of *Orlando Furioso* into modern English verse is now available and the reader can there seek out the characters Manricardo and Martano, claimed as forebears of Braggadocchio and Trompart. He can 'delight' in comparing and contrasting and in devining the deepened moral intention in Spenser's concepts, 'in place' in the Book of Temperaunce and the Moon, in the whole developing exposition of the virtue.

Prothalamion (1596)

1

Calme was the day, and through the trembling ayre,
Sweete breathing *Zephyrus* did softly play
A gentle spirit, that lightly did delay
Hot *Titans* beames, which then did glyster fayre:
When I whom sullein care,
Through discontent of my long fruitlesse stay
In Princes Court, and expectation vayne
Of idle hopes, which still doe fly away,
Like empty shaddowes, did aflict my brayne,
Walkt forth to ease my payne   10
Along the shoare of siluer streaming *Themmes*,
Whose rutty Bancke, the which his Riuer hemmes,
Was paynted all with variable flowers,
And all the meades adornd with daintie gemmes,
Fit to decke maydens bowres,
And crowne their Paramours,
Against the Brydale day, which is not long:
    Sweete *Themmes* runne softly, till I end my Song.

There, in a Meadow, by the Riuers side,
A Flocke of *Nymphes* I chaunced to espy,   20
All louely Daughters of the Flood thereby,
With goodly greenish locks all loose vntyde,
As each had bene a Bryde,
And each one had a little wicker basket,
Made of fine twigs entrayled curiously,
In which they gathered flowers to fill their flasket:
And with fine Fingers, cropt full feateously
The tender stalkes on hye.
Of euery sort, which in that Meadow grew,
They gathered some; the Violet pallid blew,   30
The little Dazie, that at euening closes,
The virgin Lillie, and the Primrose trew,
With store of vermeil Roses,
To decke their Bridegromes posies,
Against the Brydale day, which was not long:
    Sweete *Themmes* runne softly, till I end my Song.

With that I saw two Swannes of goodly hewe,
Come softly swimming downe along the Lee;
Two fairer Birds I yet did neuer see:
The snow which doth the top of *Pindus* strew,   40
Did neuer whiter shew,
Nor *Ioue* himselfe when he a Swan would be
For loue of *Leda*, whiter did appeare:
Yet *Leda* was they say as white as he,
Yet not so white as these, nor nothing neare;
So purely white they were,
That euen the gentle streame, the which them bare,
Seem'd foule to them, and bad his billowes spare
To wet their silken feathers, least they might
Soyle their fayre plumes with water not so fayre,   50
And marre their beauties bright,
That shone as heauens light,
Against their Brydale day, which was not long:
  Sweete *Themmes* runne softly, till I end my Song.

Eftsoones the *Nymphes*, which now had Flowers their fill,
Ran all in haste, to see that siluer brood,
As they came floating on the Christal Flood,
Whom when they sawe, they stood amazed still,
Their wondring eyes to fill.
Them seem'd they neuer saw a sight so fayre,   60
Of Fowles so louely, that they sure did deeme
Them heauenly borne, or to be that same payre
Which through the Skie draw *Venus* siluer Teeme,
For sure they did not seeme
To be begot of any earthly Seede,
But rather Angels or of Angels breede:
Yet were they bred of *Somers-heat* they say,
In sweetest Season, when each Flower and weede
The earth did fresh aray,
So fresh they seem'd as day,   70
Euen as their Brydale day, which was not long:
  Sweete *Themmes* runne softly, till I end my Song.

Then forth they all out of their baskets drew
Great store of Flowers, the honour of the field,
That to the sense did fragrant odours yield,
All which vpon those goodly Birds they threw,
And all the Waues did strew,
That like old *Peneus* Waters they did seeme,
When downe along by pleasant *Tempes* shore
Scattred with Flowres, through *Thessaly* they streeme, 80
That they appeare through Lillies plenteous store,
Like a Brydes Chamber flore:
Two of those *Nymphes*, meane while, two Garlands bound,
Of freshest Flowres which in that Mead they found,
The which presenting all in trim Array,
Their snowie Foreheads therewithall they crowned,
Whil'st one did sing this Lay,
Prepar'd against that Day,
Against their Brydale day, which was not long:
    Sweete *Themmes* runne softly, till I end my Song. 90

6

Ye gentle Birdes, the worlds faire ornament,
And heauens glorie, whom this happie hower
Doth leade vnto your louers blisfull bower,
Ioy may you haue and gentle hearts content
Of your loues couplement:
And let faire *Venus*, that is Queene of loue,
With her heart-quelling Sonne vpon you smile,
Whose smile they say, hath vertue to remoue
All Loues dislike, and friendships faultie guile
For euer to assoile. 100
Let endlesse Peace your steadfast hearts accord,
And blessed Plentie wait vpon your bord,
And let your bed with pleasures chast abound,
That fruitfull issue may to you afford,
Which may your foes confound,
And make your ioyes redound,
Vpon your Brydale day, which is not long:
    Sweete *Themmes* run softlie, till I end my Song.

7

So ended she; and all the rest around
To her redoubled that her vndersong, 110
Which said, their bridale daye should not be long.
And gentle Eccho from the neighbour ground,
Their accents did resound.
So forth those ioyous Birdes did passe along,
Adowne the Lee, that to them murmurde low,
As he would speake, but that he lackt a tong,
Yet did by signes his glad affection show,
Making his streame run slow.
And all the foule which in his flood did dwell
Gan flock about these twaine, that did excell 120
The rest, so far, as *Cynthia* doth shend
The lesser starres. So they enranged well,
Did on those two attend,
And their best seruice lend,
Against their wedding day, which was not long:
 Sweete *Themmes* run softly, till I end my song.

At length they all to mery *London* came,
To mery London, my most kyndly Nurse,
That to me gaue this Lifes first natiue sourse:
Though from another place I take my name, 130
An house of auncient fame.
There when they came, whereas those bricky towres,
The which on *Themmes* brode aged backe doe ryde,
Where now the studious Lawyers haue their bowers,
There whylome wont the Templer Knights to byde,
Till they decayd through pride:
Next whereunto there standes a stately place,
Where oft I gayned giftes and goodly grace
Of that great Lord, which therein wont to dwell,
Whose want too well, now feeles my freendles case: 140
But Ah here fits not well
Olde woes but ioyes to tell
Against the bridale daye, which is not long:
 Sweete *Themmes* runne softly, till I end my Song.

Yet therein now doth lodge a noble Peer,
Great *Englands* glory and the Worlds wide wonder,
Whose dreadfull name, late through all *Spaine* did thunder,
And *Hercules* two pillors standing neere,
Did make to quake and feare:
Faire branch of Honor, flower of Cheualrie,   150
That fillest *England* with thy triumphes fame,
loy haue thou of thy noble victorie,
And endlesse happinesse of thine owne name
That promiseth the same:
That through thy prowesse and victorious armes,
Thy country may be freed from forraine harmes:
And great *Elisaes* glorious name may ring
Through all the world, fil'd with thy wide Alarmes,
Which some braue muse may sing
To ages following,   160
Vpon the Brydale day, which is not long:
    Sweete *Themmes* runne softly, till I end my Song.

10

From those high Towers, this noble Lord issuing,
Like Radiant *Hesper* when his golden hayre
In th'*Ocean* billowes he hath Bathed fayre,
Descended to the Riuers open vewing,
With a great traine ensuing.
About the rest were goodly to bee seene
Two gentle Knights of louely face and feature
Beseeming well the bower of anie Queene,   170
With gifts of wit and ornaments of nature,
Fit for so goodly stature:
That like the twins of *Ioue* they seem'd in sight,
Which decke the Bauldricke of the Heauens bright.
They two forth pacing to the Riuers side,
Receiued those two faire Brides, their Loues delight,
Which at th'appointed tyde,
Each one did make his Bryde,
Against their Brydale day, which is not long:
    Sweete *Themmes* runne softly, till I end my Song.   180

Prothalamion

1	2	3	4	5
		(planet) Jove Leda	angels (planet) Venus	
				Peneus Tempe Thessaly
	nymphs	Leda 2 swans	nymphs silver	nymphs 2 swans
flowers	like brides		brood -heavenly borne	
	flowers		2 Venus birds	
			generation 'somers heat'	
Against the Brydale day which is not long Sweete Themmes runne softly till I end my song	Against the Brydale day . . . was	Against their Brydale day . . . was	Even as their Brydale day . . . was	Against their Brydale day . . . was
I	2	3	4	5
	females	swan unity & diversity procreation	concord	wedlock

6	7	8	9	10
(planet) Venus (Cupid)	planet Cynthia (Moon and Queen)		(Mars?) Hercules	
Nymph's song concord peace plenty	the river many swans 'bridal day'	they all	Essex hero (Devereux)	Essex Hesper 2 gentlemen
procreation				
love			'happiness	praised
love's dislike friendship's ... guile X		London Spenser family Leicester family old woes new joys	fame some other muse	2 faire Brides appointed tyde
'Upon your Brydale day ... is'	Against their wedding day ... was	Against the brydale ... ... is	Upon the Brydale ... ... is	Against their Brydale ... is
6	7	8	9	10
Venus	moon, change on earth	regeneration	prime virtue	completion 5 × 2 double wedding

Prothalamion

Or

A Spousall Verse made by

Edm. Spenser.

IN HONOVR OF THE DOV-

ble mariage of the two Honorable & vertuous

Ladies, the Ladie Elizabeth *and the Ladie* Katherine
Somerset, Daughters to the Right Honourable the
Earle of *Worcester* and espoused to the two worthie
Gentlemen **M.** *Henry Gilford*, and
M. *William Peter* Esquyers.

The title is thought-provoking. 'Prothalamion' is a word coined by Spenser. The precedent was Epithalamion, a wedding-song, literally 'a song outside the bed-chamber'. This, 'a spousall verse' is a song leading to the bridal-chamber—on the way to the wedding. In those days the ceremony of espousal or betrothal preceded the wedding by some weeks and was binding.

A poem for an eminent occasion, *Prothalamion* (1596) was probably printed primarily for private circulation and its composition may have been invited. There is no formal dedication; this would be noticed as unusual. On the title-page there is the honouring of the marriage and the brides; but the expected tribute to a patron will be found woven into the poem itself.

This ceremony of betrothal took place in a great house of London, the home on Thames-side of Robert Devereux, Earl of Essex, who acted as host. In this same house, then Leicester House, Spenser had been frequently present as a young man when in service of the Earl of that title. Essex, stepson to the dead Leicester, had in the mid-August of the year mentioned, 1596, returned covered in glory from the naval expedition to storm Cadiz, in which he commanded the land forces, Raleigh those of the sea. The daring exploit against Spain won wide popular acclaim but Elizabeth was reported as not altogether satisfied with the outcome; Essex was under a cloud. The espousal ceremony here celebrated took place, then, between his return and the date of the double wedding, which was to be held, also in Essex House, on November 8. Nearer than that to the date of the espousal it is difficult to come.

DEVICE AND PATTERN The poem is conceived in a time-honoured pattern of lyric: the poet goes forth from court or town into the

Essex House (rebuilt) south-west of St Clement Danes Church: detail from Hollar's 'View of West Central London, 1658'.

country and participates in, or witnessess by ear or eye, an experience of love and the season. (In the Middle Ages such a lyric would be called a *pastourelle*, a *chanson d'aventure* or a *reverdie* (a regreening) and would usually belong to the season of spring.) Here it is a vision with a song in it—a vision of bridal journey on the Thames. In all probability there was an actual progress by water of the two brides, upstream with the tide to Essex House, and the celebratory lyric imitates the action tracing the course of the progress but rendering the inner truth of the ceremony and blessing the brides with poetry.

The Thames was the natural highway for Londoners and was

renowned for its multitude of swans. Within the last decade or so there had been two poems written featuring the swans of Thames, one topographical, one showing the swans meeting to choose their king and queen. In Spenser's poem the swan is the operant image. The brides are birds: 'bride' and 'bird' were interchangeable in earlier English by virtue of the linguistic process called *metathesis* and the 'bird'/'bride' pun was one often found in poetry (it operates today in slang). The brides, in snow-white attire and moving with formal grace on the water, are swans. The swan image could unfold into a multiplicity of delightful meanings. The ceremony unrolls. Celestial powers appropriate to the action are indicated through 'likening' or invited into the celebration through invocation. These powers are both mythological and planetary, and as this appears to be astronomical poetry number may be significant.

To review the poem stanza by stanza: in (1) the poet has wandered out leaving behind him the discontent of court. (The court lay often at Greenwich on Thames-side and from there Spenser dated his *Fowre Hymnes* in that year.) First to meet his eye is a troop of girls gathering flowers on the riverbank, 'nymphs', 'like brides'. The flowers, we note, belong not to the factual season but to the theme, being vernal, virginal, bridal or amorous (2). Moving up-river are two fair swans, whiter than Leda who was loved by Jove in swan form (3). These swans, seeming 'heavenly borne' or Venus's birds but given their origin in a name-conceit—Somersheat—are (4) greeted by the nymphs with flowery tribute scattered on the water as if on 'a Brydes Chamber flore' (5); there are echoes of Peneus, Tempe and Thessaly.

The sixth stanza is a song sung by one of the nymphs, an invocation to the power of love to bless the bridal, to Venus for love, peace, concord, plenty and procreation (6). The progress is swelled by a multitude of swans—nature joins in through the attendance of Venus's birds; but the two fair birds excel the rest as Cynthia does the lesser stars (7).

From thence they all proceed; London is reached and the dimension of time embraces the past. 'Merry London' was the poet's most kindly nurse and the great house they are approaching brings fond memories of Lord Leicester (8). Suddenly the ninth stanza opens with thunder of heroic praise for Essex, son of the noble house, bringing lustre to Elisa's name (9). The noble lord, richly followed, issues from his high towers like the morning star Hesper (Venus). The two bridegrooms, like the starry twins of Jove in the heavens, pace forth to receive the two fair Birds/Brides whom they will now espouse. As the swan-birds step ashore they become Brides (10). (Magic of transformation comes by contact with a different element: think of Malbecco in *The Faerie Queene* transformed into a bat as he fell in air, or the 'sea-change' of Ariel's song in *The Tempest*.)

Far more has happened than the passing of a bridal procession by barge to Essex House. Can we follow the devising? Look first at the poetry working through number. The poem has 10 stanzas, the 10 of completion and perhaps also 5 × 2 for a double wedding. There is a single figure as the poem opens, and female figures in (2); (3) is unity and diversity and Jove mates with Leda. The swan was notable as the bird of three elements. In (4) Venus enters the poem with a second pair of swans, a four of concord, while (5) has the bridal chamber of wedlock. 6 is the number of Venus *par excellence*. (7) tribute is given to Cynthia, moon and Queen and 7 is the prime number of change in the sublunary regions. 8 has regenerative force and (8) has the family of the poet and of Leicester, with new joys for old woes. 9 is a principal figure of virtue: the stanza has eighteen lines, 6 × 3; a Venus number.

Now look at the swan as device, the integrating factor in the 'making'. It comes in stanza (3). From Jove's loving in swan form of Leda sprang Castor and Pollux, who as stars are named for the bridegrooms later in the poem. (These heavenly twins were associated also with Phœbus Apollo, God of Poetry, as signifying intellectual intent.) Swans in their whiteness are bridal, pure, unspotted. And the swan was a notable figure for a poet; the swan sings as it dies. Spenser has in modesty 'submerged' this aspect of the swan image, but it lets itself be felt: 'some other brave muse will sing' heroic praise of Essex—not himself as he had hoped. This is his last poem.

Number has been shown to be at least apt, as aspect of the poem's decorum and order. Is it more? Is *Prothalamion* astronomical poetry? In the style of the times the day appointed for such an important ceremony would be carefully chosen as propitious. And poetry and ceremony can direct the beneficent influence of the heavens, as they did with Ronsard's verses for the marriage of the Duc de Joyeuse in 1581. It is highly probable that if the full planetary orientation of the *espousal day* could be established the poem would yield its full cosmic meaning. But we do not know the date. We can discern that there is taking place among heavenly powers an action beneficent to the human beings concerned. Venus a planet blessing the bridal, obviously, and propitious to Essex as Hesper. Venus reconciled to Mars in 10 perhaps; certainly Cynthia under 7 capable of effecting change in human affairs. There is no Zodiac sign overtly present but the powers reigning over the period of time when the espousal must have fallen were the Virgin—and the Scales! Everyone would know that.

VERSE-FORM AND MEANING The *Prothalamion* stanza is based on the Elizabethan dance-song stanza of three traces: A lines 1–5, A' 6–10, B 11–12, B' 13–14, C 15, C' 16, and coda—the refrain. Each trace matches its pair in metrical form, but not, here, in rhyme scheme. Throughout the poem the stanza has a new rhyme after the first tracepair is ended, which gives a 'turne' within the stanza. There is interlacing of rhyme, between A and A' sometimes, always between B and B', B' and C. The refrain is linked to its stanza by syntactic continuity, which conditions the preposition with which each refrain begins. These links strongly and delicately serve the onward flow of the stanza. The fresh rhyme at line 10 gives a 'turne' and the refrain is a 'stand'; the form of the stanza suggests in little that of the Ronsardian ode, which is that of the contemporary English 'dance-pair' or *double-danse* of France. If I am right in this, the form is linked to the meaning indeed, a dance-pair form for the song of a double wedding.

The graceful movement of the stanza thus devised has been acclaimed, as has the haunting quality of the refrain. A refrain belongs to its stanza and to the poem as a whole. Subtly employed a refrain may be present as an element verbally identical throughout the poem but it will reflect sense differently each time it appears. Spenser's refrain for *Prothalamion* is two lines long. The second line is virtually identical throughout; but the first line, though similar throughout, is varied in all its elements save the resounding 'day', 'not long' and the connective 'which'. All other elements vary in consonance with their stanza, but also in that they carry onwards and help to direct and develop the whole poem's meaning.

A rough diagram may serve to make the reader conscious of the relation of form to meaning.

A noun with its adjective and a demonstrative or possessive bear the weight of the meaning (as we saw in the 'April Ode') but here the qualifying preposition is working hard too. The day is bridal except in (7) where Cynthia appears and it is 'wedding day'. Why? And why there? In a sequence well established there is nothing so emphatic as a sudden and unique variation.

It is only fair at this point to recall to the modern reader what every literate Elizabethan knew, that 'the wedding day' on 17 November meant for Englishmen the Anniversary Feast of the Queen's Accession, as we have seen on p. 41, remembering the day when she had wedded England with a ring. It was a general holiday and marked by high ceremony and jousting. Stanza (7) speaks earlier of the young couples' 'bridale daye' and fitly moves attention on to 'their wedding daye' in the refrain; but, with the mind moving onward in time and the important entrance of Cynthia, the noticeable 'wedding-day' in the refrain could not but sound the note of Eliza's 'wedding day'. And Cynthia, the moon and Queen, comes under 7 with its power of change in sublunary regions. Surely in a poem of love and concord, with a river running onward through time, a change towards 'happinesse' is augured and wished for Devereux, whose name-conceit is spelled out as *devenir heureux*' (become happy) in stanza 9. Essex is to be restored to the Queen's grace, as his valorous exploits deserve, before the wedding day, before the Accession Feast, in a period of time reigned over by the Virgin—and the Scales? The thunder of applause in stanza 9 is deeply meant.

The summing-up of aspects of high Renaissance style will be the same as it was for the 'April Ode'. There cosmic rhythm was external in the *Calender* scheme. Here also I suggest the perspective is astronomical but implicit in the poem. Then, apt to the matter of 'bless the bridal', we have the great Renaissance theme of time to be conquered through love and procreation or through poetry giving 'deathlesse fame'. Spenser sings again to the water's movement but the undersong is of time and the river now nearing the sea—within reach of 'the appointed tyde'. The poet can slow the running of the river till his song should be ended, but time and tide will soon run out for the swan-poet's singing.

Part Three
Reference Section

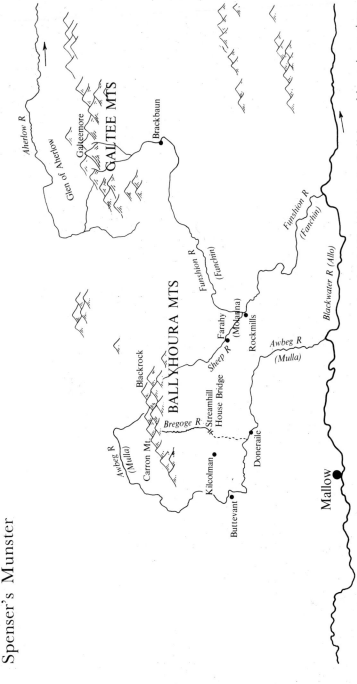

Spenser's Munster

Tipperary

Ahertow R

Glen of Ahertow

Galteemore

GALTEE MTS

Brackbaun

Funshion R (Fanchin)

Funshion R (Fanchin)

Funshion R (Fanchin)

BALLYHOURA MTS

Blackrock

Farahy

Sheep R

(Mologna)

Rockmills

Awbeg R (Mulla)

Blackwater R (Allo)

Streamhill

Carron Mt.

Bregoge R

House Bridge

Awbeg R (Mulla)

Kilcolman

Doneraile

Buttevant

Mallow

On the modern map the Funshion River (Sheep R) has one source stream (coming by Farahay) in the Ballyhoura Mountains, a sister therefore to Bregog and Mulla; the upper reaches of the Funshion descend from Galteemore (Arlo Hill).

No Gazetteer for Spenser

'Nor any footing fynde for ouergrowen gras.'

The Faerie Queene VI x 41

Spenser's life in England or in Ireland has left no certain trace behind, no house that was his, no base for a 'museum' such as has been made for Milton or for Wordsworth. In London we can visit the church of St Margaret, Westminster, where Edmund Spenser married Machabyas Chylde. The poet's school has long since disappeared from its site in Suffolk Lane, which still 'runs crookedly from Cannon Street to Upper Thames Street North, close by London Bridge'. Smithfield, the district where it was reported the poet was born, is not far away. The site of Leicester House (Essex House of *Prothalamion*) can be indicated roughly on a modern map (see p. 173). The journey of the swan brides can still be followed along the Thames by river craft. Greenwich Palace, from which he dated a letter, may be viewed from the outside, but the earliest building now surviving is Jacobean.

In Westminster Abbey, in the south transept, Spenser was buried 'near Chaucer' in what is called the Poets' Corner. The monument that we now see is the restoration effected in 1778 by Mason, a friend of the poet Gray (who belonged to the same college as Spenser.) The earlier monument was erected some twenty years after the poet's death by the Countess of Dorset.

Farther afield in England it is the same story. Of Spenser's Cambridge College as it was in his days nothing remains. Pembroke College was extensively rebuilt in the nineteenth century. The portrait of the poet preserved there was presented by Mason—the same who restored the monument—but the authenticity of that portrait is in doubt. (To get an idea of a 'small college' of Spenser's student days one can look at the old part of Queens' College, which is close at hand.)

Of houses in which Spenser resided or spent his days only the Bishop's Palace at Rochester is extant. Of great houses where he was, we believe, graciously received Wilton is near Salisbury and Penshurst Place is in Kent. Althorp in Northamptonshire, home of the Spencers whose daughters were his kind patronesses, exists today, but it has been much altered by later owners.

Rumours that 'the poet Spenser lived here' attend houses in two regions. One is at Alton in Hampshire: Aubrey was informed that 'Mr. Spenser lived sometime in these parts, in this delicate sweete aire, where he enjoyed his Muse and writt good part of his verses'. But Aubrey had a most believing mind. The others are in 'the northparts', the Pendleton district of north-east Lancashire. Here Spenser associations converge. The Countess of Dorset came from this area. A John Spenser was traced by early biographers who left this region for London and could, by age, have been the poet's father. At Hurstwood an old family of Spencers had lived since 1292 and were flourishing in the poet's day; their home was the house called 'Spencer's' (not Hurstwood Hall, but near it). Their coat-of-arms on a panel 'curiously carved' was formerly at 'Spencer's' but is preserved at Ormerod Hall. It shows them kin to the ancient baronial Despensers, with which the Althorp family also claimed kinship. As the poet was keenly interested in 'the noble familie of which I meanest boast myself to be' it seems to me highly likely that he at some point sought out the Spencers of Hurstwood. Certainly a family tradition dating from the seventeenth century claims that the poet lived there for some time. His favourite seat is pointed out, on a bold headland on the banks of the Brun above Hurstwood; and at Rock cottage on the Brun 'once lived the widow's daughter of the glen, Rosalind of *The Calender*'. However that may be, legend to this day makes claim that the poet lived and wrote at 'Spencer's' and at 'The Hollins', at Pikehill near Burnley.

In Ireland, again, no footing is to find. At New Abbey no stone now stands on another. At Kilcolman all trace is lost of 'my house' which Spenser built when *Colin Clout* was written; but the old castle of the Desmonds stands splendid in ivyclad decay. One window of it used to be shown as 'Raleigh's window', and at the time of Raleigh's visit 'my house' might not yet have been finished and the family lodged in the old castle meanwhile. Sad to say the present *dominus terrae* of Kilcolman does not encourage human visitors as he has created a bird sanctuary there. But in Dublin it is possible to view Dublin Castle, which was Spenser's headquarters for his official work under Lord Grey.

O pittious worke of MUTABILITIE!

But the lovely countryside remains, almost entirely unspoiled and unpolluted. And—the desecrated Liffey apart—all the streams of water whose running echoed in the poet's mind, to whose fall he tuned his notes and whose names and natures he celebrated in the pageant of Book IV. The whole beautiful region of Munster resounds in Spenser's poetry

> And all that Mountain which doth over looke
> The richest champian that may else be rid
> And the faire Shure in which are thousand Salmons bred.

Forest, mountain and pastureland spread out round Kilcolman, with, near at hand, the 'Mulla' with its alders and the waterside where the calling of frogs disturbed the poet. In distant view the Galtee Mountains ('Old Mole') and Aherlo, Arlo 'pronounced Ahr-low with a long A like a sigh'. This is the terrain of *The Cantos of Mutabilitie* and the river fable within it; it is the countryside of *Colin Clout's Come Home Againe* and of its river fable too. The mountains and streams are there to be found today. Their naming was devised by the poet, in contact, obviously, with Irish 'place lore'. From the Glen of Aherlow he made 'the hill of Arlo'. He understood 'mole' as hilltop, as in Kilnamullah ('the church of the summits') the old name for Buttevant. 'Mole' may also have had the submerged sound-meaning of 'bald'—hence 'Old Mole'. From 'Old Mole', the range of the Galtee and Ballahoura mountains especially Galtymore the highest peak, descend the 'daughters of Mole', the rivers 'Mulla' and 'Molanna'. Spenser's 'Mulla' ('Mulla mine') is the Awbeg (illustrated on p. 62) on which stands Buttevant (Kilnamullah); it is a tributary of the Blackwater.

'Molanna' of the river fables is the stream Altychraan or Brackbaun, rising on the side of Galtymore among rocks shaded by oaks, as the poet says. This stream becomes the Funcheon: 'Molanna' loves 'Fanchin' and is united with him (as Thames weds Medway). The villain of fable is not far away, the stream Bregoge, rising in a glen on the side of Corrinmore hill, joining the Aubeg near Doneraile. 'Bregog' is a name of lies and deception: 'breug', a lie. In dry weather it shrinks in a stony bed; in the fable it is 'whelmed with stones' and 'loses its name', the penalty of oblivion for foul lust. Spenser's 'Allo' is not the stream of that name on the modern map but the Munster Blackwater, which apparently was called the Allo in earlier times. In Spenser's poetry it 'rises in Slewlogher steep' (Slievelougher) and in the fable it is one with the Blackwater. All these may be traced and enjoyed; their very nature has been rendered in poetic truth.

But in this quest the saddest thing is the vacant look that can meet an enthusiastic enquiry after traces of the poet:

> The woods did nought but ecchoes vaine rebound
> The playnes all waste and emptie did appeare
> Where wont the shepheards oft their pypes resound.

Spenser was an incomer.

Short Biographies

ARIOSTO, LODOVICO, 1474–1533. An Italian poet who escaped from the study of law to study classical literature and language. He was a diplomat but attained little worldly success. In 1503 he wrote a continuation of Boiardo's *Orlando Innamorata* as *Orlando Furioso*; published in 1516, it won instant fame at home and abroad; translated twelve times into French it was rendered in English by Sir John Harington. His romance epic was a 'model' for *The Faerie Queene*. For Spenser's 'overgoing' and Ariosto's poetry, see Graham Hough, *A Preface to The Faerie Queene* (1962).

DU BARTAS, GUILLAUME SALUSTE, SEIGNEUR, 1544–90. A Protestant poet who learned from the Pléiade but 'served the Christian muse' turning to the Scriptures for his subject-matter. His *Judith* (1573), his *Uranie* and *Furies* were translated for the Scottish court, the last two by King James himself. *La Sepmaine ou la Creation en Sept journées* (1578) was immediately popular and widely translated; Joshua Sylvester's version in English *Bartas His Devine Weekes and Workes* made him popular in England. This is cosmic poetry but not disciplined in form. Nevertheless the success of the *Sepmaine* may have confirmed Spenser in his decision to cast his epic in cosmic mould.

DU BELLAY, JOACHIM, 1525–60. Of the new poets of France it was du Bellay who influenced Spenser most closely. He began with Petrarchan sonnets in *Olive* (1552) but soon mocked the excesses of the neo-Petrarchan style. He served his cardinal uncle, the French ambassador in Rome; the impact on him was profound, the fallen greatness, the ruins, the corruption of society. These he expressed in *Les Antiquetés de Rome*. He loved his native Anjou and his pastorals are real 'country' poetry. His treatise *Défense et Illustration de la Langue Francaise* (1549) was the manifesto of the Pléiade poets, the most important study of poetry in the century.

BOYLE, ELIZABETH, 1576? –1622. Spenser's second wife, honoured in *Epithalamion*; daughter of Stephen and Joan Boyle of Bradden, Northamptonshire, not far from Althorp. She and one of her brothers moved to Ireland, probably because her kinsman Richard Boyle was prominent in Munster. To Spenser she bore one son, Peregrine. After Spenser's death she married Roger Seckerstone (1600) and later Captain Robert Tynte (1612), having children by them. She was well educated, writing a fine Italian hand. Her relations with Sylvanus and Katherine were not happy. A fine portrait effigy on the Tynte tomb in Kilcredan Church, County Cork, was destroyed in 1925.

BURGHLEY OR BURLEIGH, WILLIAM CECIL, FIRST BARON, 1520–98.
Secretary of State from 1550 and served Elizabeth from her Accession
to his death. Her most trusted statesman, he advised her wisely on
home and foreign policy. A generous patron of serious works in law
or history, he had little time for poetry. He never looked with favour
on Spenser, perhaps because he was satirised in *Mother Hubberd's Tale*.
Spenser's plea for serious consideration of his epic in a prefatory
sonnet (1596) went unheeded, and at the close of Book VI Of Courtesie
the poet laments the unrelenting hostility of a 'great peer'. Portrait
in the Burrell Collection, Glasgow—reproduced in *The Elizabethans*.

CASTIGLIONE, BALDASSARE, 1478–1529. A diplomat active among the
great families of northern Italy and sent on a mission to Henry VII
of England. 'One of the world's best cavaliers', he died heartbroken
at accusations of treachery. His great book *Il Cortegiano* described
the perfect courtier and mirrored the ideal of courtly life. Published in
Venice in 1514 it was translated widely—into English by Sir Thomas
Hoby in 1561. It includes the best discussion of Neoplatonic love.

ESSEX FAMILY. Lettice Knollys, Countess of Essex, later Lady Leicester
—a distant cousin of the Queen. She had by Essex a daughter Penelope
Devereux (beloved by Philip Sidney) and a son Robert Devereux
who became Earl of Essex on his father's death in 1567. Before that
date Lettice's name had been linked by gossip with Leicester's who
married her secretly in 1578. She was famous for her voluptuous
beauty and scornful regard; she was referred to by Elizabeth as
'that she-wolf'. Offence taken at slighting references in *The Calender*
may have cost Spenser the favour of Leicester. Her behaviour after
Leicester's death was scandalous and she is omitted from Spenser's
celebration of the Dudley family in poetry. Portrait on p. 46.

ROBERT DEVEREUX, EARL OF ESSEX, 1567–1601, became prime favourite with the Queen after Leicester's death and during Raleigh's
'disgrace'. His personality and conduct were flamboyant if unwise.
Celebrated for his 'heroick parts' in a prefatory sonnet to *The Faerie
Queene* (1596) and in *Prothalamion*. The poet's death saved him from
witnessing Essex's failure in Ireland and his later rebellion and
execution. Portrait in the National Portrait Gallery, reproduced in
The Elizabethans.

GREY, ARTHUR, LORD GREY DE WILTON. 1536–93. Born in the English
Pale in France, trained as a soldier. Employed under Cecil; served
in the expedition in the north, in the siege of Leith against the French
in Scotland. Succeeded to the title in 1562, residing at Whaddon
House, Buckinghamshire. Involved in a quarrel and imprisoned
in The Fleet, having offended Elizabeth—but Burleigh his ally.
Appointed Lord Deputy in Ireland and bidden not be overstrict
in matters of religion. Very soon bested in battle at Glenmalure on

the 'Oure'. Proceeded against forces from the Pope and Spain holding Smerwick fort. Conduct of the siege, surrender and massacre at Smerwick criticized. Denied support in troops, he begged to resign. Returned overwhelmed with debt contracted in Ireland, and in royal displeasure. Held minor appointments; was a commissioner for the Trial of Mary Queen of Scots. 'Arthegall, Artegall'.

HARVEY, GABRIEL 1548?–1630?. Fellow of Pembroke Hall then of Trinity Hall; a friend of Spenser. 'Hobbinol' in the pastorals. He published *Letters* and works in Latin, taking part in controversy with 'the university wits'. A scholar of ancient and modern languages and literature, a keen critic of Spenser's poetry; his commentary has been preserved in annotations on texts. Conceited, egotistical and ambitious, a declared admirer of Machiavelli: his encouragement may have pushed Spenser towards overreaching discretion in comment on state affairs and personalities in *The Calender*.

LEICESTER, ROBERT DUDLEY, EARL OF, 1532–88. A friend of Elizabeth before she became Queen, he was prime favourite during the early years of her reign. On her accession she knighted him and made him Master of the Horse, and at that time contemplated marrying him. She came to see this as undesirable in a sovereign and in 1563 proposed he marry Mary Queen of Scots. In 1564, now Earl of Leicester and master of vast lands given by the Queen, notably Kenilworth, his ambition was unbounded and his ostentation remarkable even in that age. He married for a second time in 1573, but never acknowledged this marriage. (This liaison was glanced at in Shakespear's *Midsummer Night's Dream*.) Up to 1577 his relations with continental powers had been veering, as best suited his interests; but he firmly opposed a French match for the Queen and was now notably Protestant in declared sympathies. After the crisis of 1579, discussed in the text (pp. 45–7) Leicester was restored to favour and his presumption was at its height. Sent as Commander of Forces to the Netherlands in 1585 he there got himself elected Lord Governor to the Estates General, but Elizabeth, enraged, recalled him. He urged the execution of Mary Queen of Scots and was commander of the armies at the time of the Armada. He died the next year, aged fifty-six—and 'after his death was soon forgot'. Throughout his career Lord Burleigh was critical of him. Portrait in the National Portrait Gallery, reproduced in *The Elizabethans*. See page 20.

MAROT, CLÉMENT, 1495–1544. Poet of France of the generation before the Pléiade he wrote lyrics in medieval forms; but in contact with Renaissance culture in the French court he composed elegant and delightful pieces, songs, pastoral eclogues and addresses to the king. He had sympathy with the reforming party and translated forty-nine Psalms into verse. For Spenser he was a 'model', but to be surpassed in 'overgoing'. In the *Calender* the November and December Eclogues 'imitate' Marot's elegy for the Queen Mother of France and his 'Eglogue du Roy' (1539). Spenser could find precedent in Marot for several aspects of his policy on language.

'MANTUAN', BAPTISTA SPAGNUOLI MANTUANUS, 1448–1516. Born at Mantua of a Spanish father; entered the Carmelite Order of Friars and held high office in it. His Eclogues in Latin first printed in 1498 were in imitation of Vergil's but with satiric comment on his times, lively dialogue and energetic invective, These were in common use as a Latin textbook in Elizabethan grammar schools and 'imitations' in the *Calender*—July, September and October—would be immediately appreciated. Mantuan's *Eclogues* were edited by W.P. Mustard (1911) and translated by G. Turbervile (1567) edited by D. Bush, 1937.

MULCASTER, RICHARD, 1530?–1611. Born Brackenhall Castle on the Scottish border. Educated at Eton and Christ Church, Oxford; M.A. 1556. Schoolmaster in London; first Headmaster of Merchant Taylors' School 1561–86. Held various livings. High Master of St Paul's School 1596–1608. Distinguished scholar of ancient and modern languages but an enthusiast for the English language. His writings on education were 'probably based on experience he already had when Spenser was his pupil': *Positions wherein . . . Circumstances be examined . . . necessarie for the training up of children* (1581, ed. R.H. Quick, 1888) and *The First Part of the Elementarie* (1582, ed. E.T. Champagnac, 1925); *The Educational Writings* (abridged ed. J. Oliphant 1903). Commentary in C.S. Lewis *English Literature of the Sixteenth Century*.

O'NEILL, HUGH (THE O'NEILL') EARL OF TYRONE, 1550–1616. An orphan of the O'Neills in danger of his life from family feud, eligible to be elected chief, befriended by Sir Henry Sidney, brought up in England in the hope that he might be an influence for peace. This did not work as he never forgave Elizabeth for not pushing his claim earlier. He played one loyalty against another, now leading rebellion, now protesting repentance. Leader of the Tyrone rebellion of 1598, he resisted English expansion for nine years, wore out the Queen's authority, and broke generals like Essex. He aimed at the stature of a Renaissance prince based on his lordship in Gaeldom. After Mountjoy's victorious campaign he surrendered and was humiliated; he tried to treat with King James, but fled in 1607, dying an obscure exile in Rome. He is represented in Faunus of the fable in *The Faerie Queene* Book VII.

PETRARCH, FRANCESCO (Petrarca) 1304–74. Distinguished poet and scholar, 'inaugurator' of the Renaissance in Italy. He was born in Arezzo but resided in France at Avignon and Vaucluse. He assembled libraries and collected manuscripts of classical authors, discovering Cicero's *Familiar Letters*. He was a priest and venerated classical genius for perfection of intellect and civilization, but sacred inspiration for 'eternal welfare'. His great love poetry for 'Laura' arose from love for a real lady, but Laura is also 'eternal fame'. He wrote distinguished letters on classical models, splendid odes on noble friends and later 'Triumphs' of Love, Chastity, Death, Fame, Time and Divinity. His love-poetry broke with medieval traditions and celebrated the ideal lady in the landscape of perfect beauty. The influence of the new poetry spread throughout Europe and was felt vividly centuries after, though imitation brought exaggeration of his mode of poetic expression. He was a friend of Boccaccio.

RALEIGH (or RALEGH), SIR WALTER, 1552–1618. Son of a notably Protestant squire in the west country, one of four brothers or half-brothers who earned knighthoods. In his 'teens he saw service with Protestant forces in France; studied at Oxford and perhaps at the Middle Temple in London. He served for some years in Ireland with Lord Grey with whom he 'assorted ill'. Returning in 1581 he was by 1582 at court and in the Queen's favour, attained perhaps through the cloak incident. He remained first favourite for a decade, rewarded with money, offices and land, and backing expeditions to North America. Knighted in 1583, Captain of the Queen's Guard from 1587. His first fall from favour came in 1589, perhaps from too great presumption with Her Majesty. Granted Sherborne Castle and published a *Report* on Grenville's sea fight. Again disgraced because he 'seduced' a Maid of Honour, Elizabeth Throckmorton, whom he had married in 1591. Supplanted by Essex, he was out of favour at court until 1596. He took part in the Expedition to Guiana in 1593 and to Cadiz in 1596. He published the *Discoverie of Guiana* in 1597 and took part in the Islands Voyage.

He was never in favour with King James, who imprisoned him in the Tower, where he wrote his *Historie of the World*. Released only for an unsuccessful expedition to South America. Executed in 1618. He was an intellectual as well as a man of action; his London home a centre of scientific discussion with a practical end. A friend of other soldier poets, Gascoigne and Gorges, he wrote powerful lyrics never published—including his 'Ocean to Cynthia' for the Queen. A loyal friend to Spenser, who championed him in his poetry. Adored by men he led in action, he was never a popular figure, being hated for his pride. Portrait in the National Portrait Gallery, reproduced in *The Elizabethans*. See page 70.

RONSARD, PIERRE DE 1524–85. An aristocratic poet of humanist education, turned by deafness from a diplomatic career to poetry. Chief of the Pléiade, the group who created in France the poetry of high Renaissance style. He used as models Pindar and Anacreon,

Horace and Petrarch, publishing in 1552 the influential volume of sonnets and odes *Les Amours*, which had musical settings. The Pléiade regarded poetry as an 'arduous and exquisite endeavour' but had faith in the native tongue of France as a medium, needing only to be 'enriched'. His importance is in lyric and elegiac poetry. His ambitious heroic poem the *Franciade* made little impact. Spenser learned from his serious devotion to poetic art and his command of metre; but he never attempted to 'overgo' him.

SKELTON, JOHN 1460?–1529. 'Laureated' at Oxford before 1490 (in the tradition of Petrarch's crowning). He studied at Cambridge and entered Holy Orders in 1498. Tutor to Prince Henry, he met Erasmus; later Rector of Diss in Norfolk. He lampooned Wolsey and suffered for it. In old style he wrote a morality play *Magnificence*—recently performed in London. But he is best known for his 'free rhythm' informal verses, convivial or satiric, which were one forebear of the 'rough rhythm' pieces in the *Calender*. Spenser acknowledges this when he took over the pastoral name used by Skelton, Colin Clout.

SIDNEY, SIR PHILIP (1554–86). Son of Sir Henry Sidney, a successful Lord Governor of Ireland before 1579. Philip (1554–86) was educated at Shrewsbury and Oxford, entered diplomatic service under his uncle the Earl of Leicester, accompanying him to Paris. On an extended tour he met great humanist scholars, studied horsemanship, was painted by Veronese. Proposals of marriage for him ranged from European princesses to highest aristocrat. For Penelope Devereux he wrote 'Astrophel and Stella', bringing Renaissance poetry in high style into England. He accompanied his father to Ireland and served as ambassador in Europe. He discussed classical metres with Spenser in 1579, composed his 'Defence of Poesie' about 1580 (printed 1595). For his sister Mary, who became Countess of Pembroke, he created his pastoral romance in prose *The Arcadia* (1580), later recast. She was a patroness of poets, thanked by Spenser. Philip was knighted in 1583; married Walsingham's daughter, Frances. He became Master of the Ordnance then Governor of Flushing. While on service in the Netherlands died of wounds after a skirmish at Zutphen.

A model of the Renaissance courtier, soldier, poet, statesman. Spenser dedicated his *Calender* to him; but there is little trace of friendship thereafter, though the Knight of Courtesy in *The Faerie Queene* may mirror him. Spenser's elegy for him has not the ring of personal devotion. Portrait in the National Portrait Gallery, reproduced in *The Elizabethans*. See page 86.

SPENSER FAMILY. Edmund (c. 1552–99): Parents not certainly known; married Machabyas Chylde in 1579, by whom he had a son Sylvanus, born c. 1582, and a daughter Katherine, probably younger. Sylvanus served heir to Kilcolman. It is unknown when Edmund's first wife died; his sister Sarah came to Ireland, married and settled in Munster. Edmund married in 1594 Elizabeth Boyle (see separate entry) by whom he had a son Peregrine (1595?–1642). Peregrine attempted a career in London in 1618 but returned to Ireland, marrying a step-daughter of his mother's. He held the Castle and lands of Renny. Descendants of the poet held Kilcolman until about 1700, when the lands were sequestered because they were Roman Catholics.

TASSO, TORQUATO, 1544–95. An Italian poet who wrote his first epic at seventeen, gaining instant recognition and his father's permission to dedicate his life to poetry and philosophy. His *Jerusalem Delivered from the Turk* of 1575 confirmed the early promise but mental illness ended his career in 1579, preventing his 'crowning with laurel' that the Pope had intended.

Bibliography

The list follows the general plan of the present volume; for books that are currently available to purchase the publisher is named.

Text

For a happy entry into Spenser reading: *Edmund Spenser: Selections from the minor poems and The Faerie Queene'* ed. Frank Kermode, New Oxford English series.

The single volume, *The Poetical Works of Edmund Spenser*, ed. J. C. Smith and E. de Selincourt, Oxford University Press, 1912, Oxford Paperbacks 1970. This is the most useful volume though the print is small. There are no explanatory notes, but it includes the *Letters* by Spenser and by Harvey. The glossary is valuable as it records variation in spelling, which aids the exploration of a word's spread of meaning; line-references are given and the word's force in any poetic context may be checked. It omits *A Theatre*.

The complete works are available in the library edition: *The Works of Edmund Spenser: A Variorum Edition, 1932–49* ed. Greenlaw, Padelford, Osgood and Heffner, Oxford University Press, John Hopkins Press. Ten volumes, including *The Life* and *Index*. This edition summarizes commentary on Spenser up to 1946, but the most important interpretation of the poetry has been done since then.

The Faerie Queene ed. J. W. Hales, Dent, Everyman Paperback, two volumes. This has a glossary but no notes.

A new edition of *The Faerie Queene* is in preparation by A. C. Hamilton, Longman Annotated Poets.

For the minor poems: *Complaints* 1928, *Daphnaida and Other Poems* 1929, *The Shepherd's Calendar* 1930—all ed. W. L. Renwick, Scholartis Press. These have very helpful notes, but the woodcuts of the *Calendar* are omitted. Also see A. Kent Hieatt and Enid Welsford.

The Life of Edmund Spenser by Alexander C. Judson, 1945. (Volume 10 of the Variorum Edition) is the standard work, to be supplemented by 'Spenser and the Countess of Leicester' by Charles E. Mounts in *English Literary History* volume 19, Baltimore 1952.

Background

The Elizabethans, introduced by Allardyce Nicoll, Cambridge University Press, 1957, is invaluable, being an ordered compilation of passages from contemporary works and documents illustrating all aspects of Elizabethan life, with many portraits, maps and illustrations of places.

The English Icon: Elizabethan and Jacobean Portraiture by Roy Strong, 1969, Routledge and Kegan Paul, New Pantheon Books, has many relevant portraits, including Lettice Knollys, Countess of Leicester, and Lord Grey.

Also useful is *Shakespeare in his Own Age*, volume 17 of *Shakespeare Survey*, Cambridge University Press, 1964. Chapter 8 'The Commonwealth' by Philip Styles is important. (Re-issued, paperback, 1976)

Two historical studies are: *Elizabethan People, State and Society* ed. J. Hurstfield and A. G. R. Smith, Documents of Modern History, Arnold 1972 and *Science and Society in the Sixteenth Century* by Alan G. R. Smith, Library of European Civilisation, Thames and Hudson, 1972.

W. T. MacCaffrey 'England, The Crown and the New Aristocracy' in *Past and Present* No. 30, the Past and Present Society, 1965. Social mobility and patronage are studied.

John F. Danby, *The Poets on Fortune's Hill*, Routledge and Kegan Paul, London 1952, re-issued as *Elizabethan and Jacobean Poets*, 1964. Patronage and poetry are discussed.

The Queen

Roy Strong, Julia T. Oman, *Elizabeth R: Evocation and Spectacle*, Secker and Warburg, 1971. For costumes, jewels, letters, and tributes.

M. C. Bradbrook, ed., *The Queen's Gårland*, Oxford University Press, 1971. An anthology of pieces for and about the Queen.

Frances A. Yates, *Astraea*, Routledge and Kegan Paul, 1975. The imperial theme in the sixteenth century, on the Cult of the Queen and Empire.

E. C. Wilson, *England's Eliza*, Harvard University Press, 1939. The earliest in this field.

Background of ideas

E. M. W. Tillyard, *The Elizabethan World-Picture* Chatto and Windus 1943. Available in Penguin (Peregrine) edition. An easy introduction.

Ricardo J. Quinones, *The Renaissance Discovery of Time*, Harvard University Press, 1972. A specific study. Also see A. Kent Hieatt and Enid Welsford.

Castiglione, *The Book of the Courtier*, translated by Sir Thomas Hoby, 1561. Introduced by J. H. Whitfield, Everyman's University Library, 1974.

Castiglione, *The Book of the Courtier*, translated and introduced by George Bull, Penguin Classics 1967.

For Ireland

W. L. Renwick, ed., *A View of the Present State of Ireland*, Oxford University Press, 1970. Spenser's *A Vue*.

D. B. Quinn, *The Elizabethans and the Irish*, Cornell University Press, 1966.

Sean O'Faolain, *The Great O'Neill*, Mercier Paperback, 1970.

Grenfell Morton, *Elizabethan Ireland*, Longman, 1971.

Pauline Henley, *Spenser in Ireland*, Cork, 1928.

John Derricke, *The Image of Ireland*, Dublin, 1581: reprinted ed. John Small, Edinburgh, 1883.

For general literary reference

C. S. Lewis, *English Literature in the Sixteenth Century, excluding Drama*, Oxford University Press, 1954. Details are included of poets or writings mentioned in passing in this Preface.

C. S. Lewis, *The Discarded Image: An Introduction to Medieval and Renaissance Literature*, Cambridge University Press, 1964.

W. L. Renwick, *Edmund Spenser: An Essay on Renaissance Poetry*, Edward Arnold, 1933.

Paul J. Alpers, ed., *Elizabethan Poetry: Modern Essays in Criticism* (especially the article by Martha Craig, 'The Secret Wit of Spenser's Language').

Frank Kermode, *Renaissance Essays: Shakespeare, Spenser*, etc., Fontana, 1973.

William Nelson, *The Poetry of Edmund Spenser*, Columbia University Press, 1963. This volume studies all the poems.

Paul J. Alpers, ed., *Spenser: A Critical Anthology*, Penguin, Gives comment on Spenser from his own times till today, with details of contemporary criticism.

Graham Hough, *A Preface to the Faerie Queene*, Duckworth, 1962. For Spenser and Italian romance.

Barbara Reynolds (translator) English, *Orlando Furioso*. Penguin Paperback Part I, 1975. Verse translation in two parts. Part II, 1976.

Rosemary Freeman, *The Faerie Queene: A Companion for Readers*, Chatto and Windus, 1970.

Maurice Evans, *Spenser's Anatomy of Heroism*: A commentary on 'The Faerie Queene', Cambridge University Press, 1970.

C. S. Lewis, *Spenser's Images of Life*, Cambridge University Press, 1967. For illuminating comment on special passages and aspects.

A. C. Hamilton, *The Structure of the Allegory in the Faerie Queene*, Oxford University Press, 1967.

Harry Berger, *The Allegorical Temper*, Yale University Press, 1967. Shows how to read allegory 'from the inside'.

For interpretation of works of Spenser as 'astronomical poetry'

Alastair Fowler, *Spenser and the Numbers of Time*, Routledge and Kegan Paul, 1964. Shows the importance of this for 'The Faerie Queene'. This approach was first used in the following volume:

A. Kent Hieatt, *Short Time's Endless Monument*, Columbia University Press, 1960. This is the text and study of 'Epithalamion. Reissue, Port Washington, N.Y. 1972.

Enid Welsford, *Spenser: Fowre Hymnes and Epithalamion*, Oxford University Press, 1964. This disagrees with Hieatt. Subtitled 'A Study of Spenser's Doctrine of Love', it is the best introduction to that subject.

General Index

Index to Spenser's Works